Lilacs in the Rain

by
James Peinkofer

ROOFTOP
publishing

Rooftop Publishing™
1663 Liberty Drive, Suite 200
Bloomington, IN 47403
Phone: 1-800-839-8640

This book is a work of non-fiction. Unless otherwise noted, the author and the publisher make no explicit guarantees as to the accuracy of the information contained in this book and in some cases, names of people and places have been altered to protect their privacy.

This story is real and chronicles events that occurred during the 1940s and 1950s in and around New Haven, Connecticut. Some of the characters, events, and circumstances are fictionalized to add to the story's impact and narrative flow.

First published by Rooftop Publishing 10/02/07

Publisher: Kevin King
Acquisitions Editor: Nick Obradovich
Senior Editor: Lesley Bolton
Cover Design: April Mostek
Book Design: Jessica Sheese
Production Manager: Aaron Schultz
Senior Publicist: Shannon White

ISBN: 978-1-60008-073-9 (sc)

Library of Congress Control Number: 2007936387

Printed in the United States of America
Bloomington, Indiana

This book is printed on acid-free paper.

Acknowledgments

There are many people who have assisted in allowing this book to come to life and to you I'd like to express my sincere thanks.

To Nick Obradovich, Kevin King, Lora Bolton, and Lesley Bolton, all of Rooftop Publishing, thank you for taking on this project. It is a vital part of child welfare history and an important legacy.

To the families of three infant girls killed in the 1940s and '50s by Jaspers, thank you for sharing your memories, emotions, and suggestions. Stephen Hubbard, now you know the full story. Marcy Kapsinow, thanks for helping me get the ball rolling. Sheilah, you are tenacious and a fighter for the rights and protection of children. Joan, your spirit and warmth and music have carried you gracefully through these many decades.

To Marvin and Bruce Schaefer, though there was no justice in your case, your story is now told. May it protect other infants and children, as you have wished.

To the memory of Robert Salinger, MD, thank you for being a life-saver and stepping up so many years ago to take a stand against Jaspers.

To the following physicians—Thomas Chiffelle, Michael Kashgarian, Lawrence Michel, Carter Stilson, and Morris Wessel—I am indebted to each of you for having shared your personal accounts of the Jaspers case.

To Sergeants Harold Berg (retired) and Joyce Illingworth, thanks for your help in getting background information on the Jaspers case.

To Sister Deloris Liptak and Maria Medina, thanks for your assistance in obtaining detailed background information about the Sisters of Mercy and St. Agnes Home.

To librarians Allison Botelho (New Haven Free Public Library), Hilary Frye (Connecticut State Library), and Marcia Jacoby (formerly of Hagaman Memorial Library – East Haven), and Meredith Haddock (Library of Congress) for your research assistance.

To Francis Looney for your insight into the realm of child welfare in the 1950s.

To Betty Doyle for sharing personal information about the Jaspers' home life.

To Bob, Karen, Alec, and Nicole Peinkofer for your love, interest, and encouragement in this project.

To Alda and Richard Peinkofer for your guidance and love over the years.

To my wife, Tina, for your love, smiles, and support that keep my dreams alive. To my son, Jacob, who makes my heart happy and never fails to keep me guessing.

Dedicated to:

Cynthia, Jennifer, and Abbe—may you finally be at peace.

Prologue

As I stood in the hallway of the apartment complex, dripping wet from the spring rain, I nervously waited for door 3G to open. I had never met a serial killer, male or female, and I wasn't sure that I wanted to on that June day in 1999. My brain raced, and I was filled with a variety of emotions that made me gulp and nervously wipe water from my forehead and eyebrows. I had studied the woman behind this door using every source of information I could find about her. She had some notoriety among child-abuse medical professionals since she was the featured perpetrator in the original medical journal article that named shaken baby syndrome as an entity in 1972. I had talked with her victims' parents who had known her over forty years before. I knew what questions I wanted to ask her, and I knew what I wanted to get a glimpse of—her hands. These were the lethal weapons that she had used in her eight-year reign of terror on a multitude of tiny babies in the often-affluent homes in and around New Haven, Connecticut.

The woman behind this apartment door had shaken, twisted, squeezed, and slapped babies in the 1940s and '50s—killing three and injuring twelve others. Did she even remember her victims' names? I would attempt to remind her of the names while at the same time, lay to rest a multitude of questions that I had scurrying around in my head. One question that I fortunately did know the answer to was why she did what she did. Her history, presented so long ago, allowed me to put the pieces together. She had known, and later admitted, that what she did was wrong, but after her first murder, because of her volatility, this knowledge hadn't stopped her from striking out. This was the true nature of a serial killer, having no remorse and no ownership for her nefarious deeds.

Now, I just had to meet her, knowing that no one had looked at her the way I had for decades. This was a national story that quickly got swept away. But I brought it all back. The dead babies were calling out to me. They needed to rest. Their stories needed to be shared.

The apartment door opened …

CHAPTER ONE

"What the Hell Happened to Her?"

"What the Hell Happened to Her?"

10:00 p.m.
Thursday, August 23, 1956
New Haven, Connecticut

As Abbe Kapsinow lay dying, her mother, Sheilah, was heading out the door of Muriel Esposito's house. She had had a restless feeling for the entire duration of her three-hour visit, even though it was nice to link up with another woman and talk. During her visit, Sheilah complained to Muriel about Virginia Jaspers. "I don't know what it is, but I've never felt comfortable with her or that she was all that competent with what she is doing. I'd have never left Abbe alone with her if I knew that Allen wasn't there. I really will not miss her in the least. Only one more week or so, and then she can go. She is one baby nurse that I wish I never had."

"When are the other children coming back home from your parents?" asked Muriel.

"I think I'll bring them back on Saturday morning. I'll be ready for them then. Marcy was so scared of Virginia when she met her. Really, they both were, but Marcy couldn't help but stare at her. I want to keep from having Virginia do too many things with the kids; I don't want to upset them. Look ... I need to get going. It's late, and I'm a little worried about the baby. Thanks for having me over, and let's get together again *really* soon."

Sheilah left Muriel's house and walked on Woodin Street toward Laurel Court. The warm summer wind blew the maple, elm, and poplar trees as she proceeded through the darkened neighborhood. The dark did not scare Sheilah much, since she felt there was nothing around to threaten her. That was one trait that she had inherited from her father, or it was something she had learned. *Be afraid when you need to be; don't be caught up in what's not there.* The echo of her father's voice blended with the creaks of the trees as they swayed in the night wind. As Sheilah turned onto Brookside Avenue from Laurel Court, she felt a cool breeze that caught her off-guard and gave her a shiver. *Strange*, she thought, *it's nearly 70 degrees outside.* Sheilah then felt an instant rush of panic. *Abbe.* Though her back began to ache from the stress of walking, she ran the last two blocks to her home.

Sheilah quickly surveyed the living room as she burst through the front door. She did not see Virginia, nor did she immediately see Abbe, since the bulky arm of the couch kept her from view. Moonlight pierced the blinds and illuminated streaks on the wall. Sheilah walked toward the dark kitchen. Before she reached the entrance, she heard a slight wheezing, as if a small bird was slowly chirping in distress. Sheilah turned and was horrified at what she saw. She screamed, "My baby … Oh God, my baby!"

Sheilah stumbled over to the edge of the couch to be next to Abbe. The tiny girl had blood bubbling from both nostrils. Her left eye was open slightly, and her breathing was labored. The chirping sounds came from deep inside her as she struggled for each breath. Sheila's eyes and head moved back and forth along her baby's body, trying to survey what damage had been done.

"Allen! Where are you, you son of a bitch?!" she yelled, still looking at Abbe. Sheilah stood, looked around the living room, and spotted the telephone. She ran and grabbed her purse that had been dropped on the floor when she entered the apartment and raced back over to the phone.

Sitting on the floor, she rummaged through her purse with one hand and dialed the operator with the other.

"This is the operator. May I help you?"

"Yes, Operator! My baby is dying! Please, I'm trying … damn it! I'm trying to find the number of … uh … a doctor that they gave me for my baby when I was in the hospital … and … and—"

"What doctor is it, ma'am?"

"Damn it, Operator! I'm looking!" Sheilah yelled into the phone as she dumped her purse contents on the well-worn rug. "Here it is! Dr. Michel."

"Dr. Michel what?"

"No, that's his last name. Hurry! It's Dr. Laurence Michel."

"I'll connect you."

Sheilah ran back to Abbe and lightly picked her up off the couch and cradled her in her arms. She skidded back toward the phone and heard a woman speaking through the receiver. Sheilah winced as she painfully positioned herself on her still-sore left hip to talk on the phone.

"Hello, Dr. Michel?"

"This is his wife. How may I help you?"

"It's my baby … It seems like she's dying or something. Please get me the doctor!"

The operator had contacted Michel at home since all operators had a listing of home phone numbers for physicians for emergency use.

Ten seconds later, the doctor answered, "Hello, this is Dr. Michel. Who is this?"

"Doctor, my baby isn't well at all. This is Sheilah Kapsinow, mother of Abbe—Oh God! She's only ten days old."

"Ma'am, where do you live?"

"65-H Brookside Avenue … It's on the west side of town."

"What's wrong with the baby?" asked the doctor scribbling down her name and address on the back of an envelope on his desktop.

"She is bluish colored, and there is blood in her nose. She's breathing funny, too."

"Keep her warm. I'll meet you at your house soon. I'll leave right away."

Sheilah remembered to hang up the phone, as she didn't want to miss getting a call.

"Allen!" Sheilah yelled. She sat up on her knees and leaned forward to get a better view of the kitchen and dining room.

A confident-sounding voice responded from deep in the kitchen. "He isn't here."

"Virginia? What do you mean, he isn't here?"

"He hasn't been here since just after you left."

"Then … then … you …" Sheilah stuttered in her confusion as she tried to decipher the rush of thoughts that now flooded her head. "What the hell happened to her?!" she shouted.

"She wasn't hungry. She didn't want her bottle," Virginia said as she was now slowly pacing, standing just inside the kitchen entranceway.

"What are you talking about? She was hungry when I left!"

"She was having trouble taking the bottle, so I … I laid her on the couch."

"And you didn't call anyone? What the hell is the matter with you?" Sheilah said as she stood up to confront the nurse face to face, holding Abbe in her arms.

Virginia retreated, put her hands up, and walked back into the kitchen toward the storage closet. Sheilah thought for a moment about following the nurse into the kitchen, but instead, feeling exasperated, she turned around and went toward the living room door and proceeded to walk outside. On the porch, she craned her neck looking for the doctor. She looked down at Abbe, whose tiny face glowed in the light of the past-peak full moon. Her breathing was more regular, but she still heard the soft shrill. Sheilah heard distant car noises and saw several lights, but none turned down her street. *Where is he?* she wondered, her heart racing.

Laurence Michel had been a board-certified pediatrician in New Haven for the past four years. His practice was growing, and he enjoyed the variety of patients he had. He would often charge a reduced rate for poorer families, and he was well aware of the Brookside Avenue apartment complex, since many factory workers lived there. He had been out to several of the apartments on occasion for various upper-respiratory complaints in infants and children. As he drove to the Kapsinow home, he wondered what he would find. More often than not, house calls were more of a time to calm over-anxious parents than true medical emergencies. He had seen a host of patients during his residency years in the late 1940s in Brooklyn at Kingston Avenue Hospital and Jewish Hospital. Car accidents, near drownings, cancer, appendicitis, and other conditions were diagnoses that gave him a good start in the field of pediatrics. He continued to be amazed at the potential for recovery in young children—they bounced back from tragedies much better than adults. He was worried about the Kapsinow baby, though. It didn't sound good. He almost called an ambulance before he drove off from his house, but he wanted to check out the scene first. Parents would too often call him in the middle of the night, worrying about the sounds that were emanating from their children's bodies, when the simple diagnosis would be stridor or croup or something of that nature. He knew that he could always call an ambulance if needed.

Several minutes later, Dr. Michel pulled up in the Kapsinow driveway and jumped out of his car with his black kit in hand. Sheilah met him on the lawn, still holding Abbe.

"Come on, let's take her inside. I need to examine her."

Abbe was carefully placed back on the couch. The doctor listened intently to the baby's heart rhythm with his stethoscope, which had recently hung around his neck. He felt her fontanel on top of her head, which was firm and slightly bulging instead of soft and pliable. He checked her eyes with the scope and took her pulse. He didn't like what he saw, felt, or heard and knew the baby was in respiratory distress.

"Call the operator and ask that an ambulance be sent here immediately. She needs to get to the hospital."

Sheilah ran to the phone and dialed.

While she was talking, she thought she heard the doctor say, "I only hope we're not too late."

Virginia's large figure was outlined in the darkened kitchen as she stood against the back doorway. With expressionless eyes, she watched the two people hover over the baby and make a fuss. It had happened again. Virginia was fine. *They don't know me. They won't find out what happened—they never do. I'm safe.* When the ambulance drove up to the front of the house, no one came to ask her anything. *I'll stay here,* she thought. The flashing lights bounced off the walls and reflected off her glasses. The thin layer of sweat on her forehead glowed an evil red.

CHAPTER TWO

"Oh, Isn't She Just Precious?"

June 1948
Guilford, Connecticut

Walking in the front door of their brand-new house, twenty-five-year-old Virginia Jaspers cheerfully pumped the hands of her new clients. They were only her fourth. No one knew, not even Virginia, that they would be her first deadly encounter—the first in a string of lies and deaths that would ultimately captivate a nation and forever change the lives of many families.

Her hulking presence initially took Allen Hubbard and his wife by surprise. She was six feet tall and, by what Allen could calculate, she was easily over two hundred pounds. You didn't see many women, or even men, with such a build. Allen blinked and said, "You must be Miss Jaspers. Please, come in."

It was June 1948, and New Haven, Connecticut, was the area where this tragedy unfolded. It was a typical coastal town that was home to an anything-but-typical university. Yale University brought both employment and commerce to New Haven. Though the college town had dwindled in size because of the summer recess, it was still lively. The area also was home to a large Jewish population, many of whom were still recovering from the recent blows of the Holocaust atrocities of World War II. More and more Jews immigrated to New Haven after many had initially settled there in the late 1770s.

Virginia Jaspers was a pediatric nurse, unlicensed and under-trained. She was part of a running list of nurses kept by town doctors. Jaspers and others on this list went into couples' homes to live and care for their new arrivals. Often for weeks on end, the nurses would become a part of the family. No one doubted their credentials; no one thought twice about them caring for their babies. Many of the parents were well-to-do, and hiring a pediatric nurse was more of a status symbol than anything else. Some couples didn't know the first thing about baby care, so they would hire out to have an "expert" to guide them in the process. Still, others had older children to care for, and a nurse on hand was an important part of getting the family through the first month.

The Hubbard's daughter, Cynthia, arrived in June of 1948. She was their first, and she was welcomed with exuberant intensity. Allen worked as an engineer, while his wife, Eleanor, stayed at home. They had planned on not having any help with their new baby, but Allen's father insisted. "What you need is one of those baby nurses that are always advertised in the paper," he suggested.

Allen was making good money but didn't want to squander it where it didn't need to be squandered. His father said, "Hell, I'll go fifty-fifty with you." Allen was curious about why he was going to such lengths to get them extra help with the baby, but he let the process unfold.

Virginia Jaspers showed up at the Hubbards' door when Cynthia was three days old. Her first words to the couple were, "Now, where is that baby?" Allen motioned toward the living room with an outstretched index finger without saying a word, still overwhelmed by the young woman's size. He heard, "Oh! There is that girl. Let me snatch her up."

He watched as the pediatric nurse crept up toward his baby's bassinet having dropped her equally oversized purse in the middle of the floor. His eyes followed her mammoth hands curve toward each other like, well, like they were going to wrap around the neck of some kind of prey. These foolish thoughts were wrested away with a shake of his head, and the sound of his wife saying, "Careful, now."

Virginia's method of baby-handling appeared anything but careful. Cynthia's head bobbed backwards as she was lifted out of her secure environment still in slumber. "Oh, I've cared for hundreds of babies in my life. No need to worry, folks," the nurse replied.

Allen, skeptical, wondered how she had cared for so many babies having graduated from her home-nursing program just two years earlier.

"Oh, isn't she just precious?" The large woman plopped onto the Hubbards' new davenport, which still had six payments left. Allen smiled glibly and asked, "May I get you something to eat or drink?"

"Well, maybe a little something," came the reply.

Eleanor Hubbard went into the kitchen and soon reappeared with three small donuts on a glass plate and a large glass of milk. Virginia's eyes widened noticeably. One hand cradled the slumbering Cynthia's head and one hand plucked donuts. Each donut received two bites which were followed by a slug of milk. Allen felt like he had a stopwatch, timing the nurse to see how quickly she would consume the goodies. He gauged that it took less than one minute for Virginia to join the "clean plate" club.

"Thank you. They were delicious."

Eleanor asked, "Would you like some more?"

Virginia looked down at her plate and glass and said, "Well, I *do* have more milk."

Three more donuts were munched in the same fashion, followed by a semi-stifled belch.

"Excuse me. My father always says that a burp is the sign of a good meal!"

Allen's head moved backward slightly, and he just stared at the woman. His thoughts went to the young woman's father. It was such a contradiction to what he had just witnessed. William Jaspers was a Connecticut state senator. He was tall and bulky but never played the slob. He seemed to have just enough class without being overly zealous in his role as a senator. One thing Allen did know was that Mr. Jaspers had clout and plenty of it. It stymied him to think that the person in front of him, who had popped down six donuts without blinking, was cut from the same fabric as the impressive state senator. He then wondered if she still lived at home and what home life was like and …

"Allen, is anything wrong?" asked Eleanor.

"No, nothing. I was drifting in my thoughts. I'm sorry."

Just then, Cynthia began to cry. Virginia said, "Where's the bottle? This girl is hungry!"

Allen wanted to add, "You should know," but he thought better of it. Knowing that William Jaspers was her father, he knew that any type of mistreatment, however slight, might cost him his job. He was a very influential man with many connections. This was one of the reasons they chose the name of Jaspers as an infant nurse from the list their doctor had provided.

"Isn't she the daughter of the state senator?" they asked Dr. Olmsted.

"Oh, yes," he replied. "Though I haven't suggested her much as a baby nurse as she is fairly new to the field. She is quite a large woman, you know."

At the time, Allen and Eleanor thought that this arrangement would subtly place them in a more favorable position in society among their friends.

"Now, you go on about your business, folks. I'll get a bottle going on the stove, and the baby will be okay in a few minutes." The infant nurse looked down at the child as she walked swiftly to the kitchen. "Won't you, dear?"

One week passed, and Virginia became a regular part of the Hubbard household. Allen would often catch himself staring at her in amazement while she ate and conversed at the dining room table. He took in her large, bulbous nose, her abundant lips, and her crystal-blue eyes, which hid behind a pair of dark, plastic horn-rimmed glasses. She *was* quite ugly. Her weekly nursing fee of $63.00 was reasonable, but her vast appetite strained Allen's weekly bankroll. He was impressed that she restrained from snacks and other food during her hours on duty with Cynthia. It was the times afterward when he was left shaking his head in amusement at the sight of her guzzling soda and eating large bowls of ice cream. He mentioned his concerns about her food consumption to Eleanor.

"Oh, now look at the size of the woman! She has to keep up with her weight, and she's doing no harm at all." Allen had no response and let the conversation die a quick death.

Virginia's quirkiness became a part of her charm. She handled Cynthia well. She interacted with the Hubbards' guests, and she kept the household in a general state of levity. Allen grew to enjoy listening to her chatter about the latest movie ("I'm crazy about them!") or the key players on the *New Haven Register's* society pages ("I can't believe she is getting married—I went to school with her!").

During each day when Allen was at work, Eleanor would spend time helping Virginia with Cynthia's care while listening to her many stories about her high school days or months of training at St. Agnes Home up in West Hartford. Eleanor was aware of Virginia's need to be sociable and knew that this was the right business for her. The infant nurse was able to place herself around other adults by caring for their children. Virginia seemed to be a lonely heart underneath all the outward gaiety.

One night, after Cynthia was fed, Allen and Eleanor decided to retire to their small parlor to read the newspaper and work on a crossword puzzle. Allen heard the pounding first. It was a sound like someone was beating a rug, only at a rapid pace.

"What the hell is that?" he asked.

"Oh, Allen, it's only Virginia burping Cynthia."

Eleanor was used to the infant nurse's heavy-handed style with Cynthia. She knew that was the method Virginia used to help "get the bubbles up." She thought back to several days ago when the nurse tried to teach her the style. "One needs to be firm when burping a baby and use even blows to the back." Eleanor had chuckled inside at that comment, because Virginia sounded as though she was repeating a rote phrase she had learned at St. Agnes when the nuns taught her aspects of childcare. Eleanor tried the pounding as Virginia had detailed but couldn't bring herself to be as hard as her teacher.

Allen heard the nurse coming their way, the pounding seeming to become louder. He stood to face her, dropping his newspaper to the hardwood floor. Cynthia let out a tiny belch and then began to cry.

"There you go!" Virginia gleefully cheered and stopped the pounding. She then asked, "And how is the society page? Remember to save it for me."

Allen glibly smiled and commented, "That's quite a wallop you give the baby. Are you sure that is good for her?"

"Well, Mr. Hubbard, one needs to get the bubbles up, and firm, even blows to the back will do that for you."

Eleanor completed the phrase in her mind as Virginia was saying it. She knew it too well, though it was the first time Allen had heard it.

"Well, how about taps instead of blows," Allen said smiling.

Virginia didn't respond with words; instead, she walked up to Cynthia's father and gently handed her to him. She looked at the floor sullenly and ambled out of the room.

"Now, Allen. See what you did," Eleanor objected.

"I don't want her hitting Cynthia," Allen snapped in response.

"She isn't hitting—she is burping her. It was a shock to me when I first saw her do it too. The poor thing is just heavy-handed. Look at the size of her in comparison to Cynthia."

Allen looked down at his angel, who was now fidgeting to get to sleep. She would be thirteen days old tomorrow. Allen thought about her short life so far. For him, thirteen days passed by so quickly, but for his daughter, the period was her whole lifetime. His thoughts overwhelmed him. Such strong emotions had welled inside his heart since she was born. They were different from any he had ever felt before. He knew about the concept of motherly love, but this love was his own, a personal love that no one else could touch—a fatherly love. He couldn't express these feelings in words to his wife and especially not to his coworkers during the day. It was private, between him and Cynthia. She had her whole world in front of her and her whole life ahead of her. Allen just wanted to protect her, in a way. He wanted …

"Allen, what are you thinking about?"

The words interrupted his meditation. "I was thinking about how special this girl is."

"She is. I am sorry I scolded. Virginia looked so criticized when you suggested that she tap Cynthia. I know you were looking out for the baby's well-being."

Eleanor walked over to Allen and placed one hand on the left side of his face and the other hand on Cynthia's bald, quiet head. It was a family moment—one that didn't need comment from either adult.

"Allen, she does handle the baby quite well. St. Agnes must have taught her something."

"I love you, Eleanor. And I love being your husband and a father to our child. I'd better go say something to Virginia. Think she'll forgive me?"

"I'm sure."

At 3:00 a.m., Virginia loudly clearing her throat awakened both Allen and Eleanor. It was clear to Allen, even in his grogginess, that it was an I-don't-want-to-bother-you-but-I-need-to throat clearing. He shot up in bed in their darkened room and was alarmed at the sight of Virginia Jaspers' outlined silhouette. Her hulking figure was backlit by the hall light, and she was simply pointing behind her. The couple sat in their bed and watched the infant nurse as she continued to point and make stammering noises.

"I ... the ... well ..."

Allen, immediately frustrated by this lack of dialogue, belted out, "Jesus Christ, Virginia! Tell us what's wrong."

The nurse put her large hand to her mouth and seemed to whisper, "The baby ... kitchen."

Allen and Eleanor raced out of bed and ran down the hallway stairs to the entrance of the kitchen. The lights were on, and the refrigerator door was open. The couple both made audible sounds as they saw their baby on the floor in front of the sink. They both raced to her, and Eleanor snatched her up to her chest. Cynthia was cold. Her eyes were halfway opened.

Allen grabbed her from Eleanor and repeated, "Oh, my God. Oh, my God." Tears came freely to Eleanor's eyes, and she began to shudder and dropped to her knees on the cold floor. Allen's mouth went over Cynthia's, but he took in her nose as well. He blew life-saving air into her clear, pink lungs. The baby didn't move or even cry out. Allen cursed as he gave his daughter another puff. Nothing. He had watched a fellow serviceman save the life of a peer five years ago when he was stationed in the Philippines, but now he couldn't remember how it was done, especially to an infant, his own daughter.

He knew she was dead, and he stopped to look at her. He coughed several times and allowed his tension to be overtaken by sorrow.

The clomping of feet descending the stairs interrupted the couple's grieving and furious rescue efforts. Allen whipped around still holding desperately to his limp daughter. He could only mutter, "How? How?"

"Ohhh!" Virginia wailed. Tears flowed down and over her reddened cheeks like trout streams.

"Come on, Virginia! What the hell happened?"

The nurse squeaked out, "The baby just stopped breathing. I set her down and went to get you folks."

Eleanor swiveled slowly around and placed a hand on Allen's warm back and asked, "Virginia, tell us what happened."

Their guest completed her descent to the kitchen floor from the stairs and sat in a chair that moaned under her weight.

She gulped several times. Her eyes stared downward and flitted back and forth like she was watching a scurrying mouse. After a deep sigh, she began.

"She had been hungry tonight and had been up several times crying. I fed her and walked with her each moment she was awake. I was having trouble sleeping myself, as well. The last time she cried, she sounded a little different."

"How, different?" inquired Allen quietly as he looked at the floor, arranging the tiled pieces in various ways in his mind.

"Well, like a small whistle that a child would blow. *Toot, toot, toot.* Like that. Anyway, I picked her up and walked with her again. Maybe she had a bubble or too much food. She seemed loose like a rag doll when I got to the kitchen. I knew something was wrong, so I set her down and got you folks."

The three of them sat there in silence with the dead infant. They were each in their own world. Allen said to his wife later that day that he would have given anything for the whole thing to have been a bad dream. It was Virginia who broke the five-minute silence.

"Shouldn't we call a doctor, or something?"

"Too Goddamned late for that!" Allen cried out, fresh tears starting to well and run their course.

"Allen," said Eleanor, reaching to touch his hand. Her chest rose and fell several times in quick succession. Her pain was great, greater than anything she had felt in her lifetime.

"I'll call Dr. Olmsted. He'll tell us what to do," Allen offered.

He slowly got to his feet. His body felt like it had been used as a punching bag in a prizefight. He was the one who didn't have the strength to fight back. He ambled to the telephone and picked it up off the receiver. He inserted his shaking finger slowly into the cold hole of the dial plate and made a clockwise movement from the "0."

"Exchange 3-7-2."

"One moment please," came a sleepy voice.

After three rings, another sleepy voice whispered, "Hello."

"Dr. Olmsted. Allen Hubbard here. There has been a tragedy at the house. Our little girl, Cynthia, is dead." Allen burst into tears and covered his mouth so he could hear some guiding words.

"I will come right over. I am so sorry."

Allen hung up the phone and walked over to his wife. He knelt beside her to put his arms around her. Eleanor was now holding Cynthia in her arms. The couple rocked back and forth and cried. They seemed to be soothing each other and their dead infant at the same time—a family moment, as Allen had thought earlier that evening.

Virginia dared not watch the scene. She felt like she would explode or something if she did. Instead, she watched a tiny spider scurry across the kitchen floor. As the bug got near her, she slowly raised her size-14 shoe and just as slowly lowered it over the spider's body—no splat, no crunch, just quiet.

CHAPTER THREE

"Her Brain Was Just Too Fragile"

June 24, 1948
Yale University Pathology Department
New Haven, Connecticut

The third-floor office Dr. Thomas Chiffelle used overlooked the peaceful, tree-protected grounds of Yale University. He stood at the long, open window and watched nature flit about; carefree squirrels and bluebirds enthusiastically enjoyed the warm breezes outside. He stood there for some time thinking about the baby. She was barely seven pounds, so tiny. He remembered that during the autopsy, he had paused briefly to look at her perfect features, his eyes gliding down her simple arms to her hands and fingers and to her paper-thin fingernails.

From the window, he walked to his typewriter that he had obtained through the university. Although used, it was new to him, and it worked well enough. He didn't have a secretary to transcribe his recorded notes, like most of the older pathologists on campus. Anyway, he liked to work alone. He wouldn't have to second-guess the spelling of the medical terms that he had recorded on tape several hours earlier. He had perfected his typing skills in medical school. This helped during his residency as he had many "posts" to do. Now, one year later, no longer a resident, he was able to take more time to type and prepare his reports. Being on staff at Yale was a welcome change for Thomas. He felt as though he was able to stand on his own two feet, not being mentored by someone and not feeling under the gun to be perfect.

Yet, striving for perfection in his posts was an acquired internal drive handed down to him by Dr. Amos Wilson. In medical school, the once "doddering, old coot" became the icon of what Thomas Chiffelle strived to be. He constantly heard the old pathologist's words, *Remember, you are looking at each post-mortem examination objectively, as an extension of your knife. Yours is not to wonder the etiology of the deceased's fate. Yours is to document what you see and how the person died. In cases of murder, let the police, attorneys, and judges figure out the rest. With pretty girls on the table, keep your hormones on the other side of the door; they are just dead pretty girls. With babies, put your feelings aside—they are just small versions of the adult body.*

Thomas had autopsied several babies during his residency, but the one from today somehow seemed to captivate him. The baby's name was Cynthia Hubbard. She was thirteen days old. She had died at 5:07 that morning. The autopsy was performed at 1:30 p.m. All the way through, he thought, *Keep it clinical.* He sat down and reviewed the typing that he had started an hour ago. The baby had developed well in her short life and was well-nourished. She had perfect skin, a slightly distended abdomen, and equal pupils. She was, essentially, an apparently normal infant. He turned back to his typing and began the section known as "Gross and Microscopic Evaluation." The girl's organs in her thoracic and peritoneal cavities were in great shape. There were no gross lesions or abnormalities. Under the microscope, he noted some problem areas:

Heart—considerable edema of the myocardium with widening of the interstices and one small focal hemorrhage; lungs—extreme congestion with pink, acellular edema fluid filling the alveolar spaces; adrenals—marked congestion of the wide reticular zone with early atrophy and many necrotic cells; ovaries—many congested vessels and several follicular cysts lined with granulose cells; bone marrow—scattered large number of eosinophilic myelocytes; thymus—presence of clusters of eosinophilic leucocytes in the wall and surrounding venous channels.

The only major source of concern in the baby's thoracic cavity was her liver. He typed:

In the center of the right lobe near the bilus of the liver is a small tear in the liver substance forming a small space loosely filled with fresh blood. Microscopic—The conspicuous feature is the presence of multiple small and large tears in the liver. The ragged, irregular lining is heavily infiltrated with neutrophilic and eosinophilic leucocytes. In two places, the hemorrhage has extended and dissected around the large venous channel thereby separating it from the surrounding liver substance.

He stopped typing to consider how the baby got the tears in her liver and then shook his thoughts away as he focused on the area of her body that was the source of her demise—her head.

He remembered when he examined the baby's head that he had noted how the fontanelles bulged. He knew from Dr. Olmsted's report at Grace New Haven hospital that the girl's lumbar puncture had been bloody, indicating cerebral subarachnoid hemorrhage. When Thomas removed Cynthia's skull and underlying membrane, he wasn't prepared for what he saw. The sight took him by surprise as he cut the firm, bulging dural membrane and quietly muttered, "Son of a bitch," as copious blood mixed with some brain matter poured out into the top part of her open skull and onto the table. The mostly unclotted blood that had remained on the surface of the brain had pooled bilaterally. He stared and wondered what the hell had made this mess and then again quickly shook these thoughts away and prepared for the microscopic view.

Microscopic—There is considerable recent hemorrhage underneath the pial membrane and lining the ventricular cavities. The parenchyma is congested, edematous, spongy, and torn. Many small and large perivascular hemorrhages are seen. The ganglion cells are pyknotic and shrunken. Many have disappeared. In the cerebellar cortex, blood cells line the surface, and small hemorrhages are seen in the parenchyma.

Thomas then removed Cynthia's eyes and carefully studied the underlying optic nerve. He noted:

Microscopic—Optic Nerve—There is congestion and edema of the nerve, but otherwise no significant changes in the fiber tracts. There is considerable recent hemorrhage surrounding the optic nerve in the perineural connective tissue. Retina—There is extensive hemorrhage throughout most of the inner fiber layer of the retina and scattered recent hemorrhages in the inner nuclear layer.

Thomas stopped typing. He pulled the final sheet from the typewriter and studied what he had created.

"Autopsy Number 8023," he said.

11:30 p.m.
June 24, 1948
Dr. Chiffelle's Home
New Haven, Connecticut

Thomas Chiffelle couldn't sleep. He tossed his down pillow about as lightly as he could so as not to wake his wife. He reflected on his day, and the one question that had dogged him during his working hours persisted to follow him to his sleeping hours. It was as if the question was challenging him. He felt it call, "Thomas, how could this be?" A night specter indeed! He finally turned and asked, "Honey, I'm sorry, can I talk with you, please?"

A sleepy voice in the dark responded quietly, "Yes, dear, of course."

"Well, I know I'm not supposed to let autopsies affect me, but the one from today bothers me."

Thomas's wife turned to him, her eyes blinking gently in the moonlight streaming in through the bedroom window. "Tell me."

Thomas propped himself up on both arms as he lay on his stomach. He began, "It was a baby. She was only thirteen days old."

His wife moaned in response. "Those cases must be extra hard."

Thomas said, "Well, they aren't supposed to be. Each case, I usually look at objectively. It isn't for me to say why they died, just how. But this tiny girl, who looked perfect on the outside, had massive internal bleeding.

There was no trauma that was reported to me. So, I listed the cause of death as subarachnoid hemorrhage due to congenital abnormality."

"In lay terms, that means what?"

"It means bleeding in a certain area of the brain because of a structural weakness she was born with."

"Okay, what's wrong with that?"

"Well, there was bleeding in other places and abnormal swelling too. It was the swelling of her brain that did her in. I found a lot of cells called neutrophilic and eosinophilic leucocytes. These are found in people who are fighting off an infection, such as a cold, or who are responding to trauma. So, the baby has a bug of some kind, and her body is defending itself when she dies. Her liver had a tear in it. Livers just don't tear, even baby livers. Her heart was congested as well as her lungs, adrenal glands, and little ovaries."

"You looked at her ovaries?"

"Of course, it's one of the standard areas of the female anatomy that is part of the autopsy. She would have been a healthy birthing mother one day."

"That's sad."

Thomas paused to look at the lines in his pillow. He slowly continued. "There was even bleeding behind her eyes." There was another silent moment as Thomas turned toward his wife's upward gaze. "Maybe it was all the pressure she had in her head that was the cause of the bleeding."

His wife gently touched his arm and asked, "What is it that is really bothering you about this girl?"

Thomas looked down again at his pillow. "I think it's because it looks like a truck hit her inside her tiny body, and I made my report to Dr. Olmsted, the girl's pediatrician, that she was born with a weak brain. The family, I guess, had a practical nurse in their home, and she was the one that was caring for her when the problems started. Maybe she dropped her accidentally or something. I mentioned something to Olmsted about these concerns, but there is nothing to do about it. He read my report and is going to speak with the girl's parents tomorrow."

Thomas's wife guided his head with her hand and gave him a tender kiss. "Sounds to me as though you did your job."

"Yes, I did, but ... never mind. Anyway, thanks for listening to me. Good night."

"Anytime you need me. Good night."

Chiffelle turned back toward the window and hugged his pillow. The moonlight streaming in didn't bother him. His eyes were wide open; he was deep in thought. Sleep came to him two hours later.

June 25, 1948
Dr. Olmsted's Office
New Haven, Connecticut

Richard Olmsted sipped on his first cup of morning coffee while perusing some patient charts. A knock on the door brought forth his nurse's voice. "Dr. Olmsted, the Hubbards are here to see you."

"Okay, send them in," he replied, and he gulped down a few more drinks of his lukewarm black coffee.

His brow furrowed slightly as he prepared for the Hubbards' entrance. He didn't like to give news like this but had prepared for this discussion after talking with Chiffelle yesterday.

Allen and Eleanor entered the doctor's office. Allen removed his hat; Eleanor's was pinned to her hair and remained gracefully in place.

"Take a seat, folks," Olmsted began. "How are you doing?"

The Hubbards awkwardly nodded.

The doctor knew he should just dive in and start the conversation without the niceties, so he began. "Mr. and Mrs. Hubbard, the autopsy showed that Cynthia died of a cerebral hemorrhage apparently caused by a congenital weakness. This means she was born with an abnormality at birth. Her brain was just too fragile."

The Hubbards sat and listened, as though wanting more information.

Olmsted looked back at them and then down at the floor. "I'm sorry I don't have more to tell you. It was one of those tragic things."

Allen spoke up. He needed to before he left. "Could something like this have happened from, well, from burping her?"

"No."

Eleanor stood and went over to the young doctor with an outstretched hand. The doctor took her hand and smiled. He said, "I'm really sorry for your loss."

"Thank you."

As the Hubbards left, Richard sank into his large, padded chair. He couldn't tell them about the other internal injuries, how he was now feeling that the baby was dropped or something. He could only talk with a colleague or two about this. He scrawled out a quick message to himself:

"CALL SALINGER."

VIRGINIA BELLE JASPERS
July Twenty-fourth

Activities: Dance Club (1, 2, 3, 4);
Photography Club (2); Glee Club (2);
Traffic Squad (1, 2); Junior Prom
Committee (3); Sports Club (4).

"Ginny" . . . takes life slow and easy . . .
mania for movies . . . "crumb bun" . . .
future baby tender . . . books.

CHAPTER FOUR

Future Baby Tender

June 1942
East Haven High School
East Haven, Connecticut

William and Grace Jaspers beamed as their eighteen-year-old daughter walked across the stage in the auditorium of East Haven High to accept her diploma from the school principal. It was a happy moment. Many of the peculiarities of Virginia Belle Jaspers' sixty-foot walk on the stage that Saturday afternoon went ignored by her parents—such as the sight of her standing between Ed Jarmie, who was five-foot-six, and Evelyn Johnson, who was five-foot-two, as she waited to cross the stage, or the clumping of her shoes as she walked, which echoed in the back of the auditorium, or the wince on the face of Mr. Jennings, the principal, as Virginia clenched his hand in a congratulatory handshake, or the eyes that bulged on poor Mr. Keating, the diminutive assistant principal standing next in line, who was briskly hugged by Virginia.

The Jaspers only chuckled. Other parents around them whispered and chuckled too. It was something the Jaspers had grown used to by now. Virginia had always been a healthy girl. She was large from the start, weighing in at 9 pounds 8 ounces at birth. Her mother had to be "put out" due to the pain of the delivery. Virginia once heard her mother say to someone in a phone conversation, "It was like giving birth to a calf. It was just too much to bear."

As a toddler, Virginia's large size often got the best of her. Walking was difficult for her. She was clumsy and would often teeter even at age three. Her intake of food was great too, but her mother kept up with the demand. At age five, the Jaspers were advised to put Virginia on a diet. "Less servings of milk and bread," the pediatrician recommended. This proposal lasted a few days, as Virginia's mother couldn't withstand Virginia's constant requests for more food.

One place where Virginia excelled was her speech. She was a source of constant chatter. This pattern emerged rapidly by the end of her second year of life. Her parents, when not holding a conversation with her, would typically find her talking with her toys, singing songs to them, and looking in the mirror. When guests visited the Jaspers' home, Virginia relished playing the role of host. People were amused at the merriment of such a little girl. Many felt inwardly sorry for her and would remark on their way home that it was too bad about the way she looked. Virginia was never an attractive girl. To most people, she was not even homely. Her size and her facial features were more male than female. Both her hands and feet were big, as though she was pieced together with the wrong parts.

Though Virginia's excellence in the area of conversation was marked, her intellectual abilities fell far behind. She had struggled from grade school to the time she walked across the East Haven High School stage. Mathematics was a subject that was most difficult for her. Reading was the only area where she transcended her classmates. At home, she read for hours on end. At dinnertime, when her mother would call to her room, she would reply, "Just one moment, I'm almost finished with this chapter." Her parents would typically find her asleep in her darkened room with her flashlight glowing under the covers of her bed. When in school, Virginia was the first to raise her hand when the class was asked to give oral book reports. Both boys and girls would roll their eyes at the sight of the little giantess with glasses standing in the front of the room swaying back and forth while telling the story of Johnny Appleseed or Rip Van Winkle.

Verbal harassment from her peers began early. Names like "horse" and "elephant" were cast her way almost daily toward the latter part of elementary school. In fourth grade, after several repeated days of pestering from classmates, she ran home crying.

"What's wrong, dear?" her mother asked her.

Virginia blubbered out, "The children are just awful. They tell me I'm ugly and call me names. I can't go to school again."

Her mother held her in her lap and let her cry for a while. She soon had Virginia blow her nose and wash the tears from her face.

"Now, dear, let's talk with your father when he gets home from work. In the meantime, I think you should ignore the other children. As Grandma Jaspers was fond of saying, 'When you feel the lip start to sag, stiffen it up with a smile.' Doing something like that and not allowing the others to bother you will set them straight."

When William Jaspers heard of the harassment, he went to the school principal the next day. He simply said to the woman, "I want this problem to end." The problem was rectified by the principal coming to Virginia's class and lecturing about there being hell to pay if anyone was caught bothering Virginia, or any other student, again. Similar incidents involving Virginia never arose in that school again.

When she was in middle school, a new school, the harassment returned. This time, there was a physical altercation. It was late fall, and for much of the new school season, Virginia had been taunted by a circle of boys. Several times a week, after school, her eccentricities seemed to draw them to call her cruel names. Though inwardly, Virginia's heart would pound readily at the sight of the boys approaching her, she remained nonplussed outwardly. She would smile bravely and walk head up and straight toward the direction of home. She'd tell herself, "Mother would be proud!"

One day, a small boy from the circle moved quickly toward Virginia to begin his insults when he surprisingly pushed Virginia from the back. Her books scattered aimlessly, her body lumbered forward, and she collapsed to the ground. The boy stared at her, feeling a mix of disbelief at what he had accomplished and pride. Virginia's dress had flown up to her thighs on impact and the boy said, "Elephant legs, too!" The circle cackled with glee, not noticing Virginia's expression transform into one of rage. No one expected her to move so quickly. The boy's neck was between Virginia's hands in an instant. It was as though she was encircling a Coke bottle. She squeezed intensely and slowly. Her anger had built rapidly, and she soon had the boy on the asphalt ground. Virginia sat on the boy's small hips, her weight crushing his equally small penis. His eyes bulged. He tried to speak, but nothing came forth.

The shaking began almost immediately. Virginia's hands were still around the boy's neck as she quickly began shaking him violently. The back of his head smacked the asphalt as Virginia shouted, "Don't ... ever ... call ... me ... a ... damn ... name ... again." The other boys watched in horror. They couldn't move, or dared not to, for fear of this monster-come-to-life turning on one of them. They watched as Virginia slowly extracted herself from the boy's seemingly broken frame, collected her things, and walked away sobbing. The back of the small boy's head was bleeding, and his eyes fluttered upward several times before he too began to cry. His companions helped him to his feet, and he wobbled back in the direction of the school building to get some help. He would be out the rest of the week with a slight concussion, though not enough to hospitalize him, according to the doctor who examined him at home that evening.

Virginia told her parents about the calamity at school, and later that day, William Jaspers was on the phone with the school principal to explain the abuse his daughter had been put through and to insist that it stop.

The principal responded, "I was going to call you this evening. Do you know that your daughter almost put a boy in the hospital? That could be grounds for dismissal."

Jaspers chuckled and remained even-keel about the incident. He said, "I realize the boy was hurt. Sounds like he deserved it from the way that he and his punk friends have been harassing Virginia. Any court of law in the country would justify this act as self-defense. He pushed her down for God's sake! Don't threaten us with dismissal. Stop the harassment of my daughter, or you'll be looking for work."

The principal knew that Jaspers was in cahoots with many school board members. He responded, "Yes, sir. I'm sorry for the trouble Virginia has been having. It won't happen again." A click of the phone on the other end closed the conversation.

High school brought no problems for Virginia. Teens were compliant with teachers for the most part, families were stable, and the country was not yet in the throes of a world war. The young girl's stature made her appear much older than she was. At fourteen, she matched several of her male peers in height; two years later, she towered over most of the boys and reached her peak height of six feet. Her giddiness was perpetual and most of the children in her class accepted Virginia as she was—an anomaly. Kids who were lifelong members of the community quickly brought any new students at East Haven High up to speed.

"Stay away from her, and don't tease her. She killed a kid in middle school, and her old man paid hush money to make it go away," was one of the tall tales that kept some children from even getting close to Virginia.

In ninth grade, Virginia joined the dance club. Many of her peers snickered when they saw her clump through the doorway of the theater room the day of the first meeting. Males who were paired with her either groaned or rolled their eyes. Two of the boys quit in fear of being coupled with Virginia. Yet, this was an area where she actually excelled; she continued to dance throughout her high school stay. Sometimes, she would practice her dance steps at home with her father or younger sister. They both enjoyed this time with Virginia and tolerated her occasional missteps and laughter in good fun.

On weekends, Virginia sought out babysitting jobs. The act of caring for children seemed natural for Virginia. As a four-year-old, she would push dolls all about the neighborhood in a miniature-sized carriage that her father had bought for her soon after the birth of her younger sister Betty. Jaspers had not wanted his daughter to be left out in the flurry of caretaking that accompanied a new baby. Virginia seemed very comfortable with the new role. Visitors to the Jaspers' home would grin widely at the sight of this oversized young girl talking to and caring for a raggedy doll. As she got older, the caretaking responsibilities turned profitable. For Virginia, a quarter or fifty cents here and there added up and made for great spending money. Much of her income was used on trips to the downtown ice cream parlor or picture show.

In her teens, Virginia would sometimes stay overnight at the houses of her "clients," as she called them. She had read a story in her mother's *Good Housekeeping* about a woman from Hartford, not seventy miles away, who had a baby tender service for new parents. This woman would typically stay several weeks in her clients' homes while performing the hands-on duties of a caretaker. The magazine went on to say that such services were springing up throughout the country, and training was available in certain states. In Connecticut, the training center happened to be in West Hartford at a place called St. Agnes Home. The piece didn't reveal the details of the program, but Virginia surreptitiously clipped the article from her mother's magazine and tucked it away in her already-bulging keepsakes binder that she kept under her bed.

Openly, Virginia exclaimed, "Wow, what a great job! Virginia Jaspers—baby tender. That's what I'll be after I graduate!"

Throughout the summer of her seventeenth year, Virginia continued to babysit in the East Haven vicinity, keeping a close record of her contacts as prompted by her father. She did not share her occupational aspirations with her family until just after the school year started. She had written to St. Agnes Home, and one of the Sisters of Mercy, who ran the home, wrote back and detailed the baby nurse program that had been established there. Virginia was so excited that at dinner on the night she received the information about St. Agnes, she squirmed noticeably in her chair.

"Virginia Jaspers, why are you dancing about?" asked her mother. Betty, sitting across from her, snickered into her hands.

"Yes, Ginny, what's going on?" her father pushed.

"Oh, Mom, Dad, Betty, I, well, I ..."

"Go on," came her parents' reply.

"I want to go to a baby nursing program at St. Agnes Home in West Hartford next summer after I graduate. I love children, and this will give me the chance to establish myself as my own business." She said the last sentence exactly as she had memorized it from the *Good Housekeeeping* article.

This made William Jaspers chuckle. "Own business, huh?"

Virginia's mother seemed a bit uncertain. She said, "Tell me more."

Virginia went on to describe more of the details of the eighteen-month program. William glanced over at his wife at the opposite end of the table. She had a concerned look on her face.

"Honey, what are you thinking?"

Virginia's mother's eyes glanced quickly from the salt and pepper shakers to her daughter and said, "Well, dear, you haven't had a lot of experience with young infants, so maybe this would be a good thing for you."

The Jaspers knew that college was out of the question. They believed that their elder daughter would not be the most erudite of their children and had not been sure what life held for Virginia after high school.

"Anything that you decide upon is fine for us, Ginny," said Virginia's father.

The large girl now beamed in her chair, looking off toward the ceiling while the rest of her family returned to their meal. She pictured herself strolling down Main Street, East Haven, or even New Haven, pushing a carriage, wearing the latest fashions, humming a tune. Oh! She couldn't wait for that day. It would be hers. It would be.

September 1942
West Hartford, Connecticut

Virginia Jaspers settled nicely into her dormitory room at St. Agnes Home for Unwed Mothers. She would not have a roommate. She would go to classes daily with ten other girls who were there for the eighteen-month training. She would visit her family on holidays.

After putting her sheets and blanket on her bed, she poofed her pillow and plopped down on the firm mattress. She closed her eyes to nap, but before she drifted off, she reached her large hand down slowly to the floor to grasp a book. After she searched blindly for thirty seconds, her thumb grazed the corner of the object of her search—her high school yearbook.

She slowly raised the book to her belly and turned open the pages. The newness of the paper and ink wafted into her nostrils. She flipped quickly through the yearbook and soon found her picture surrounded by her peers: Ed Jarmie, Ruth Judge, Evelyn Keyes, and Rita Kelly. *How beautiful I look*, thought Virginia.

The feeling that a new yearbook brought was indescribable. It was a book that one had to look at again and again. She read over her senior statement. She was pleased. It noted her participation in dance club and gave a list of her hobbies that she was involved in during high school, but the thing that she was most proud of was listed next to last: "Future Baby Tender."

Comforted, she carefully laid her book down on the floor, so as not to harm it, closed her eyes, and drifted toward slumber. There were no sounds to her dreams, no crying, just Virginia holding babies and laughing in the brilliant sunshine.

CHAPTER FIVE

"Why Is She Sending Us These Things?"

December 1950
Guilford, Connecticut

The wind outside was picking up, and Allen Hubbard shivered slightly as he watched the new snow wisp about the ground. His perch was in the library inside his home. It was 1:30 a.m. The baby was back to sleep, as was Eleanor. It was quiet in their house. Though he had to get up for work in five hours, Allen's mind buzzed. He knew why. He had a feeling he couldn't shake, and the accompanying thoughts were horrifying at times. He kept these to himself; he couldn't share these with Eleanor. After all, he was just being irrational. Why worry her with his crazy thoughts? Still, he was nervous—nervous about tomorrow. She's coming back … those hands … that pounding … the baby's cry. Allen grabbed the sides of his head as if to tear the inner voices away. He audibly uttered, "It will be okay; let it go." He turned slowly from the frosted window and walked quietly back to his bedroom. The uneasiness lingered, but he knew sleep was near to calm him, if only for the time being.

Virginia Jaspers' reentrance into the Hubbards' home was not as grand as the first time. The baby nurse seemed a bit hesitant to Eleanor when she arrived sharply at 10:00 a.m. the next morning, almost as though she was attending a funeral home viewing. Virginia's handshake, which nearly enveloped Eleanor's petite hand, was almost limp.

"Where's Mr. Hubbard?" asked Virginia as she stepped onto the hallway rug.

"Why, Virginia, he's at work. It's Wednesday."

Virginia tittered behind the hand that was quickly placed over her mouth. "That's right, I'm so sorry. Well, then, where's the baby?"

Eleanor led Virginia into the living room where Stephen lay sleeping in his bassinet. He was one month old.

"Oh, he is a darling," commented Virginia more confidently. "Has Mr. Hubbard been playing football with him yet?" Virginia cackled loudly, which caused little Stephen to stir, though he did not cry. He quickly settled into slumber once again.

"I'm sorry. I'm just teasing," Virginia said, still chuckling uncontrollably.

Eleanor looked at her and smiled. "I know you are, dear. Let's go into the kitchen so we won't bother the baby."

Allen arrived home promptly at 5:20 p.m. He was extremely tired from being awake so much last night with his thoughts. Beyond that, he felt slightly more confident with the decision to have Virginia back into their home for their new baby. The decision was ultimately his, though Eleanor had initiated the idea. She could use a break and a helping hand with Stephen, and Eleanor thought that using Virginia Jaspers again would make her feel better after the initial tragedy. "Why, how would you feel, Allen, if you were the nurse at someone's home and the baby just died? You'd feel terrible. I think this is something we owe her."

Allen reflected on those words as he hung his black hat on the worn hat rack in the foyer of their home. He remembered his hesitancy, which he still felt, about bringing Virginia back. He …

Virginia clomped from the living room into the hallway where Allen stood lost in his thoughts. She was holding Stephen, giving the hungry boy a bottle.

"Oh!" came from her mouth. Her eyes were immediately averted to the floor and then came back again to Allen's face. His smile showed that all was okay.

"I thought I heard someone come in the house," Virginia said, smiling now too.

"Welcome back, Virginia."

The transition for Virginia was, as it turned out, an emotionally easy one. It was due, in large part, to the kindness of the Hubbards. Another couple might not have been so trusting and forgiving. But Allen and Eleanor took an easier approach toward life and enjoyed their new son Stephen and the quirkiness that the baby nurse brought along with her.

The months passed quickly; Virginia continued to eat excessively, interacted gaily with the Hubbard guests, and lavished young Stephen with toys. She frequently took pictures of him with the new Kodak she had bought with her own savings.

"Don't you just love photos?" she inquired of Allen and Eleanor, who were huddled over a card table working diligently on a puzzle one night. "It's just so exciting waiting for the pictures to arrive at the pharmacy. I can hardly stand it!"

The two nodded in agreement and smiled, not looking up from their focal point. Virginia sat on the davenport clumsily flipping through her latest batch of scalloped prints, her eyes wide. Stephen played happily in the thinly netted playpen at Virginia's feet. The baby would often try to pat the feet of his nurse, especially when Virginia tapped her feet in excitement at one of the photographs she especially liked.

"I hear that Troy Donohue will be making a guest appearance at the Strand Theatre this weekend. I am going to be one of the first in line, and you can bet that I'll have my Kodak close by. He is so darn dreamy!" (Troy Donohue never did make it to the Strand, though Virginia stood outside the theater that rainy Saturday night, camera in hand, for two hours until she realized that the famous actor must have had another engagement or he came down with a cold or something.)

The subject of Cynthia's death never resurfaced during the time that Virginia cared for Stephen, though it was obvious to all three adults in the home that the subject was one that lingered nearby, like a silent dark specter hovering overhead.

One night, when he heard Stephen crying, Allen called out from the kitchen, "Virginia, would you see what Cynthia needs?"

There was silence in response.

"Virginia?"

Allen poked his head around the entryway of the kitchen, just as Virginia was slowly moving in his direction. The two almost collided and visibly lurched backward with uncomfortable suddenness.

He looked quizzically at the baby nurse. "What?" he asked.

Virginia's eyes darted to the floor, a safe haven for her soul lay there, somewhere. Her eyes rapidly filled with tears. "You … you said … Cyn … thia," she managed in a whisper.

Allen started to quietly protest, "I …" But then he sank back against the kitchen wall with noticeable emotion on his face.

"Oh, God, Virginia, I'm sorry. I guess she has been on my mind recently."

"It's fine, Mr. Hubbard. I think about her all the time as well."

Allen walked by Virginia slowly on his exit from the kitchen. His eyes were sad. He lifted up his right hand slowly to gently console the large woman, but he instead brought his hands together to console himself. Virginia didn't notice the gesture on Allen's part, as she was lost in her own world of remembering, and she continued to stare at the floor—her sanctuary.

November 1951
Guilford, Connecticut

On the day that Stephen turned a year old, Allen and Eleanor received several birthday cards and small gifts in the mail. The Hubbards decided to celebrate the occasion on a small scale and have festivities with just the three of them. Eleanor baked a miniature chocolate cake for Stephen and had purchased a pint of vanilla ice cream from the market. She loved the thought of Stephen digging into his birthday cake and squealing with delight at the joy of getting messy with something delicious. Eleanor would savor that moment when it arrived sometime after dinner that evening.

Allen was looking forward to coming home to be with his family, as he had had a particularly difficult day on the job at the New Haven airport. During the drive home, he tried to shake off the slight row he had had with one of the chief mechanics that afternoon. Allen hated conflict, but when it was necessary, he wouldn't back down from the beliefs that he held.

"I don't ask for much," he muttered aloud while waiting at a stoplight. He continued speaking while he accelerated after the light turned green. "I told him there was a limit to the parts that we order, and it's like he doesn't hear me."

Allen cut the conversation off short, because he knew that such rambling was going nowhere and only creating more stress for himself.

He soon glided smoothly into his driveway with his car. He looked up after shutting off the engine to see Eleanor in the front window holding Stephen. He smiled greatly in response to Eleanor flapping the baby's arm in a waving motion. Allen could almost hear his son screeching with innocent delight. All of the day's problems melted from Allen's heart as he took in the scene. Glowing inside, he quickly stepped from the car and jogged to the front door.

Dinner was delicious. Stephen had squeezed mashed potatoes between his fingers before putting the off-white lumps into his mouth.

Eleanor grinned and said, "Just think what he will do with the cake!"

Allen chuckled. "Were there many pieces of mail today for our birthday boy?"

Eleanor put down her napkin and walked into the living room where the packages and letters lay in a neat stack. She brought them all to the table and set them down in front of Stephen. Effortlessly, she grabbed a washcloth that was kept at the table for all meals and wiped the baby's hands and mouth.

"I think we can open the cards, but let's let Stephen open the packages."

Allen moved the tray away from the boy and pulled his highchair closer to the table.

"Don't you think he's a little young for opening presents?"

"Let's see."

Stephen pulled on a big corner of brown paper that his father had ripped slightly for him and shook it back and forth carefully. He smiled at the newness of the game. Allen reached over to help him finish the project, and a white card fell to the floor. Allen picked the card up and read aloud:

With Love to Stephen, Your Friend Ginny

"Ummm," said Allen. Inside was a baby doll, dressed in a pink gown. The baby's eyes stared forward blankly. Stephen reached out and smacked the baby's forehead three times.

"No, no," cautioned his father. "Be nice to the baby."

Eleanor laughed. "Allen, he's too young to know what he's doing."

"Well, you're never too young to start knowing right from wrong," was his response.

Both thought the doll was an odd gift, although neither said a word. Eleanor then opened the card from Virginia. She shared it with Allen, who looked at it questioningly.

"Why is she sending us these things?" he asked sternly.

Eleanor gently touched the back of Allen's hand. The gesture was enough to cause Allen to lift his head up from looking at the glassy-eyed doll. She smiled and said, "Allen, Virginia will probably never have children, so it's as though she is taking on her clients' as her own. These presents are a symbol of connection that she desperately needs in her life."

Allen smiled lightly and nodded. He looked back at the doll and set it down in the torn brown paper on the floor. Stephen laughed joyfully and kicked his feet forward.

"Look's like you want some more presents, partner," his father said to him. Allen reached across the table for the next package and began the process of opening another magical object that would bring countless hours of joy to his son's heart.

CHAPTER SIX

"I Just Love What I Do!"

June 1949
East Haven, Connecticut

Jane Jaspers brushed the front walk furiously to and fro with the green-handled broom. The silly song "Mairzy Doats" played through her head, and she found herself whistling along. She'd heard it this morning emanating from the radio in Ginny's room. That was before her daughter left—off to another "client" as Virginia loved to announce. She would be there two weeks. It would be different this time, because the baby's parents would be gone. Thinking about this, Jane stopped her broom in mid-sweep, for only a brief interval. *How could a newborn's parents up and take off like that?* she queried in her mind. That was Jane's main concern, not that Virginia couldn't handle the responsibility, but why would these people leave their baby to go on a trip to Acapulco? *What kind of world are we living in?*

Her thoughts continued to zip through her brain with a flash here and there of a baby lying prone, cold as steel, quiet, at peace … Jane muttered aloud, "Silly thoughts," refocused her attention, and quickly returned to the job of cleaning the front walk. *What happened had passed—a terrible thing for the Hubbards and for Virginia,* her thoughts concluded.

She expected Senators Hanson and Altmont to come home with her husband William any time now. A week-long senatorial session was just finishing in Hartford, and Jane was very excited to play host to these important gentlemen. Tonight would be the tenth time since William had begun his political pursuit in 1947 that she had held a dinner for others in public office. As she walked back through the front door of the house, she paused to clip the broom on the holder that William had made for her in the breezeway. She smiled as she brushed off the fringe of her skirt, and she stopped to check her hair in the living room mirror.

Jane felt good about her life. She had two grown daughters still at home, a husband who had been a Connecticut politician for over two years, a nice house in a nice town—what more could a woman ask for?

She checked on her "famous roast," as William once deemed it. She turned the oven to warm and straightened up. "Ready," she announced aloud to the quiet house. Ten seconds later, she heard her husband's car pull into the driveway. Life was good.

July 1949
East Haven, Connecticut

"Betty, what the hell is this thing doing on the kitchen table?" called the booming voice of William Jaspers. The five-foot-eleven-inch man with the barrel chest stomped over to the bottom of the stairway in the living room leading up to the second-floor bedrooms.

"Betty!"

"Yes, Daddy?" came the reply. Betty, Virginia's nineteen-year-old sister, galloped down the hallway and down the stairs like a filly coming out of a barn for the first time.

"Yes, Daddy?" she repeated as she stood composed in front of her father.

"That horn in the middle of the kitchen table!"

"Oh, Daddy, you silly thing! That is my cheerleading megaphone. I left it there for two seconds while I changed into my uniform. And it will disappear in a flash 'cause I'm off to practice right now."

With that, the youngest Jaspers skipped over to the kitchen table, grabbed the megaphone in one hand, picked up a cinnamon donut from the plate next to it with the other hand, and headed toward the front door. As she passed by her father, Betty stood briefly on her tiptoes and pecked him on the cheek. She waved behind her as she headed out the front door. William Jaspers had to smile. He hadn't been angry, and his daughter knew it.

Betty was everything that her older sister Virginia wasn't. She was beautiful, slender, graceful, intelligent, and outgoing. She was looking forward to her sophomore year at college. Betty's admission into the school the year before was a proud moment for the Jaspers. She had gotten into the school on her own merit, though her father did know several people in the admissions department. At the end of her freshman year, Betty was eligible to try out for the cheerleading team, to which she was accepted as a member after the first round.

To her father, it seemed like Betty was always gone. *She is nineteen, going on twenty. I guess she needs to lead her own life*, the elder Jaspers contemplated. His family felt so disjointed these days. Virginia had her own work, and Betty had her college work and activities. This was exactly the arrangement that William thought about when his children were youngsters, the ducklings leaving the nest and all that. But now, it felt different from how he had anticipated it would be. It was almost too quiet, although he believed that the quiet was something he would get used to. Retirement was right around the corner, and he looked forward to a peaceful remainder of his life.

William Jaspers did insist on one thing when it came to family stability: Sunday dinner with all family members present around the dining room table. He remembered one Sunday a few months ago, Betty said she wanted to be excused from dinner, as some of her friends were gathering for a picnic lunch at the park in Hamlin. Jaspers put his foot down and said, "Betty, as long as you are living in this house, you will be here for Sunday dinner."

There were no "buts" in response; Betty knew better. It didn't matter if she was nineteen; she was still a member of the Jaspers' household. Betty was too familiar with the demeanor of her father when he was resolute. This characteristic was one of the things that made him an effective state senator. When he was steadfast with an issue, he held firm and swayed other politicians to join rank.

William Jaspers had had what he believed to be a "well-balanced" political career over the past four years. He had been a member of the Connecticut House of Representatives in 1947, and he then successfully became a member of the Connecticut Senate for the 1949 term. As a Republican, he held staunchly to the issues that he thought mattered most to the voters who elected him to office. He remembered that promise he had made to the people of the state of Connecticut each time a policy came up for a vote. Jaspers often stood at the center podium of the state capital building pounding his fist in disagreement or raising his hands high like a preacher when he wanted a bill of his passed.

In 1947, during his term in the house, he served on the Forfeited Rights Committee and the Public Utilities Committee. It was the latter of the two committees that mattered most to him. Technology had been booming around him since World War II had ended. It was hard to keep up with all the proposals on the house floor that focused on what monies would be designated for which utilities and other special projects that were emerging throughout the state. Even though he was a "junior" (what the elders of the house called neophyte representatives), he was also the clerk of the Public Utilities Committee.

In the late summer of 1948, Jaspers began his campaign for state senator. He felt the need to cross over to the senate, because he felt as if he could have more influence on how his interests would fare with his constituents. He won the state senate seat easily from "that horse's ass Democrat" Stevens.

Being a state senator gave William Jaspers more poise among his political peers. On the streets of East Haven, when he would walk the family pet terrier, Susie, townspeople would wave to him and say, "Hey, Senator Jaspers!" He felt proud, as did his wife and daughters.

William Jaspers would serve two terms as a Connecticut state senator. In his first term, Jaspers served on the Aviation and Labor Committees and the Public Welfare and Humane Institutions Committee. Eight years later, Jaspers' involvement with public welfare would be a glaring irony due to the fact that his daughter would ultimately be identified as a *threat* to child welfare.

CHAPTER SEVEN

"We Have Some Bad News to Share"

"We Have Some Bad News to Share"

December 1951
New Haven, Connecticut

Joan Brainerd looked out at the snow falling steadily from the window of her medium-sized home on Prospect Street in New Haven. Here it was, almost a week after Thanksgiving, and tonight was the first snow. Just an hour ago, she had noticed a flake or two flitting past her kitchen window. Now, the snow had picked up significantly. She tried not to worry about Willard. She expected him at 7:00 p.m., and she saw that the grandfather clock showed the time as 7:15 p.m. The slight twinge of nervousness that started to envelope her caused her to hum aloud. Humming always helped. Whether it was pre-concert jitters or another sort of uneasiness, a happy tune worked wonders.

"Oh, I thought I heard something," a voice said, which broke her pensive silence.

"Yes, Virginia, I was humming one of the songs that I'll be singing in two weeks in New York."

"Oh, okay," stated the large woman, closing the half-opened French door that led to the kitchen and the half-eaten bowl of maple nut ice cream sitting on the table.

Joan's outside stare never wavered, even after her thoughts and tune were interrupted. She looked toward the New York skyline, which was barely visible in the distance. She wondered what the audience would be like and how she would perform. Joan was never one to be filled with angst prior to a performance. Her debut performance at the Yale Bowl last spring was a great success; a thousand or more people had been in attendance. She had learned to keep her nerves under control, so as not to influence the quality of her singing. The Bowl performance was also a boost for her music career. It led to this upcoming engagement in Queens. Handel's *Messiah* was a perfect selection for the Christmas season. As a soloist, she would also earn a healthy compensation for her work and practice. This time in her career was exciting because even though she had returned to music only one day a week, she felt that things were taking off again. It filled her with joy. Yet, standing at the window, her joy was somehow incomplete. Maybe it was because Willard was late, or maybe it was the fact that she would be gone away from Jennifer for the better part of two days. It was a feeling of guilt that she had never experienced before. It was as though she was turning her back on a good friend—something she'd never done before. Yet, this was a different feeling, a deeper one. Far overshadowing …

Joan's intense contemplation was broken by Jennifer's wails, which filled the room. Virginia had her baby cradled in one arm as she trounced over to Joan with a big smile.

"Your turn," the nurse announced, continuing to smile.

Joan looked at her quizzically as if Virginia had just tagged her in a game of hide and seek.

Virginia's eyebrows arced downward as she said, "Don't you remember? You said you wanted to feed the baby next."

To Virginia, it *was* a game, Joan subconsciously realized. This made her feel somewhat uneasy.

"Yes, of course, Virginia, I'd well forgotten."

The smile returned to the large woman's face as she dutifully handed Jennifer over to her mother. Joan headed to the kitchen for the bottle that Virginia had left on the stove. The water in the pot was steaming busily, though not yet boiling. "Should be just right," Joan heard in the background. Yes, that was one thing that Virginia did do quite well, heating a bottle to the right temperature.

"Are you going to add the cereal?" Virginia inquired.

Joan turned the stove's left knob slowly to the right and watched the flame extinguish. Virginia's question confused her for a moment, and then she remembered that earlier in the day, the two had discussed adding powdered cereal to Jennifer's nighttime bottle. Virginia had been elated sharing this "new technique" that she had recently learned from a peer infant nurse. Joan felt that it was too early for Jennifer to begin eating any kind of solids and had even confirmed this with Dr. Stilson when she telephoned his office several hours ago.

"No, I think not, Virginia. I checked with Dr. Stilson today, and he said that we should give Jennifer a few more weeks before we introduce cereal into her formula."

"Okaaay," answered the nurse, slowly dragging out the simple reply. She was frowning when Joan passed her on the way to the living room.

"Thank you for thinking of it, though."

Joan liked having Virginia's help in the home, but she was increasingly concerned about Virginia's fluctuating moods. Joan had called another woman who had used Virginia as a nurse as a reference. Virginia was often melancholy and even cried on the job at times. Joan wondered why she was so very sad. Whenever she noticed Virginia crying, her inquiries always elicited the same answer, "I don't know, just a low day, I guess." Joan thought, *I wonder why someone like her would take up work going into a home with people who were at their happiest? It was as if she didn't have a life of her own.*

Joan found a comfortable spot on the davenport back in the living room to feed her still-crying and hungry daughter. Feeding her baby allowed Joan to look deeply into the little girl's bright-blue eyes and experience the magic that happens for that moment. Joan thought of a phrase she had learned from an old teacher about how the eyes are the windows of the soul. *What a precious little soul you are turning out to be,* thought Joan.

August 1951
New Haven, Connecticut

The sound of a newborn crying woke Joan Brainerd up from a horrible nightmare. *My God, how tragic. I'm awake. I'm safe. My baby is with me.* Thoughts raced through Joan's head as she opened her eyes and sought her bearings in a very strange place.

She propped herself up on her pillow and looked around at the white walls of Grace New Haven Community Hospital. A nurse rapped quickly on her door and moved toward her briskly.

"Well, you *are* awake. How d'ya sleep? Oh, I know that it's not like home, but we try here."

Before Joan had a chance to answer, she lifted her head and looked at the bassinet next to her bed. Her brow suddenly creased as she realized it was empty.

"Where …?" she began to ask and then realized she knew the answer. She didn't have a baby. It was stillborn yesterday after Joan experienced hours of painful contractions and bleeding. The sudden memory of this sent Joan's head reeling back to her pillow.

"I know, hon, it's a tough time for you now. I've been through it too," empathized the nurse.

Joan just lay there and cried. She didn't know what to say or even feel. There was a numbness that covered her like a cold receiving blanket. The nurse filled her water glass, patted her leg, and calmly left the room.

Her thoughts turned to the words that her obstetrician had uttered to her six months ago when he diagnosed a problem. *You are Rh-negative and have a condition known as erythroblastosis,* the doctor relayed. Joan, being the curious type, hastened to learn more. She visited her local library, and through a succession of books and afternoons, she learned that what she had were anti-Rh antibodies that could have fatal effects on a fetus. Her husband, Willard, was not Rh-negative. The obstetrician thought that she shouldn't get too "worked up about it." Joan thought that she'd beaten this medical condition by making it to her eighth month of pregnancy, but when she started spotting yesterday morning, she knew that the incompatible blood exchange had actually won.

She hardly moved from her hospital bed that morning, except to use the bathroom to urinate or change the bulky, bloody pad that soaked itself with Joan's blood every few hours. One time when she hobbled back to bed, she paused to look out her window, which overlooked a copse of trees just past the parking lot six floors below. She noticed that the edges of the trees were turning faintly orange-red. Autumn was near. It was not unusual for this time of year and this area of the country. But seeing the trees brought forth a strange sense of reality. *How can life go on as normal?* she contemplated. She thought about her townhouse where she and Willard lived. Three other women in the townhouses that surrounded theirs were pregnant too. Joan closed her eyes and fell lightly on her mattress. New tears quickly formed. She knew why she cried. These were the tears of envy that her mother had always warned against. In the next several months, all the women would deliver their babies and take them home to warm cribs, happy faces, and enough love to fill a concert hall a thousand times over. Joan was devastated. She lay there and sobbed.

Soon, her husband, Willard, knocked gently on her door. She didn't hear him, and he let himself in since he heard her crying and quickly went to her side. "There, there," he faintly comforted.

"I'm sorry, dear," stammered Joan. "I'm thinking of all the babies that will be around us soon and the fact that we won't have one." Joan continued to cry. Willard calmly took in the moment and gave her some time to grieve.

He was the first to break the lapse in conversation by announcing, "I have some good news."

Joan lifted a handkerchief to her eyes, blinked at her husband, and said, "Whatever do you mean?"

Willard had a habit of jumping in the direction of goodness, rather than wallowing in the sad and dismal. He'd once told her that it was on account of his Jewish upbringing that the world often looked rose-colored to him. It was a trait that made him proud, yet one that Joan felt was unrealistic.

"Darling, I spoke with the doctor today. He said that if we can't have children, that we should adopt. He said it was fine by him."

Joan looked off toward a distant wall and thought. *Fine by him? He didn't just lose a baby, nor is it his decision.* Joan was beginning to understand and dislike the arrogance of many doctors. Yet, she was feeling very maternal. She had experienced pregnancy and all that came with it for months up to this point and was greatly looking forward to being a mother. She looked at Willard and nodded in agreement with the idea. *It won't be the same,* Joan thought, *but maybe I can grow to love a baby that isn't mine.*

"Doctor Parker said that he would stop by your room tomorrow morning at 10:00 to speak with us about the process of adoption. I'll be here at 9:15 to help you pack up your things."

Willard pecked her on the cheek, turned, and left Joan's room. She didn't mind. It was his style. On the surface was where her husband was most comfortable living his life. The conversation had been a bit much for Joan. So much had happened in such a short time. Her eyes gazed out her window and took in the blue August sky. A breeze whipped a solitary leaf up to her level. *Yes, autumn is upon us,* she thought. Nearby, a newborn baby cried.

At 9:30 the next morning, Willard Malkan was in the middle of tidily packing his wife's belongings in their deep brown Samsonite, when there was a hurried knock on the hospital door. Dr. Parker strode into the room, full of energy and caffeine, and said, "Excuse the intrusion on you folks, but I have something very strange going on in my office."

Joan looked at Willard for help in figuring out the doctor's riddle. Willard continued to look at the doctor wide-eyed, as if waiting for a punch line.

Dr. Parker continued, "There is a couple in my office, that if I turn them around from the back, look exactly like you two. He wants to go back to Yale and study some more, and she has to work. She is seven months pregnant, and the baby is due in October. They're Catholic, and they don't intend to keep the baby, so maybe you'd be interested?"

He had relayed this information so quickly that Joan briefly considered asking him to repeat himself.

"Did you hear that, Joan?" Willard asked, now staring wide-eyed at her.

Joan nodded and smiled feebly.

"So, I take it you're interested?" the doctor asked.

"Sure, we are! Right, honey?"

Joan again didn't know what to say. She was very pleased about this opportunity but still had this gnawing emotional pain deep in her soul from her miscarriage. She gulped lightly, smiled past her pride, and said, "It would be wonderful."

The only thing that gave Joan a sense of sanity was her family and friends encouraging her to return to her music. They suggested, "Now that your pregnancy is over, why don't you go back to your music?" Joan didn't take such comments as insensitive; she understood people's intentions. They were hoping to give her suggestions to thrust her back into something she loved, rather than have her sink into the darkness of grief. Even though the people closest to Joan didn't give her much credit, she was emotionally strong and was feeling better each week. The music came back slowly. First, it was humming some classics aloud. Then, she and Willard attended a few recitals. Finally, she accepted some local singing engagements.

September passed by quickly, and in October, the plans for Jennifer's adoption began to take shape. Willard asked Joan one morning about buying clothes and furniture for their new baby.

Joan replied, "I'm hesitant to do too much, Willard, since the mother has three months to decide to keep her child or not." This was in accordance with the adoption laws of the 1950s. Joan had been told that every birth mother had ninety days to reconsider giving up her baby for adoption. Many an adoptive parent became a casualty in the process. Joan had heard of such cases.

"Let's just try to treat it like a little visitor."

Jennifer was born on October 16, and five days later, Joan and Willard met with the Mother Superior of the Sisters of Mercy in Grace New Haven Community Hospital. The office was dark. A shaft of light came through a two-inch space in the blinds. The Mother Superior worked diligently on the Malkans' adoption paperwork. Willard wrote a check, while Joan took in the aura of the office from her large cushioned oak chair. *Too many crucifixes*, she thought.

"And what name should I put down for the baby?" asked the elderly nun.

The couple had discussed this over the past few weeks. Willard liked the name Jennifer as a first name, and Joan chose Leona as a middle name in honor of her beloved granny Leona Tobias. As Willard dictated, the nun transcribed.

"Well ... that should do it just fine. Are there any questions?"

Joan's head was swimming with hundreds of questions, and she felt slightly nervous. Her mind couldn't bring forth any burning issues, so she shook her head from side to side amicably.

"No, I don't think so," answered Willard.

"Well, remember that on December 31, there will be the legal case where the mother will finally decide that she wants the adoption to go through. And then in mid-January, it will become final, since that is ninety days from today. If there are no other questions, then let's bring in your baby," said the Mother Superior as she picked up the handle of what looked like a dinner bell and set it ringing. The couple were both taken aback and jumped a little in their seats. The office door creaked open, and a novice nun dressed in white brought Jennifer right to Joan and placed the baby in her arms.

The Malkans grinned widely as they watched the tiny girl yawn and move her mouth. "She's so small," said Joan.

"You know, folks, the mother never once looked at the child. That is the way we think it should be, you know. Less of a chance for the mother to get heart-tied to the baby."

Joan and Willard seemed to not hear what the Mother Superior was saying. It was truly a miracle that they had the chance to be parents again after such tragedy had entered their lives. They watched their new daughter sleep and thought about all the wonderful times that lay ahead. It seemed that fate was now smiling on them.

Friday, December 14, 1951
Queens, New York

Joan had just finished the first of two performances of Handel's *Messiah* at Queens College auditorium. It was an exhilarating experience with a full choir and orchestra. And she, Joan Brainerd, was the featured soloist. It was truly a dream come true. She must have thanked the conductor Don Victor a hundred times for inviting her to perform.

"Oh, it went very well, dear. Full house. How are things going there?" Joan was tickled as she spoke with her husband on the phone from her room at the nearby hotel.

"Things are fine. Glad all went well."

"Oh, marvelous! How is our dear baby?"

"Fine, too. Ginny has put her down to bed. Why, she played patty-cake with her tonight."

"Oh, what fun!" replied Joan. She missed Jennifer very much, but the thrill of the evening seemed to diminish the urge to have the baby with her.

"I'll be ready for you on Sunday. I'm looking forward to coming home too." It had been planned that Willard would drive down with Virginia and Jennifer on Sunday morning to pick Joan up at the hotel.

"Okay, I love you. Good luck tomorrow. See you bright and early Sunday."

"Bye, dear. I love you too."

Saturday, December 15, 1951
Queens, New York

Joan spent the day resting her voice. She was able to visit some of the sights that she had missed while living in New York studying music right after college in the 1940s. Part of her enjoyed this brief break from

Willard and Jennifer. She believed that the baby was being well cared for, so Joan was able to relax in a way that she hadn't experienced in the two years that she had been married. She was twenty-seven years old, and she wanted a moment for herself, however selfish it seemed.

When the lights faded to half, Joan knew it was time to begin. The orchestra tuned momentarily and applause escalated as conductor Donald Victor strode to his podium. As she stood in the left wing, Joan's heart raced a bit when the curtain opened revealing the oratorio's chorus. She was eager for the performance. As the opening notes crescendoed, Joan and the other soloists walked on stage to their awaiting music stands. The house lights were left to half in order to give the soloists the maximum amount of light to read their music.

As she took her position, Joan noticed a few members of the audience taking their seats. Her eyes went to a trio moving slowly down the left aisle, as if coming toward her. She continued to follow them with her eyes as they sat in the empty reserved front row. Her smile rapidly changed to a frown when she noticed that the three people were Willard, her mother, and her stepfather. Joan's heart picked up a faster beat beyond the pre-concert jitters that she had been experiencing. Her legs felt weak, and her body sweaty. She gazed at Don, who was about to cue her. He noticed the concern in Joan's face and continued to lead and cue. Joan didn't miss a beat, though her first note was somewhat tremulous. As she sang, her concentration was interrupted with thoughts, such as *What the hell is going on? Where is Jennifer? Where is Virginia? Why is my family here?* During a break from singing, Joan looked down at her husband and parents. Curiously, their eyes were not on the stage; instead, they stared at the floor. *They are sad. It must be Grandma Tobias. Something happened to her.* Halfway through the two-hour performance, Joan noticed movement in the right wing. She looked out in the direction of the movement and noticed a policeman standing there looking right at her. Joan closed her eyes and thought, *Something is terribly wrong.*

CHAPTER EIGHT

"Can You Tell Us What Happened?"

December 15-16, 1951
New Haven, Connecticut

Carter Stilson looked at the baby in her crib and looked at his watch. *TOD—7:15 p.m.; cause—aspiration,* he scratched with a dulling pencil on a small notepad that had been buried in his breast coat pocket. He was left alone with her as he turned off her bedroom light and sat down in a rocking chair in the corner of the darkened room. As he slowly rocked, he heard the nurse still whimpering downstairs somewhere. *Mr. Malkan and his in-laws raced out of here about twenty minutes or so ago,* he thought. *Sixty minutes to Queens and sixty minutes back with a police escort, they should be back by 10:00 at the latest.* He then realized that he'd forgotten about the running time of the concert. "Christ," Dr. Stilson said aloud. "What am I doing here?" Willard had asked that he stay with Jennifer until they returned with Joan. "Okay," Stilson said hesitantly. *Okay,* he thought, now rubbing his temples and closing his eyes. Slowly, he moved his circling fingers down to his ear canals. He found the soft holes and pressed his fingers into them just to keep out the Goddamned whimpering downstairs.

Joan rushed backstage immediately after the soloists' final bow and found her husband, her parents, and the police officer standing together.

"What on earth is going on?" asked Joan.

"Ma'am, perhaps we should step over here away from people," said the police officer as many members of the chorus shuffled by, staring at the curious huddle.

Joan was diffident and said, "No, I want to know what is going on. I've been dying inside for the past two hours!"

Willard looked at her with sad eyes and said, "You are not going to believe this. The baby died in the nurse's arms. They are holding the doctor and the nurse and are waiting for us to drive back."

Willard grabbed Joan's hand and started walking toward the stage door. Joan felt sick. *This must be a terrible dream*, she thought. *Oh God, not again. Wake up! Wake up!* She blindly followed her family to the car and was directed to the front seat. Her parents sat in back and Willard trotted to the driver's seat. The police officer turned on his lights and siren in his cruiser, and off they sped toward the throughway.

Willard didn't know his car could go 80 miles per hour. There was silence in the car the whole way back to New Haven. Willard had prefaced the trip as they got in the car by saying, "The doctor will explain everything when you get home." Joan took it to mean, "Don't ask me a thing about what happened."

The police cruiser had turned off its siren on the throughway but kept the flashing lights going. As the cars pulled up to 638 Prospect Street, the passenger door of the Malkans' car was open. Joan jumped out of the vehicle without closing the door and ran into the house. Several firemen from the station across the street were in the living room. Virginia was still crying and was sitting on the davenport where Joan and Jennifer had enjoyed many happy hours. Dr. Stilson was slowly making his way downstairs from the baby's room, his eyes blinking to adjust to the light.

"What happened?" Joan asked as she approached him.

"I am sorry for your loss, Mrs. Malkan. We believe that your baby choked on her cerealed formula."

"Virginia," she said brusquely.

The nurse cowered a bit as if she had been scolded. "I thought we agreed that the cereal was okay."

"Okay, Virginia, just tell me what happened."

Everyone had heard the story before, except for Joan, so the rest just looked away from the nurse as she spoke.

"Well …" started Virginia, blinking and sniffling. "I … I sat down with the baby a few minutes before Mr. Malkan came home. She was awfully hungry and seemed to like the cereal that was in the formula. She sucked away at that bottle like there was no tomorrow." Virginia smiled a bit as if she was reminiscing about times gone by. She then realized how she looked and quickly returned to a sad countenance.

The nurse continued her story. "I tried to burp her well, but it seemed that she was too full to burp. I knew there was a bubble inside. It was no use, so I set her down in her bed and went to make some coffee. I checked on her right after that, and she was choking, and she had some formula on her face. I picked her up to pat her, and I noticed she was kinda blue. I ran to call for help." She then started to cry.

Dr. Stilson picked up where she left off. "The fire department from across the street somehow got the call, and they came right over. She was dead by then. They then called me. Your husband was home by that time."

"I called your mother and stepfather, and they came over," interjected Willard. "I knew that you would want to see Jennifer before she was, you know, taken away. I asked the doctor to wait, while we drove to get you. I also called the police to escort us."

Joan tuned out the rest and went to the stairs leading up to Jennifer's room. She paused at the first step, her hand resting lightly on the banister. She felt pulled to run up to her baby's room, but at the same time, she was very scared about what she might see. Her feet moved cautiously one step at a time. The entire room full of people watched her ascend. When she reached the threshold of Jennifer's room, Joan extended her left arm slowly to the right and touched the light switch. When flipped up, the switch activated a small lamp that sat on a small baby dresser. Joan had originally asked Willard to set it up that way in order not to have harsh overhead lights glare on their daughter as she slept or when she was awakening. Soft lights were the mood of the home.

The dim light went on, and Joan looked over the crib to view her daughter. Her initial thought was that Jennifer looked completely serene. It looked as if there were nothing wrong with her. It was as if Joan was there to wake up this beautiful sleeping baby. There were no marks, no blemishes. Someone must have wiped her face, because it was clear. There was a crusted mix of formula and cereal on her sheets. Joan reached her right hand into the soft bed to touch her daughter. Her hand rested on the girl's chest; it was cool and didn't rise and fall as it should. Joan's hand crept toward her baby's face. The back of her fingers caressed her cheek. *Smoother than silk.* Joan stood for a long while just studying Jennifer, her long eyelashes; her wispy, thin hair; her soft button of a nose. *I want to remember everything about you.* Tears formed in the corners of Joan's eyes and dropped on her baby's sheets. "I love you," she said aloud, as she leaned over and placed her lips on the dead girl's cold mouth for the final time.

She had choked on her cereal. Choked. Cereal. Virginia. Autopsy. What the hell happened? These thoughts raced through Joan's head as she tried to sleep. It was no use. She turned slowly and watched her husband. His head turned every few minutes in fitful sleep. She wondered when they both would be able to rest again. *Such madness. It wasn't fair. Why did this have to happen to us?*

Joan carefully swung her legs around to the floor and sat on the edge of the bed waiting to rise. Glancing at the ticking clock, she knew that a few hours of sleep were all that she could ask for that night. It was 3:30 a.m. She crept downstairs and rested her head on the davenport wishing someone would hold her like she had held Jennifer. She wished that someone would whisper in her ear that everything was all right. Tears formed instead.

Joan reflected on the hours before when the firefighters, Dr. Stilson, Virginia, and her family sat around not saying anything about what happened. But she remembered, just before she went to see Jennifer, that the non-family members had a look in their eyes. It was almost a look of embarrassment—that they too thought something went wrong, that the accident was not an accident. Joan had nothing but a feeling to go on, but she needed to have this thought in order to make sense of what happened—almost to give God an out for allowing this to happen. No, it wasn't an act of God; rather, it was something far deeper and more nefarious. Her thoughts were coupled with the feeling that she didn't want to ruin someone's reputation over a false accusation.

Joan stayed in the living room until she heard the newspaper dully hit the front door at 5:50 a.m. There would be no headlines of her daughter's death. The world would go on as it did yesterday. She and Willard were alone—again.

December 18, 1951
New Haven, Connecticut

An awkward knock on the door startled Joan from her conversation with her mother, who had come for an afternoon tea visit. She immediately knew that it was Virginia and went to retrieve her purse and open the door. Cracking the door halfway, Joan held up Virginia's purse to her.

"Oh…" was the reply.

"I thought that you might be coming by today for it," Joan said blandly.

Virginia's large hand came up and encircled a good portion of the handle. "I mistakenly left it here Saturday night."

"Yes, Virginia."

Joan looked into the nurse's blue eyes; Virginia, in return, evaded any personal connection. Joan had never seen her so sullen. A quick image of a bulldog with glasses flashed across Joan's mind. That fit Virginia to a tee, a sad, long face. *What happened?* Joan's mind screamed suddenly. She felt an overwhelming urge to grab Virginia by the coat and shake her until she confessed. She had the answer. She was there and was responsible for all this. *If my baby fell on the floor, just tell me!*

"If my …" Joan started.

"Huh?" came the reply.

"Forget it. Is that all you need?"

"Yes. I'm sorry to trouble you. I'll be going now." With that, the nurse turned and clunked off the steps as Joan closed the screen door. Her head rested against the cold doorframe after it was closed. She too was cold. She was also anxious and tired.

"Who was that?"

"It was Virginia, Mother. She'd forgotten her purse on Saturday night."

"Oh."

Joan moved quickly into the dining area, where her mother patiently waited for her. The tea felt good on her lips, and immediately, she felt warmed. She looked at her mother and noticed that she was staring out the window.

"What are you thinking about?"

"Oh, Joan, I'm just thinking about what Willard is going through, the preparations and all."

"I wouldn't know. He just told me that he would take care of everything."

"Well, he mentioned to me something about a brief service for her and that he was working with your stepfather."

"Mother, he specifically told me not to worry about these details and that he didn't want me to know."

"I know, dear, but don't you have the right to know?"

"Maybe I'm becoming callous as I get older, but since Dr. Stilson said there wouldn't be a need for an autopsy, Willard and I agreed that Willard would take care of everything. I've said my goodbyes."

"Joan, I know that we know what happened, but shouldn't there have been an autopsy?"

"Damn it, Mother! Jennifer choked. It was because Virginia talked me into adding cereal into her formula, because she learned it as a trick to get babies to sleep through the night from that stupid nun's school she went to. She choked on it, because she was too young. She choked. She couldn't breathe. Her heart stopped, and her brain went dead. No wonder she was blue when Virginia found her!" Joan forcefully downed the rest of her tea. She stood up and went into the kitchen with tears streaming down her face. "I'm sorry, Mother," she said as she set her cup in the sink.

"I understand, Joan."

Do you? Joan thought.

CHAPTER NINE

"Why Is She Just Watching Us?"

December 19, 1951
Bridgeport, Connecticut

The wind howled outside and blew the snow around in tiny circles around the dull-green ground. Willard was pleased that he was inside where it was warm, yet the sadness of this mission encircled him like the dancing snowflakes outside. As he waited, he studied the names of the Mountain Grove Crematorium. Small plaques of raised bronze letters and numbers marked the cement recesses of ash and bone chips. Florsheim footsteps on the marble floor thirty feet behind him broke his concentration. He turned and was presented with a metal box. He said a brief, "Thank you," and headed out the door to his waiting Chrysler, cradling Jennifer against his abdomen as if to protect her from the storm.

December 31, 1951
New Haven, Connecticut

At 4:00 p.m., Joan and Willard crossed York Street and headed toward the south entrance of Grace New Haven Hospital to meet the Mother Superior of the Sisters of Mercy once again. Mother Superior had called Joan two days ago and asked her if she and her husband could meet with her on the day that had originally been slated as the judge's trial for the formal adoption of Jennifer. Joan knew that the day would be a heartbreaking, melancholy one, but she consented anyway.

The same white-attired novice that once brought Jennifer to them directed the couple into the Mother Superior's office. Joan quickly surveyed the room and noticed that the office seemed surprisingly brighter, though nothing of the physical environment seemed to have changed. Mother Superior presented herself with her hands clasped in front of her and smoothly glided to her desk. She reached easily across the top of her desk with both hands and grasped the couple's palms so gently. "My dears, I am truly sorry for your loss and ours—a gift from God taken away."

Joan and Willard politely smiled and uttered soft acknowledgements with bowed heads.

The nun continued, "Are you quite positive that you cannot have children of your own?"

Joan was taken off-guard and slowly sat back releasing the warm, wrinkled hand that held her. "No, Mother Superior, I'm not, but see, I have this medical condition—"

"Hmm."

"I need to speak more with my doctor. It is a blood incompatibility as you probably saw from my records when we adopted Jennifer. My doctor told me that medicine doesn't offer too much to fix this problem."

"Well, as you know, babies are quite hard to come by. I am wondering if you would talk with your doctor about seeing if you could try. If at the end of a year, you couldn't have your own child, then we would find a baby for you."

"That sounds wonderful," Willard quickly said.

"That would be fine," Joan said hesitantly. *What is going on? We lose a baby, and the sisters are now making a deal with us?*

Mother Superior concluded the meeting by saying, "I also wanted to let you know that Judge Lipton, who was going to oversee the case, formally called me. He said this whole thing was terrible, and we are going to get you a baby, if your doctor feels that you are unable."

"Well, it's nice to have the law on our side!" quipped Willard.

"Yes, indeed. Talk it over with your doctor, and we'll see how the year goes."

Joan felt queasy.

July 1953
New Haven, Connecticut

"Apples, oranges, peaches, pear, let's all go to the big-top fair. Elephants, ponies, clowns, and lights, yippee, hooray with all our might!"

Jack smiled greatly at his happy mother. He really responded to the singsongs that she made up. It helped make mealtime extra special for him, and Joan loved seeing her son so tickled. He was a happy boy. It had been quite stressful during the first few months of his life, especially during his feedings. Jack often was a slow feeder, which was fine for Joan. Each gulp provoked a sense of anxiety in her. *God, please don't let him choke.* Each nap that he had, Joan would feel his back every thirty minutes to assure herself that his chest continued to rise and fall. She was sleep-deprived, and no one could talk her into getting more rest for herself.

Her mother said, "Are you willing to be put through the tortures of hell because you're worried that he's going to stop breathing?"

"Yes, I went through months of having to have blood tests and worries that I would lose the baby, so I'll be a nervous wreck for a few more months."

Joan really wasn't sure how much longer she could lose sleep like this, but in a way, her body had adapted well. There was motivation to do so. Willard was busy at work, and she loved being busy at home.

One afternoon, on a particularly warm day, Joan's mother was over for a visit. Jack was sleeping in the living room in his playpen. The two women were sipping iced tea in the kitchen.

"Goodness, Joan, please open the window more."

"It is quite warm, isn't it?" said Joan as she moved toward the kitchen window that faced Prospect Street.

As she adjusted the shade, Joan spotted a figure sitting on a bench against a retaining wall about fifty yards away. People often sat there waiting for the bus, but this was midday, not a time for buses. The person was large and took up a great deal of the bench. Joan turned her head to make a teasing comment, but she turned her head back with a start and a slight gasp.

"What's wrong, Joan?"

"Virginia Jaspers in sitting across the street watching our house."

Joan's mother snickered and said, "Well now, why not go out and invite her in?"

"That's not funny, Mother," replied Joan.

"Well, she probably feels dreadful about having an infant in her care die. So, she's probably very remorseful and may not know how to make amends."

"She doesn't have to, because she'll never be able to."

Joan didn't see Virginia again until one Saturday in October when she was standing at the sink cleaning the morning dishes. She sat on the same bench across the street from their home. Willard was playing with little Jack in the den.

"Why is she just watching us?" Joan called to Willard.

He picked up his son and moved into the kitchen. He looked at the bench and wondered the same thing.

"Shall I go say something to her?" he asked.

"No, just let her look. It's so strange and unnerving, though."

"She isn't doing any harm, but you're right, it is creepy," Willard said as he reached up and pulled the curtains closed.

"Do you think she could ever hurt Jack?" Joan asked.

"Not as long as we are with him," Willard replied.

January 1955
Hampton, Connecticut

Joan slowly unpacked the last of their boxes late in the afternoon with Jack's help. It was a box of his toys, and his job was to place them into the toy chest in his room. He, of course, couldn't resist playing with the majority of them before they found their home in the chest. Joan smiled and stroked his hair. She let him play with the few that remained on the floor and went down to the dining room. She hummed a favorite section from Mozart's *Requiem* that had entered her head as she arranged some dishes. A knock on the front door interrupted her. Joan went and opened the inside door. She glanced at another woman outside the storm door and noticed that she too was quite pregnant.

"May I help you?" Joan asked as she opened the door part way.

"Yes, I'm Judy Sinowitz from next door. I wanted to welcome you to our neighborhood and brought you a little something."

"Well, isn't that kind! Please come in."

The woman was carrying a paper sack and handed it to Joan as she crossed the threshold into the living room.

"It's homemade walnut bread."

Joan could smell the freshly baked bread even without lifting it to her nose.

"Hmmm. I'll set it down in the kitchen and cut some pieces. Please take off your coat and have a seat."

Joan soon came back with a plateful of the bread and set it on the wooden coffee table in the living room. "I'll go get my two-year-old and bring him down to meet you. The bread will also be a fun appetizer to his dinner."

Judy politely waited until the two came down from upstairs before she helped herself to a slice of bread. Jack hungrily chewed on a piece while he sat on his mother's knee.

"It's been so hectic moving us here, but we are starting to settle in quite nicely."

"Yes, I wanted to give you all a few days to get arranged before I came over to introduce myself and welcome you."

Joan smiled and said, "This is very thoughtful of you."

"Sure thing. Now tell me about your family," Judy said.

"Well, we moved here from New Haven, after being there for many years. My husband's name is Willard, and he is going to be working regularly in New York City starting next month. This probably means that we will be seeing him less. This is Jack, who is a big helper when it comes to unpacking things. He will have a brother or sister in March."

"Oh, you don't say!" interrupted Judy. "That's when I'm due too."

"Well, it *is* a small world."

"Yes. This will be my third child. My husband, George, is hoping for another boy. We have a four-year-old girl and a boy, just about Jack's age. Having a couple of little ones with a newborn around will be quite nerve-wracking, won't it?"

"Yes, I suppose," said Joan.

"What are you going to do about a nurse?"

Joan stared down at the floor not daring to lift her head for fear of showing the shocked expression that had raced to her face. "I hadn't thought about it."

"Well, I need one. George said that we could probably afford one. He just got a new raise at the factory."

After about an hour of visiting, Judy Sinowitz excused herself and went home. Joan left Jack in the living room to play and proceeded to fix dinner. Her heart raced as she thought of anyone close to her having an infant nurse at home.

Over the next several weeks, the Malkans became fast friends with the Sinowitzs. Young Jack played well with the Sinowitz children. In March, the two women waddled on short walks together, shared stories of pregnancy aches and pains, and looked forward to the births of their babies. Several days prior to Judy going into labor, she called Joan and asked, "Are you going to have the nurse?"

Joan replied, "I don't think so. I think I'll just take care of the baby on my own."

Judy said, "You know, I've just called this agency, and I'm so excited. I have a registered pediatric nurse, and she's very cheap."

"Really?" Joan said hesitantly.

"Yes, in fact, her father is an ex-state senator. Doesn't that beat all?!"

Joan shuddered and asked, "What is the nurse's name?"

"Virginia Jaspers."

Joan gave birth to Aaron Malkan two days after little Stephen Sinowitz was born. Upon release from the hospital, Joan instructed Willard to bring her scarf and sunglasses in the car.

"Why on earth would you want to do that?" he asked.

"Because Virginia Jaspers is living next door to us, and I don't want her to see that it's me who is bringing a newborn home."

"We can't hide from her."

"The heck we can't."

Joan had so been looking forward to having her baby and happily bringing him to the family's new home, but instead, the experience was tainted and ugly. She despised the fact that she couldn't be content and had to live in fear.

When she and Willard got the new baby situated at home, Joan spoke with him.

"Please forgive me for my behavior. You probably think that I'm being irrational, but this whole thing is so strange that I feel it's unnatural. My God, Willard, she sat and watched our house in New Haven on three different occasions until I begged you to move us out of there. And now … now, she is living *next door*! We can't escape her, I swear."

Willard comforted Joan as best he could, but she felt there would be no peace until the threat next door was removed.

"Maybe I should warn Judy."

"Joan, she just had a baby. Like you, she should rest and not be caught up with troubles."

"Easier said than done."

"Besides, Virginia is not guilty of anything, so we can't risk something like a libel suit if we start telling her clients that she is dangerous when she's not."

Joan knew that further discussion with her husband about this issue would lead nowhere. She would just have to be strong and accept the hand she was dealt.

A week later, Judy came over for a visit. She took a place on the davenport, and Joan made tea in the kitchen.

"Guess what?" Judy called to her from the other room.

"What?"

"George and I are going to a bar mitzvah in Boston in mid-April."

"That's great," said Joan. "For the day?"

"No, for a couple of weeks."

"My goodness, why so long?" asked Joan.

"Well, my husband wants to spend extra time with his family up there."

"The whole family is going, of course?"

"We're taking the little ones, but the baby is going to stay here with Virginia."

The cup of tea that was meant for Judy slipped out of Joan's hand and crashed onto the linoleum floor. She was stunned; the noise of the breaking cup didn't faze her.

Judy quickly rose and went into the kitchen. "Is everything okay?" she asked.

"Yes," Joan said dully. "My clumsiness got the best of me."

Joan reached for a broom, and Judy began to blot the spill with a dishtowel.

Joan asked her, "Why are you leaving the baby for such a long time?"

"Well, George and I discussed it. Virginia is doing a fine job, though she gets kind of sad sometimes. The young ones can see their cousins and other relatives. Baby Stephen won't know any better. Having Virginia take care of him for this period will free us up to enjoy ourselves."

Joan started to say, "Yes, but …," but instead, closed off her sentence, because she didn't know how to formulate what she was thinking. She didn't know how to tell this woman that every single day with the baby nurse was one of reckless disregard for the tiny life. Joan felt as though it wasn't her place to disclose what had happened to her and Willard. So, she simply remained silent.

Joan's silence interrupted her waking and sleeping hours. Two days after her conversation with Judy, she called Judy's husband George. Joan knew she would catch him at home without her on Thursday evenings, since it was pinochle night for Judy at the community center.

"George, this is Joan." Without giving him a chance to reply, she continued. "Judy told me about your upcoming trip to Boston. You do what you think is right. I don't know, call it the ravings of a madwoman, but this is what happened to me." She then proceeded to tell him of the fatal night four years previously and of the dreadful consuming fear that had haunted her since she arrived home with Aaron. She told him that she didn't want to alarm his wife, but someone needed to be told. George agreed and told Joan that he would speak with Judy when she arrived home after cards. Joan felt relieved. A weight had truly been lifted off her, but another had been put on. She didn't want to meddle in people's business and interfere with a friend's plans, but for her, this was an extreme situation.

The next day at 10:00 a.m., there was a knock on the door. It was Judy. Her face was serious. *Now, I've done it*, thought Joan as she let her in.

Judy looked at her as she entered and said, "I'm so glad you called George last night. We're not going to go to the bar mitzvah."

Joan felt immediate relief when she heard those words.

"You know, I feel so sorry for her. I don't feel like I want to fire her for something that happened in the past."

"Of course," interjected Joan.

"But I am going to watch her like a hawk. I wouldn't want anything bad to happen to my baby."

August 1955
Hampton, Connecticut

A sudden knock on the front door caused Aaron to jump slightly while he was being held by his mother. He was just drifting off to sleep, having recently finished a bottle of formula.

Judy was let in. She had her hand to her mouth, and her face was pale.

"Joan, I just heard the most terrible thing on the radio. There was a baby across town that was smashed against its crib yesterday and now has permanent brain damage. The radio said the father was arrested."

Joan became mad. "Judy, I'm sorry, I don't want to hear it. Please don't tell me stories like that."

"I'm sorry, Joan. I forgot about your situation."

"It's not *my* situation, Judy. It should be everyone's situation. Why do things like this happen? To the most innocent?!"

Joan excused herself and took Aaron upstairs to his room. Judy showed herself out.

That night, Joan shared with Willard all that happened that morning. "Is it bad luck? What is it, Willard?"

"I don't know, Joan."

"It just keeps following us—all these bad events involving our babies or other people's babies."

Willard let his wife vent her thoughts and feelings. This had long been coming to a head, he thought. So he let her talk it out. Yet, what he didn't expect was her proposal to him.

"For a variety of reasons, Willard, I want to move again. I want to get away from this. I just don't want the memory of it. I have two wonderful boys, and I'm so grateful, but all this is so horrible. I want to go to New Canaan. My aunt told me that the house next to hers is up for sale, and it is reasonably priced. It is also halfway between New Haven and New York. You sometimes work in both places, so it would be perfect. We would also still be close to our families. I promise I'll set down roots there. Willard, I just want to forget all this."

Willard Malkan looked at his wife deeply, probably the deepest he had looked at her in years. He knew how serious she was and felt that if he didn't consent that she would take the boys and go without him. Instead of saying anything, he smiled, caressed her cheek with his hand and hugged her tightly.

CHAPTER TEN

"I'm Taking Her Off My List"

February 1952
New Haven, Connecticut

"Feeling refreshed?"

"Hardly, it rained half the time we were there."

"Well, maybe next year, you can go to the Amazon—I hear it never rains there."

"Ha ha. Very hilarious."

Robert Salinger goaded Carter Stilson inside the Olympus restaurant in downtown New Haven. It was the first time the medical partners had made it a point to get together since Dr. Stilson arrived back from his vacation in Naples, Florida. He and his wife, Jacqueline, had been gone nearly two weeks. The trip had been spontaneous; Stilson needed to get away. The death of the Malkan baby had been too much. It was time, he had decided. For reasons other than the inclement weather, the vacation had not been restful either. The doctor felt unsettled and fidgety, which was unlike him.

"More tea?" asked the waitress.

"No thanks," replied Salinger.

"Bob, we need to talk about Virginia Jaspers, that so-called baby nurse," Stilson encouraged.

"Hell, you don't have to convince me about what a louse she is," Salinger replied. "You know, right after the Malkan baby expired and I heard that you took the next train south, I knew we'd have to have this conversation."

"Yes, sorry for cutting out like that and sorry for leaving you the scrawled message about covering my patients, but I couldn't take waiting around and having those parents call me or being around more snow, etc. I needed to get out."

"That is very understandable. Besides, your patient load wasn't bad. I split it up between Wessel and me. He's a good egg when it comes to taking on a few more wheezy and pukey kids."

Stilson laughed aloud. It felt good to be talking to his partner; it had been awhile since they had just sat down and freely talked like this. He looked out the restaurant window and followed a few snowflakes as they drifted along. His silence bothered Salinger.

"Carter, remember? We were talking about a louse?" said Salinger as he waved a hand in front of Stilson's pensive face.

"Yes, I am deep in thought, aren't I?"

"Well, you don't have to convince me, but I'm taking her off my list," Salinger said as he wiped his mouth with the linen napkin. "I'm sure she's killing kids left and right."

"Are you *sure?*" implored Stilson as if seeking justification for the thoughts that had plagued him for several weeks.

"Yes. The whole damn thing started in '48, before you came on board at the office. A baby named Hubbard was killed. Dick Olmsted called me shortly afterward and told me that he was suspicious of the baby's manner of death. She died of a cerebral hemorrhage. He'd discussed the case with Tom Chiffelle, and he didn't like that the death was spontaneous and not attributed to a fall or something. No evidence of cerebral aneurysm or anything like that. We all got together and decided that the baby nurse probably dropped the infant and covered it up. We didn't tell the girl's parents because we couldn't be sure and we had no proof."

Stilson looked at Salinger. He smiled slightly, raised his eyebrows, and said, "Well, I feel better. But, I screwed up on the Malkan baby because I didn't order a post. Also, no body to dig up, since her father cremated her."

"Too bad, is right," said Salinger. "Maybe there would have been something we could hang our hat on."

"Goddamn it! Why didn't I see it?" exclaimed Stilson firmly, causing some patrons to look his way.

"Shh, it's fine." Salinger attempted to calm his partner.

"No, it's not. Basic pediatrics—vomiting is a classic sign of head injury."

"And overfeeding."

"Yes, but I was always taught about being thorough in medicine. The whole situation was crazy. I had to stay there with that nurse just bellowing downstairs and a dead baby just lying there. It got to the point that I put a blanket on the side of the crib so I could have something between us."

Salinger breathed deeply and shook his head. "Sorry you had to go through that," he said.

"It's okay."

"I guess the only thing we can do is cross her off our recommended lists and dissuade parents if they ask about her specifically. We need to be careful about being libeled, especially since her father was a legislator."

Stilson nodded in agreement. He then asked, "What do you know about Jaspers' training?"

"I don't know where she got her training. There are none around here that I know of—maybe she went somewhere around Hartford. You know, bigger city, more choices."

"More *problems*, it seems to me."

October 1942
West Hartford, Connecticut

"Remember, don't you, that she was a happenstance in the program."

"You mean a quirk?"

"Now be kind. I pray to God that she had nothing to do with that baby's death."

"Mother Superior said we shouldn't think about that when I spoke with her on the phone yesterday."

"We did train her to be the best she could with infants."

"Yes, so rest assured on that."

"Do you think this will affect the program?"

"No, Mother Superior said not to worry. There is no connection, and there is no proof that she had anything to do with it. Besides, her father was very supportive of us."

"That is true."

The two nuns continued their walk in the park throwing stale bread to the hungry birds that flocked about them. Now silent, both were caught up in their thoughts remembering a time ten years earlier when those in the pediatric nurse program had been taken aback by a very large presence.

"We're to drop the issue," one nun said.

Without looking up, the other nodded.

The leaves had all but fallen off the trees and had carpeted the ground in red, orange, and brown on the small campus of the St. Agnes Home. Sister Hildegarde and Sister Ruth walked steadfastly into the east wind, their habits blowing straight back. Several residents who were sitting at the base of the center oak tree laughed out loud at the sight. One girl put her arms out like wings and jumped up to run around the tree, making a "brrr" sound as she impersonated an airplane to the delight of her friends. The nuns ignored the mockery and proceeded on their course. They arrived at the headmistress's office promptly at 2:00 p.m. She was a nun named Bertrand.

"Thank you for coming over, Sisters. Please have a seat."

The nuns took their places, adjusted their garb neatly, and focused on the headmistress.

"I've had several complaints recently."

"Not about us, I hope," said Sister Hildegarde.

"No, of course not, you two are my best instructors. These complaints have been from students in the program about the Jaspers girl."

The two nuns looked at each other sheepishly. They knew exactly what the headmistress was referring to: Virginia Jaspers was the worst student in the history of the pediatric nurse program. She laughed out loud inappropriately. She stomped about, questioned everything, and once during diapering, she even cried in front of everyone out of sheer frustration from losing a pin. Yes, the nuns knew the troubles with Virginia. They also were very aware of the fact that she had sixteen months left in the program.

"What can we do to address these issues?" asked the headmistress.

Sister Ruth felt comfortable speaking up. "I think we will have to just work with her the best that we can. We all remember some hesitancy on all our parts when we looked at her application last winter. There were accolades from members of her community, but a concern by one of her teachers about her ability to be successful in the nursing program. Her father has a great deal of influence in her town and in the southern part of the state. He is well known to Bishop Crowley from our diocese."

"Hmm," remarked Sister Bertrand.

"I believe if we show her the basics and move her along, she will ultimately do fine. Repetition seems to work in her favor," suggested Sister Hildegarde. She inched forward in her seat and continued, "She is an emotional girl, strongly emotional, but let's take some pity on her and hope that this next year passes without too many rocky moments. If the other students have issues, we will speak to them privately. It's important that we keep our program successful here at St. Agnes. As you know, we are called the 'darling charity' of the diocese for our good work with these unwed mothers."

St. Agnes Home was built in West Hartford in the late 1800s. There was approval by the town for a two-acre plot off Steel Road. Skilled townspeople and church members initially constructed the main building. Years later, contractors erected two other small buildings for offices. The pediatric nurse training program was begun soon after the home was completed. In the 1920s, Hartford began to see more and more unwed mothers being banished from their homes. St. Agnes welcomed these young mothers and gave them an opportunity to start life anew with their babies. Unwanted babies were not aborted; instead, they were adopted through the Sisters of Mercy. In their heyday, the sisters became the state's largest adoption program, with sites in New Haven, Hartford, and Glastonbury. Hundreds of women from all over the state of Connecticut graduated with certificates from the nursing program. Some joined already established agencies in their hometowns, while others developed their own businesses.

Babies were not hard to come by for the Sisters of Mercy adoption program in the Hartford area, nor were unwed mothers hard to come by for the St. Agnes Home. Getting these girls to agree to come into the program often provided challenges. In the 1940s and '50s, nuns sold cigarettes to "wayward" pregnant girls on the street to build a rapport and entice them to the home where they could talk with them, have them become residents, and improve their lives. It was through this special community work that the sisters built a reputation that many other dioceses around the country followed. It was in 1956 that the St. Agnes nursing program came under scrutiny and was developed into a course with tighter controls and state involvement. It was in 1956 that the Virginia Jaspers' murder case broke and the St. Agnes connection was made.

CHAPTER ELEVEN

"Why Is His Leg Swollen?"

January 17, 1955
Woodbridge, Connecticut

Marvin and Norma Schaefer looked down at their son, Bruce, who was sleeping soundly in his white wicker carriage that was parked in the middle of the living room. Marvin had purchased it the day before at Sears and Roebuck. "An early spring sale," he said in justification. Norma laughed when he told her this as he struggled to get it in the front door of their two-story apartment.

"Ride!" squealed their three-year-old daughter when she first laid eyes on the carriage.

"Yes, ride for the baby. Sissy is too big for this."

"Ohh," came the disappointed response.

Marvin chuckled and went back to looking at Bruce.

Norma touched his hand and said, "It doesn't seem as though he is almost three weeks old."

"He looks much bigger," came a voice that startled the couple.

"Oh, Virginia, you scared me," Norma confessed.

The nurse, who had been surreptitiously spying on the couple, snickered slightly, her hand covering her broad grin. This incident had been another game to Virginia. For her, this type of teasing broke

79

up the monotony in her life. She justified these types of games in her mind as moments by which she could bond with her clients. For most families, she was accepted as an odd and eccentric sort of personality. As long as she did her job as a baby nurse, her idiosyncrasies were tolerated.

Marvin felt uneasy about Virginia. He was not used to looking up to a woman, and she was a good two inches taller. The day after she started as a nurse in their apartment, he joked to a coworker at the real estate office about never wanting to challenge Virginia to an arm-wrestling competition. "She'd have me on my ass in no time!"

Virginia had only been at the Schaefer household for about a week and had settled in adequately. Bruce was not on an arranged schedule for feeding or sleeping, but she was already practicing with him. She had even made a timetable for reaching certain goals with him. An example of this was feeding. Virginia instructed the Schaefers that the baby would start his feeding schedule when he turned three weeks.

"It's really quite easy, folks. You feed him every three to four hours and then start to let him go at night until he really hollers. Try to feed him only once in the middle of the night, and then, after a couple more weeks, he'll be sleepin' right through. During the day, wake him up every two hours and then let him sleep at night." Virginia beamed at her knowledge of pediatrics and smiled greatly.

Norma questioned this by asking, "Won't he be very hungry at night if he's used to eating regularly during the day?"

"Oh no, don't be silly. Babies get used to that. Remember, I'm the expert here." Virginia laughed. "They taught me very well at St. Agnes, don't you worry."

The Schaefers did worry. Bruce was to turn three weeks old the following day, and Virginia was determined to set this schedule for him. Marvin believed that the feeding and sleeping matter was slightly sadistic and that St. Agnes didn't know what the hell they were teaching. *But, far be it from me to cross a nursing school,* he thought.

"Did you remember to get a 'spring special' for your nephew's birthday tomorrow?" Norma asked her husband.

Marvin smiled, grabbed his wife's hand, and led her into the kitchen. Propped up against the door leading outside was an oblong gift-wrapped package. A large blue bow covered the top half.

"What on earth did you get him?"

"A 'spring special' pogo stick!"

"Can I try?" called Virginia.

"You are joking, right?" asked Marvin.

The nurse hadn't been joking, and her sudden change in facial expression tipped off Marvin that she was serious. The only thing Marvin thought about were pieces of the stick being strewn about the kitchen, it having collapsed violently under Virginia's weight.

"Sorry, it's already wrapped," he said trying to save face for her.

Norma changed the tone of the conversation and said, "A great gift for a nine-year-old boy! Thank you for picking it up." She reached over and pecked Marvin on the cheek.

"What time is the party tomorrow?" asked Virginia.

"One o'clock," said Marvin.

"Is little Francine going with you?"

"Yes," said Norma. "She just loves her cousin Nathan."

"Nathan … isn't that a Jewish name?" the nurse posed.

Marvin frowned slightly and said, "Yes, Virginia. The whole family is Jewish."

"Oh, that's right."

"We should be getting home around 6:00," Norma added.

"Just in time for the 6:00 feeding!" announced Virginia.

God help us, implored Marvin silently.

January 18, 1955 – 4:00 p.m.
Woodbridge, Connecticut

"You little bastard! Why don't you sleep?! You will learn this schedule," Jaspers screamed at the Schaefer infant.

Her meaty hand fit perfectly around the baby's torso. She carried him one-handed like she carried the eggplant she bought at Rover's market three days ago. Bruce screamed, coughed, and writhed as well as he could. Something was squeezing his chest, something large, something terrifying. The nurse's eyes had turned evil, and she glared without focusing. Her large feet clomped loudly as she paced back and forth inside the apartment with her prize deftly grasped in her right hand. She tried to think, but she couldn't hear herself over the baby's wails.

"Stop it! Stop it!" she screamed as she lifted Bruce up to her face. "You're gonna get a spanking. You know that, don't you? This is what happens to bad, terrible little Jew babies who don't take naps."

Jaspers placed her left middle finger and thumb together in an "O" shape, brought it up to the baby's nose, and flicked hard. New wails rang out in the air, startling Jaspers as if she didn't know what the reaction would be. She plumped down on the living room couch, turned Bruce over on her left knee, and walloped him twice on his thinly padded bottom. He coughed and sputtered for air, not knowing what this pain was that had taken him over.

The nurse stood up suddenly and knocked over the new white carriage. She kicked it aside and walked past it, muttering, "'Spring special,' ha!" to herself. Once inside Bruce's room, she stopped her marching. She still held Bruce in a one-handed grip and stood still as if trying to formulate an action plan. As the baby wiggled in her hand, she raised her arm and with tremendous force, threw him headfirst into his crib. His left leg hit the hard wooden edge of the crib as his body fell onto the soft mattress. Jaspers didn't hear Bruce's leg snap in two, because she was yelling, "Take a damn nap!"

Nothing seemed right to the Schaefers when they arrived home from their nephew's birthday party at 6:00. Both had been on edge at the celebration, since it was their first time away from their new son. At one point that afternoon, Marvin asked Norma if she thought they should call home and check on how things were going. They both decided that since Dr. Godfrey, Norma's obstetrician at Grace New Haven Hospital, had recommended Virginia Jaspers that she would do a good job, even with her peculiar ways.

"Virginia?" called Norma as she entered the kitchen through the outside door. She immediately heard Bruce's cries from upstairs. "Is everything okay?"

Marvin was carrying Francine in his arms and entered the kitchen just as Norma asked her question. He squatted down, and the little girl hopped out of his arms to the floor. He began to take her coat off awkwardly as he was looking in the direction of the living room. He heard shuffling, and then Virginia appeared in the doorway of the kitchen.

"Sorry, folks, did you say something?" she asked, her face serious.

"Yes," said Marvin, now frowning deeply. "What is wrong with the baby?"

"Oh, I … I guess he is just very tired. We played a lot while you were gone."

Both Norma and Marvin rushed over to the stairway leading up to Bruce's room. His cries were more intense, almost as if he were in pain. After they both entered his room, Marvin reached into the crib and gently picked his son up. It was then that Norma noticed Bruce's leg. He was wearing a diaper and a tee shirt—his tiny legs and arms were bare. His left thigh was twice the size of his right, and it was shade of deep red.

"Oh my God!" she cried. "Why is his leg swollen?"

Marvin straightened his arms as he held his son so he could get a look at the leg. He cringed slightly as he noticed what his wife was referring to. Bruce's cries continued as he was being held. His right leg was pushing up and down; his injured left leg was limp. The sight sickened Marvin. He handed the baby to his wife and approached Virginia as she came up the stairs. He grabbed her shoulders, which caused her to utter, "Ohh."

"What the hell did you do to him, you cow?" he yelled.

"I … I … why nothing. He was trying to take a nap."

"Did you see his leg? Look!" said Marvin, pointing out the swollen, reddened area on the baby.

"I don't know what to say, really!"

Marvin was so upset that he could not stand looking at Virginia anymore. "Out!" he said. "Out of my Goddamned house!"

He marched her into her room, grabbed her suitcase, flung it on the bed, and said, "You have three minutes to pack." He slammed her door and walked to the phone to call Dr. Salinger.

January 18, 1955
Grace New Haven Community Hospital
New Haven, Connecticut

"Your son has sustained a transverse, or midshaft, femur fracture, Mr. and Mrs. Schaefer," explained Dr. Salinger. "Dr. Frechette, the orthopedic surgeon, just let me know."

"Could you be less specific, Doctor? I want to understand what happened," Marvin asked.

"Of course, but before I do that, I'd like some more information as to what happened to your son. One nurse, who is attending to him now, told me some basic information, but I'd like more from you. It is highly unusual for an infant to have such an injury."

The Schaefers and Dr. Salinger huddled together in the small waiting room outside the radiology department within Grace New Haven Community Hospital. The light was low, which made the scene more melancholy for the Schaefers. Marvin kept swallowing in order to stifle an outburst of emotions. Norma wept freely. Dr. Salinger's kind hand rested on the couple's clasped hands.

"Doc, you've known us for years, since before little Francine was born. We're good, hard-working people trying to make a decent life for our children and us. We've been happy up till now. Everything's been great. But this ... this is unspeakable." Marvin bent his head to cry.

Norma continued, "I got this nurse's name from my obstetrician. He's recommended her for years. We needed extra help since Francine is three and still needs our attention, so we opted for a baby nurse. We could afford her as well. Anyway, earlier today, we took Francine to her cousin's birthday party in Shelton. When we got home, Bruce was screaming. We went up to check on what was happening, and I noticed how swollen and red his leg was. That Jaspers woman couldn't give us an answer as to what happened. Marvin told her to pack her bags and get out. She hurt our baby, we just know it!"

When Norma said Virginia's name, Dr. Salinger flushed slightly and looked away. Marvin noticed this and suspected the doctor knew something.

"Dr. Salinger, what do you know about Jaspers?"

"Well, Mr. Schaefer, I can't really discuss anything about her. She's not here to defend herself."

Marvin knew that the doctor was a man of good character and was well respected as an outstanding pediatrician in the community. "Doctor, please, we need information."

"I'm sorry, I can't. Let me, though, tell you more about your son's injury. It's what I think happened. A transverse fracture is also called a mid-shaft fracture, which means that your son's largest bone in his body, the femur, was broken straight across the shaft. The break was in the middle of the femur, hence the term mid-shaft. It was either broken with hands or might have been hit with something ... or your son was thrown down."

The Schaefers cringed as they heard the details of their baby's injury. They both wept. Marvin looked at the doctor and asked, "How could this have happened? We are supposed to protect our children."

"I don't know. I'm very sorry. I can tell you that he is stable and can go home in two to three days. His leg is so tiny that Dr. Frechette had to use a tongue depressor as a splint for the cast."

Marvin smiled slightly at the thought of this and wiped the tears from his eyes.

"Folks, he will be okay, really."

Marvin looked at him and said, "Doc, I need to know about the nurse. I ..."

He was cut off by a knock on the waiting room door.

"Enter," said Salinger.

A nurse slowly opened the door and said, "Doctor, a police officer is here to speak with the Schaefers."

"That's fine; we're all finished anyway."

"Doctor, I'd still like to talk with you."

"Maybe another time, Mr. Schaefer. I have many patients to see. Talk with the police, and then get to your son; he needs you."

Dr. Salinger slipped out through the waiting room door as the tall, uniformed police officer entered. He shook hands with the Schaefers and sat down. He opened his small, wire-bound notebook, took a pencil from his shirt pocket, and asked, "Now, what can I do for you folks?"

CHAPTER TWELVE

"We'd Like to Press Charges"

January 18, 1955
Grace New Haven Community Hospital
New Haven, Connecticut

The policeman scrawled notes as the Schaefers, once again, told the story of how their baby was hurt while they were away. The officer asked several innocuous questions about how the nurse got along with the baby, why he was left in her care, and so on. The Schaefers were both beginning to feel guiltier than they already had been feeling.

"I mean, folks, the child is only three weeks old, don't you think that you should have brought him with you or stayed at home?" suggested the officer.

"Excuse me, but I think that is why we hired a nurse," Marvin said defensively.

"Okay, just offering something to you."

The officer scribbled some more and then asked, "So, what would you like me to do?"

Norma spoke up and said, "We'd like to press charges."

"Now, ma'am, before we do that, we need to speak with all parties involved and see if there actually has been a crime committed."

"Officer, excuse my abruptness," Marvin began, "but you have now spoken with two of the three 'parties' involved in this situation. My son was fine when we left him this afternoon, and his leg was broken during the time we were gone. He's too young to play baseball or trip over a pipe in the ground or anything like that. A crime *has* been committed, and we'd like to press charges. It's that easy!"

"Mr. Shiffer, a crime is never easy, and there isn't a crime until a suspect has been arrested. We will do our investigation and speak with the nurse, all right?"

"Fine. By the way, the name is *Schaefer.*"

Bruce was very awake when his parents entered his hospital room. He studied them carefully and looked at the mobile that hung over his bed. Marvin lightly caressed the small cast on his leg. *Tongue depressor,* he thought and smiled as he looked at his son's blue eyes.

"I'll never let anything like this happen to you again. I'm also going to see to it that this nurse pays for what she did to you."

January 19, 1955
Dr. Robert Salinger's Office
New Haven, Connecticut

"You look tired," Dr. Salinger said as he approached Marvin, who was sitting outside his office door. It was 7:00 a.m.; patients would not be seen for another hour and a half. The office nurses were not yet to work. "Come on in," the doctor said, "we have about an hour to talk, and I think we'll need it."

Marvin followed Salinger into the darkened office. After turning on the overhead lights, the doctor stopped by the percolator to plug it in. He smiled and said, "My secretary, Ethel, sets it up the night before, since I like that overnight taste."

Marvin chuckled lightly and followed Salinger further down the halls past the patient rooms to the largest room, which was the doctor's personal office. He frequently held meetings with patients' parents in his office. A large Persian rug took up most of the center of the floor. It was beautiful with ornate, complex designs. Marvin studied it as he walked in.

"Like it?" asked Salinger. "I not only use it to make my office look good, but I use it as a tool to assess cognitive developmental abilities in my infant patients. I let them crawl around on it and observe what they do with the patterns. Parents don't have a clue that I'm doing it. It's kind of fun."

Marvin smiled and nodded and took a seat across from Salinger's desk after he was invited to do so.

"I know why you are here."

"Do you have any children yourself, Doctor?"

"My wife and I have adopted two sons; one is fourteen, and the other is twelve. I got a late start. I was forty-eight years old when we first adopted. Why do you ask?"

"I ask, because you probably are aware what a father is feeling who has been violated and whose trust has been severely broken."

"I can only imagine," Salinger responded sadly.

"Then why wouldn't you talk to me yesterday about Jaspers?"

"Wrong place, and I was caught off-guard when you asked me. I have to be very careful, since I'm a pediatrician who has been around for a long time and know a lot of people in the community."

"I understand that. I hope, though, you can also understand my position for being here today. When you left yesterday, my wife and I were basically given the brushoff by the cop who took our statement at the hospital. I need help, Doctor."

"It's understandable that your statement was viewed as … well, for lack of a better word, a convenience in this case."

"What is that supposed to mean?"

"Do you know anything about the Jaspers woman?"

Marvin looked at the rug briefly and stiffly answered, "No, except that she trained somewhere in West Hartford called the St. Agnes Home."

"Yes," said Salinger, "a very good program that graduates some very good people each year, so I've heard. But, probably to their dismay, they graduated a bad apple about seven years ago."

"Jaspers? Bad, how so?"

"Marvin ... may I call you Marvin?"

"Of course."

"Marvin, she was the main caretaker for two infants who died within the past seven years. It is my feeling that she was responsible for their deaths."

"My God! They died?" Marvin Schaefer's face went ashen. He thought about Bruce and how a broken leg was almost minimal compared to what he could have gone through. *I'm lucky to still have him,* he thought. A rush of nausea swept over him, and he wiped his brow. He had to force himself back into conversation with the doctor, in order to not risk ruining the fine Persian rug at his feet.

"I ... I ... Why didn't you tell someone?" he asked.

"I have tried in my own way. One can't accuse someone of murder without solid evidence. There were no bruises on either infant, and the second one didn't have an autopsy. That's also only part of the whole picture. Have you heard of William Jaspers?"

"Yes. I guess I hadn't put the names together. The ex-senator, right? Is he related?"

"Her father."

Marvin whistled low and thought about the influence he was up against. A revelation about the police officer's behavior came to him suddenly. "No wonder the cop seemed to be doing a half-baked job. He knew about her father."

"Probably. Her father now has a simple job as an assistant manager at New Haven Railroad, most likely to keep his income healthy until he retires. He is also the treasurer for the county. Being an ex-politician, the man definitely has connections—legal connections. I've spoken with a few detectives, one or two assistant DAs, and even a psychiatrist over the years. I couldn't get anywhere. Several years ago, I even took her off my list of baby nurses that I keep."

"I just wish that my wife's doctor had done that," Marvin remarked. "What can be done?"

"I don't know, except to wait and see what the investigation discovers about your son's injury."

"I just wish there was something I could do—I feel powerless."

The doctor stood and gathered his stethoscope in one hand and scooped up some charts to be refiled in another. "I wish I had more time for you."

"That's okay, Doc. You've helped my family and me. For that, I thank you. It's just a wait-and-see spell, isn't it?"

Dr. Salinger nodded and led Marvin to the waiting room, which was beginning to bustle with activity. He patted him on the back and said, "Let me know if I can be of further help."

Marvin walked out onto the sidewalk and turned toward the direction of the hospital to be with Norma and Bruce. The next five minutes gave him some time to digest what Salinger had disclosed to him and to think of a plan as to what he'd do if the police failed to act on his son's behalf. He turned up his collar against the howling wind. It was cold.

January 23, 1955
Woodbridge, Connecticut

"What do you mean that it was turned over to the state police?" Marvin Schaefer shouted into the phone. "You guys took our statement. Yeah … yeah … and when will we hear from them? I really want it to be today, and you get that message to them! Thank you!"

The phone gave a sharp ring as it was put down hard onto the cradle.

"Quiet, you'll wake Bruce," said Norma.

"Sorry," said Marvin, changing to a hushed tone. "Do you know what those bastards did? They sat on the case for two days and then gave it over to the state police. They said it wasn't in their jurisdiction since it happened here in Woodbridge."

"Well, honey, maybe that's their procedure for doing that sort of thing," Norma said, trying to calm her husband.

"Yeah, but the progress was held up. Jaspers could have come up with any sort of story."

"Did the state police speak with her yet?"

"Supposedly on Thursday in one of her father's offices in downtown New Haven. I'm waiting for a call back from the state police investigator, Paul Something-or-other."

The phone call that Marvin Schaefer was hoping for failed to arrive that day or even the next. By Monday morning, Marvin was pacing at work—he could not concentrate. At lunchtime, he called the state police. He found out that the investigator, John Doyle, was away until 2:00 p.m. Marvin asked that he be called at work as soon as Doyle arrived back at the station. At 3:00, Marvin called again and was told that the investigator would be gone for the rest of the day.

"I'd like to see Investigator Doyle right away."

Marvin stood at the front desk of the state police barracks that was located just outside of New Haven. His right foot tapped impatiently as he waited for a response.

"I believe he is here this morning. He usually has a Tuesday morning meeting with the captain," said the secretary politely.

"Could you please interrupt him out of that meeting? This is urgent."

"May I tell him what this is regarding, sir?"

"Yes, tell him the father of the boy who was injured by Virginia Jaspers is here."

A few moments later, the state police investigator rounded the corner of the hidden hallway and approached Marvin with an outstretched hand and a wide smile.

"Mr. Schaefer, hi, how are you? John Doyle, what can I do for you?"

Marvin's brow puckered. "Are you kidding me? I've been calling for information about my son's injury for days, and I've been put off too many times. I'd like to know what's happening."

"Let's go into my office, shall we?" Doyle said as he pointed the way back down the fluorescent hallway.

The two made their way to the office; Marvin noted pictures of ex-state police captains and civic notaries hanging on the wall as he walked past. Doyle's office seemed typical, with volumes of case files on his desk, a near overflowing ashtray, and citations on the wall. Marvin sat in an open chair across from Doyle, who sighed slightly before he spoke.

"Mr. Schaefer, you're a man who is direct and one who wants straight answers. I appreciate that, so I won't dilly-dally around the topic. We have found, after a thorough investigation, an in-depth interview with the accused, and a discussion with the state's attorney, that there is no basis for filing charges. There is simply no evidence of abuse."

Marvin sat stunned. He almost asked the investigator to repeat himself; instead, he repeated what was just revealed.

"So, you're telling me that my son wasn't abused and that you aren't arresting Jaspers?" Marvin's voice intensified as he spoke.

"Yes, sir. I'm sorry. There is nothing that can be done."

"Why did the state's attorney look at this?"

"Well, um." Doyle furtively glanced across the room. "Because, we wanted to be sure that we were not missing anything."

"Okay then, so what did Jaspers say happened?"

"That is private information, sir. Can't help you there."

"Mr. Doyle, I think I've been a patient man thus far, yet I feel railroaded here. My son was terribly injured by this large woman, and you can't even give me some basic information." With that, Marvin stood and headed toward the door. "Maybe, I'll just have to personally call the state's attorney myself."

"Okay, Mr. Schaefer, calm down. Miss Jaspers simply stated that she believes your son may have broken his leg after putting it through the slats of his crib. We verified this possibility with one of the local doctors."

Marvin shook his head in disbelief; he didn't know which question to ask first. He felt stunned by the stupidity of the whole investigation. It was near comical.

"First of all, my son hardly moves around—he's only now a month old! Secondly, which one of the local quacks did you ask?"

"Dr. Rubin."

"For Christ's sake, he's in his seventies and a general practitioner to boot! He wouldn't know pediatrics even if a stork ran into him."

"Mr. Schaefer, I'm sorry, our decision has been made."

"I'm sorry too—that we have people in power like you who make the wrong decisions for families."

Marvin turned quickly and went down the hallway toward the exit breathing heavily. His heart raced; his thoughts whirled. He failed to notice one of the many pictures on both walls as he walked by—one of William Jaspers shaking hands with the state police captain at last year's annual dinner. State's Attorney Andrew Ullman stood by left of center.

CHAPTER THIRTEEN

"It's Now Up to Us"

March 1955
Woodbridge, Connecticut

From the outside, the country club looked more like a ski lodge than a place for men in suits and amateur golfers. Marvin had only been here once before; another real estate coworker had tickets for a pro-am event that famous golfer Bobby Jones was to star in. Southern Connecticut was having an early spring this year; typically, snow lasted into April. Several golfers warmed up their swings as Marvin passed by them. He didn't feel a bit envious. He was here for important business, not for play. He hoped that Salinger would have some information for him and, more importantly, some guidance. The well-kept sidewalk wound around to the grand oak-door entrance. Marvin followed it. He was slightly nervous and did not know why. He gripped the door's handle, pulled it open, and walked in. The foyer was dimly lit, and he looked around for the doctor.

Dr. Salinger had arrived thirty minutes early. He liked to be early for appointments and strove to abide by the "better early than late" tenet. He ordered a pot of tea and sat down to watch the early morning golfers. His mind wandered as he watched men practicing outside. He thought about what he and Marvin would talk about in their efforts to stop the

Jaspers woman. He knew that all that could be done had been done on his part. He felt overly frustrated with this menace; the whole thing was a damned political scheme—her father, smack dab in the middle. *Didn't anyone care about these little innocents?* he would often question in his mind. The answers to his inquiries were plentiful and all similar: "There isn't enough evidence"; "She comes from a good family"; "She is trained, isn't she?" He had heard enough. Now, he had agreed to meet with the father of one of his injured patients. Why? Maybe it was because he felt a special connection with this man. Maybe it was because this guy had the drive enough to get something done. Who knew? *Let's just see what he has to say.*

Salinger was pouring himself a third cup of tea when he felt a tap on his left shoulder. He looked up and saw Marvin looking at him with inquisitive eyes.

"Are you doing okay? I called your name twice. Maybe you didn't hear me," he suggested.

"Yes," said Salinger, standing up to shake hands. "I'm sorry, must have been dazing, deep in thought."

"I truly know the feeling, Doctor."

"Here, Marvin, have a seat."

Marvin put his coat on the wooden rack adjacent to the table, sat down, and pulled himself in closely. The two men both leaned forward with hands clasped, as if playing competitive chess.

"I appreciate you meeting me, Dr. Salinger."

"First of all, call me Bob, all my close friends do, and secondly, I'm not too crazy about the locale, but it's the best I could come up with, since we both live in Woodbridge."

Outside, the activity of golfers became more evident. Salinger felt distracted and reached over to pull the Venetian blinds closed most of the way. He then rejoined the intimate huddle that he and Marvin had formed.

"How was your meeting with Ullman?"

"Well, when we last talked on the phone, I told you about my meeting with him scheduled for that Thursday, but what I didn't get the chance to tell you was that his secretary called and cancelled."

"Put off again, huh?"

"Yes, what is going on?"

"Well, it is both simple and complex. Number one, the whole business is political. Her father is covering for her. I am just sure of it. It didn't start with the fact that your son's injury investigation was transferred to the state police. It began a long time ago."

"Yes, tell me. Why was it transferred?"

"I can only guess. Remember I told you that I know a lot of people? Well, I also know connections. Bill Jaspers is not only an ex-senator; he is also deeply involved in civic affairs. He is very tight with the state's attorney's office, not to mention area police agencies, such as the state police. He has had some disagreements with New Haven's police chief over several issues, so he is not so tight with him. Hence, the case was transferred. Hell, his daughter probably would have been arrested if it had stayed with the New Haven boys."

"Well, what about the other baby deaths that you told me about?"

"Remember, it was orchestrated from the state's attorney's office, which chose the doctor to use and everything."

Marvin shook his head and covered his tired eyes with his hands. He stared downward in disbelief.

"And I'm stuck in the middle, without recourse."

"Unfortunately, yes. But, we needn't remain quiet about it," suggested the doctor to him.

"What do you mean?" asked Marvin.

"Why, talk with those you know who will listen: parents, legislators, coworkers, etc."

"You mean, have a kind of an anti-Jaspers campaign?"

"No, I *wouldn't* recommend that. You would, in fact, be asking for trouble. What I mean is this—whenever you hear of a couple planning to hire a baby nurse, ask them if they've checked her out?"

"That's it?"

"That's one thing you can do. Another is to dissuade people that you know who are actually going to hire the Jaspers woman. I mean, don't run in and say, 'She broke my kid's leg,' rather say something like, 'I haven't heard good things about the way she treats children, so you might want to rethink your decision,' or something like that."

Marvin listened intently and thought about what the doctor was telling him. He then asked, "Well, what about politically? Anything we can do to get the law involved?"

"That, my friend, is an uphill battle … I mean, straight up! You know what they say about not being able to fight city hall. In this case, you wouldn't be able to fight the whole state of Connecticut."

Salinger stood and stretched his legs. He looked at Marvin, who appeared very despondent. "What I did do for us is make an appointment with Chief McManus. Next week, Wednesday at 3:00. Can you make it?"

Marvin's face brightened. "Sure I can! What are you going to say?"

"He and Bill Jaspers are not the best of friends, so we have McManus on our side. We are simply going to sit down with him and detail the events of the nurse's past, as I know them. We will tell him about your case from your viewpoint. And we will ask that she be arrested if any more of these incidents occur and are tied to her. She's a menace."

"Do you think anything will change, Doc?"

Salinger put his coat on and tapped Marvin on the shoulder. He grinned slightly and said, "We'll see what we can do."

February 1955
New Haven, Connecticut

The baby looked up at the nurse. She was angry. The harder he cried, the louder she yelled at him. He jerked backward quickly as she grabbed him and began to squeeze him around his chest. Immediately, the shaking started. It was hard. He was whipped back and forth. There was nothing he could do but allow the forces to overcome him. The nurse kept shaking and shaking, until he blacked out.

CHAPTER FOURTEEN

"Get Away from Her!"

July 1951
New Haven, Connecticut

Marcy Kapsinow's cries outraged her young father. It was his nature to be outraged. He had lived an angry life from day to day. Growing up, he took his lumps and received the brunt of his parents' wrath. His anger was a place where he generally felt most comfortable. He walked around with a chip on his shoulder and not many people tried to knock it off.

He met Sheilah Rovner at a dance when she was fifteen and he had just turned eighteen. He was a smooth talker to the young girl—so smooth that he had her in the backseat of his Ford within an hour and a half after being introduced to her. Sheilah was smitten and very captivated by his tough approach to the world. She felt that she could trust him, even though he had an edge to his persona. There was something inherently sweet about Allen. Yet, the radical in him was the attraction. He had a job at the Armstrong Rubber and Tire Company; he had his own apartment, his own car, and had nothing to do with his parents. Sheilah did not have sex with Allen until she was sixteen; it was soon after this that she became pregnant with Marcy.

Sheilah's parents protested loudly. Her father told her, "No Jewish daughter of mine is going to run around and have babies with a punk kid."

Sheilah asked sarcastically, "What am I supposed to do if I'm already pregnant?"

She escaped her parents' control the best she could and married Allen. Because she was pregnant, they were not married in a synagogue. The local justice was not surprised when he agreed to wed the young couple, the girl with her stomach bulging forward. After the war, he had seen more and more young folks in similar positions. *Kids weren't the same as they once were.*

Sheilah's labor and delivery went smoothly. Her mother stayed out in the waiting area. Her father stayed at home. Allen went to a local watering hole to get drunk as an early celebration of being a new father. Marcy was very healthy and very loved by Sheilah. Allen cried the first time he held her. "She's beautiful. She's mine. I have a daughter."

His comments seemed selfish, but Sheilah understood that having a child was very important to her husband. Maybe it was because he had such a lousy upbringing that he wanted a child to make up for all that he *didn't* have. Watching him hold her and cry, even though it was with drunken tears, pleased her. *We're a family now,* she thought. She would not see Allen cry like that again until he cried at another daughter's funeral five years later. He would then never cry again.

"Why can't this baby shut the hell up?" he shouted at Sheilah.

"Because she's probably scared of you and that's what babies do," Sheilah retorted in Marcy's defense.

Sheilah spoke up for herself and the baby when she felt that it was needed. She could handle Allen and never felt threatened by him. Because of this, Allen never physically struck her. If he did, she might strike back. She would definitely walk out on him and take Marcy. Allen struck Sheilah with caustic words and loud yelling instead. He'd often wake the baby when he would come home drunk, which was nearly every Friday and Saturday night.

Sheilah grew up fast, being around her fast-living husband, plus having a baby to care for. She made the decisions in the family, paid the bills, cooked, and kept a clean home. Sheilah's religious devotion never wavered. Even though her parents, especially her father, had cooled their relationship with her, she still attended Temple Beth El and sat right in back of them. She asked her mother after each Saturday service if she would like to come to dinner at the apartment. It was not for months that the invitation would be accepted, surprisingly by her father.

While Sheilah prepared dinner and her mother fed four-month-old Marcy a bottle, Jacob Rovner said, "Sheilah, I'm sorry for my behavior in the last year. You have made a good life for yourself and your family. I am proud of you."

"Oh, Daddy, thank you," Sheilah said as she ran to give her father a hug.

As he held her, Jacob said, "But I still don't trust your husband."

Marcy's crying woke Sheilah. She sleepily groped for the light by her bed and looked at the clock. 3:30. She had just fed her an hour before. *What's wrong?* she asked herself as she put her left hand into her robe sleeve. As she moved out into the hallway, she heard muffled hostile noises coming from the baby's room, her door closed.

"Quiet, I told you!" said Allen on the other side of the door.

As Sheilah opened the door, she said, "Don't you hurt my baby!"

Allen had Marcy over his knee and was about to spank her. Sheilah reached for his hand and connected with his fingers just before he brought them down on the baby's diapered bottom. Allen threw Sheilah's hand away and shoved her shoulder.

"I'm teaching her a lesson!" he shouted.

Instead of struggling again with her husband, Sheilah ran toward the kitchen. She looked around quickly, and her eyes landed on the cast-iron skillet that hung on the stained wall. Without pausing, she grabbed the skillet and went back into the baby's room. Allen was yelling more and again had raised his hand. Sheilah shouted, "Get away from her!" as she brought the skillet down on the side of Allen's head. It grazed him but caused him enough pain to howl and let go of Marcy. She fell halfway to the floor as Sheilah dropped the pan on the floor. She picked up the baby and ran into the kitchen, shouting, "Get out and stay out!"

It took thirty minutes for Marcy's crying to subside. Sheilah cried right along with her as she sat down on the kitchen floor against the wall where the skillet had recently hung. She didn't know if Allen had left the house, nor did she care; she just wanted to be alone with her baby. She then realized that because of her husband's actions and failure to be a decent, loving father, she would truly be alone forever. As she felt her body slump back on the wall from fatigue, she made a silent vow that she would never let anything bad happen to her daughter. The two fell asleep as Sheilah whispered, "I promise you."

Allen came home two days later. It was after work. He sported a new shirt and carried with him a bouquet of flowers for Sheilah. He was bright and chipper and looked good, except for the small bandage worn on the side of his forehead.

"Hi, sweetheart!" he called to her as he approached her.

Sheilah retreated slightly as he went to kiss her, her eyes questioning his intent.

"Oh, still sore about before? Let's not fuss about that."

Sheilah was confused; she didn't know what to say.

Allen went over to Marcy who was eating mashed potatoes in her high chair. He kissed her head and said, "Hi, Peppermint!"

Marcy's mouth turned down, and her eyes teared. Sheilah knew what was coming and went to her daughter to comfort her. The baby was fully crying by the time Sheilah picked her up. Allen seemed nonplussed by the incident and was busy putting the flowers in a tall glass since there were no vases in the apartment.

"Allen, what the hell is this?" Sheilah finally said.

"I'm home. And we are celebrating."

"Well, if you happen to remember, I was very angry with you two days ago, and I am still very angry."

"Look, like I said, let's not let that get in the way of our family."

"Allen, you get in the way. Your drinking, your anger—you almost beat our daughter. Come on!"

"Sweetie, I'm sorry. I was feeling low 'cause of work stuff, and I lost it with the baby. But hey, all that's over now. I got a raise!" Allen shouted happily, which startled Marcy once again to tears.

Sheilah softly patted Marcy and said, "What do you mean, a raise?"

"Well, not just a raise, 50 cents an hour, by the way, but a promotion. Old man Tarrington croaked at home two nights ago. He was the head supervisor, so everybody else in line for a move-up was promoted. I had put in for the assistant foreman job months ago."

"How come I never knew about this?" asked Sheilah.

"Oh hell, I don't know; maybe 'cause I wanted it to be a surprise when I got it—like now!"

Allen ran over to Sheilah, grabbed her, and flooded her face with kisses. She smelled the Old Spice on his face, but not a trace of liquor. As he continued to kiss her, his hands began to grope her dress. She didn't push him away. It had been some time since they had been intimate. She felt a deep yearning for him and was warm standing in the kitchen. She reached over and placed the baby in her playpen as Allen stroked her dress up. The baby was safe. She had her husband home. He had a promotion. Her thoughts drifted as she was pulled to the floor, down onto Allen.

CHAPTER FIFTEEN

"She's Beautiful"

August 13, 1956
New Haven, Connecticut

On the night that Abbe Kapsinow was born, the citizens of New Haven were enjoying their diversions from work. They went to the state theater to enjoy the new Bing Crosby/Grace Kelly movie called *High Society*; they listened to the news on the radio or watched their $167 RCA TV about Adlai Stevenson getting the democratic presidential nomination and read their newspapers, which featured Alley Oop, Pogo, and Archie in the comics section. Life was enjoyable. There were no significant events that would stir up their particular city or even the state of Connecticut. Kids walked from school to ball diamond to home without a care. Mothers left newborns with near strangers to watch for brief amounts of time. Fathers came home punctually from work at 5:30. Twenty-one-year-old Sheilah Kapsinow lay laboring in her hospital bed. This, her third pregnancy and third labor, was much more difficult than the previous ones. She rolled from side to side as she lay, and a kind nurse patted her hand to console her. Sheilah's blood pressure rose and fell, and her doctor hinted that she might need a cesarean section.

"Doctor Freeman, please … no cesarean," Sheilah panted through her labor contractions.

"Well, Sheilah, I will give you a few more hours to dilate, and then we will have to probably have to do the surgery. You or your baby could suffer."

Sheilah nodded. She trusted Dr. Freeman, one of the growing numbers of Jewish doctors in the New Haven area. She had liked him from the first time she met him, two years ago when she was pregnant with Heide. Freeman had an easygoing manner and seemed to respect her. Yet, now, Sheilah knew that danger could be imminent. Her water had broken two hours before and she had been experiencing strong, painful contractions ever since. She had only dilated to four centimeters. "Six more to go!" the doctor teased as if he were counting laps at a track-and-field event. Her back hurt. It was really only on one side and localized. Sheilah tried to ignore that particular pain and chalked it up to labor.

The nurse left her briefly for a bathroom break, and Sheilah closed her eyes. She was tired, but the contractions kept her from being able to sleep. Her mind wandered aimlessly. She thought of Marcy and Heide. They were staying at her parents' house while she was in the hospital. She wasn't sure what her husband Allen was doing. *Probably at the gin mill*, she thought. *He'd better be staying away from Becky Tyler. Damn new secretary. Home-wrecker.* Sheilah's thoughts were wrested away with a new contraction that made her yell out sharply and briefly.

When the two hours were nearly up, Dr. Freeman came back in and examined her.

"How do you feel, Sheilah?"

"Like hell, Doctor. Ready to have this baby!"

"Well let's see how you are doing. Hmm … okay. Okay … fine, nine centimeters. We'll let you go to ten without surgery."

This was just how Abbe came into the world. Dr. Freeman lifted the tiny remaining lip of the cervix over the baby's head as she crowned and bulged from Sheilah's stretched vaginal walls. Once the head was out, the shoulders followed easily. Dr. Freeman and the nurse quickly wiped off the fluids and scant blood on Abbe's body, which was followed by a light swat to the bottom and umbilical cord clamping. Dr. Freeman looked at the clock and announced, "Time of birth—9:57 p.m."

Abbe was wrapped in a light receiving blanket and placed on her mother's chest. Sheilah looked down at her and smiled widely. She lightly stroked her newborn's nose, and the baby opened her eyes and quietly studied Sheilah's blurry face.

"Isn't she beautiful?" Sheilah remarked.

"She certainly is. You are a fortunate woman," said the nurse.

"Thank you for staying with me."

"That's what I'm here for."

This was a melancholy moment for Sheilah. She had a beautiful new baby in her arms that she immediately bonded with, and she had no family with which to share the moment. *It's okay*, thought Sheilah, *you and me and your sisters will soon be all together. We'll manage somehow.*

A sharp pain in her lower back made her wince. The pain did not cease as she looked at the nurse. It was hard to speak.

"Doctor Freeman, I think you better come back," called the nurse down the hall.

When Sheilah awoke from surgery, she felt appropriately groggy. It was hard for her to focus. Her first thought was, *Where is my baby?* She moaned as she tried to turn onto her left side, the pain intensifying as she moved. She felt confused as to what had happened. She couldn't keep her eyes open. She slept.

When Sheilah awoke the next morning, a nurse was entering her room.

"How are you feeling?"

"I'm fine, I guess. A little achy, especially on my side."

"That's to be expected. Dr. Freeman will be in to see you shortly."

Sheilah had the nurse pull the blinds and asked her what day it was.

"It's Wednesday. You had your surgery on Monday night."

"What surgery?"

"For your kidney. The doctor will be in soon to explain."

"But ... where is my baby? Where is Abbe?"

"Oh, she is in the nursery upstairs. They will bring her down so you can see her after the doctor speaks with you."

The nurse left the hospital room, closing the door quietly behind her. Sheilah looked outside and noticed several sparrows playing among the branches of the poplar tree just outside. She wondered about her other children as well and hoped they were happy being with her parents. The sky was clear with wispy clouds here and there. It looked like a perfect day. *I've lost two days with my daughter. What surgery? Oh, where is that doctor?* Sheilah's thoughts matched the clouds, random and punctuated.

Sheilah welcomed a superficial rap on the door, as Dr. Freeman entered the room.

"How is my favorite patient? I see you are mentally with us today," teased the doctor.

"What kind of surgery did I have? What happened?"

"Ah, so soon with the questions? No 'I am fine, Doctor, and how are *you* this beautiful day'?" he kidded.

"I'm sorry, I am anxious. I wake up after being down for two days, and I'm achy and don't have my newborn daughter. So, naturally, I'm asking questions."

"Sheilah, this pregnancy was difficult on you. The baby is fine, but you—your poor body went through hell this time. You basically developed a ureter infection, and it ruined one of your kidneys, which had to be removed."

Sheilah gasped and put her left hand to her mouth in shock.

"It's okay—people can survive with one kidney and do just fine. We had no choice. You were in danger."

"How long do I need to be here?"

"So soon she's leaving?" said the doctor with his best Yiddish accent. "Probably three more days."

Sheilah's head fell back against her pillow in disappointment. She immediately thought not only of Abbe, but her other children. They all needed her.

"Sheilah, the thing you need most, besides healing, is rest. You aren't going to get that trying to take care of a newborn and with two young ones pulling at you as well. Can I make a suggestion?"

"Sure," Sheilah replied glumly.

"Have your parents keep the children with them, and you and your husband hire a baby nurse that will come live with you for a couple of weeks."

"And how can we afford a baby nurse?"

"Your husband is now a foreman at the company, isn't he? So, he's making some okay money. I know a couple of baby nurses, one in particular, who are very affordable."

"I don't know," said Sheilah skeptically.

"Well, my dear, you think about it, and we'll talk tonight when your husband comes in for the baby."

"He's coming in tonight for the baby?"

"Sure, the baby doesn't need to be in the hospital. She's healthy as a little horse. She needs to be with her family."

"She needs to be with me."

"Okay, Sheilah, don't worry, the nurse is bringing her down from the nursery in a few minutes. Let's just talk tonight, okay?"

"Thanks, Dr. Freeman. We'll talk."

Sheilah watched the doctor as he left the room and then buried her face in her pillow so her cries would be muffled. This was not the way that she wanted life to be right now. Everything seemed to be falling apart right in front of her. *How could Allen take care of a newborn? Dr. Freeman doesn't know what he almost did to Marcy.* She lay in bed and waited patiently for Abbe, beautiful Abbe, with her big blue eyes and soft, round cheeks.

Allen was promptly late, of course, but brought the younger children with him, which made up for the transgression. She got big hugs from Heide and Marcy and a peck on the cheek from Allen.

"My, you two have grown since I saw you last," Sheilah said to her children who sported beaming smiles.

"Are you both being good for Grandma and Grandpa?"

The children nodded affirmatively.

"Well, good. Mommy had an operation, and I'll be in the hospital a few more days. And then I have to rest at home. So it will be about another week before you two come home for good."

Little Marcy and Heide seemed nonplussed about the need for them to stay longer with their grandparents. In a way, it made Sheilah feel happy that they were doing well. She knew that her parents were doing a good job with them. *Lord knows it's not easy with a five- and two-year-old running around the house*, she thought.

After the family had visited for thirty minutes, Dr. Freeman knocked on Sheilah's door. He shook hands with Allen and patted the children on the head.

"Your mommy is a brave lady, do you know that?" said the doctor.

The children nodded.

"She had a boo-boo on her back that we had to fix. She's almost all better, but she needs lots of rest and quiet for awhile."

Dr. Freeman pulled up a chair for him and Allen. The men sat down, and the doctor continued. "Now, as I explained to you both, you are going to need some help at home. The only reasonable thing I can think of is for you to hire a baby nurse."

Allen piped in and said, "Then, we'll do what we have to and get us a nurse. Okay with you, hon?"

Allen had never invited such input from Sheilah before, and she guessed that he was doing so because the doctor was present.

"I don't think we have a choice."

"Well, good then," said Dr. Freeman. "I'd like to recommended one lady that I keep in my register of nurses. Her name is Virginia Jaspers. She is a rather large woman and has some idiosyncrasies, but I highly recommend her. In fact, her father is an ex-state senator. Pretty nice, huh?"

"Sure," said Allen. "And you say she is pretty cheap?"

"Yes, one of the cheapest in the area. But she's a good caregiver. I've made arrangements, in anticipation that you would agree to this, for her to start this evening. She will meet Allen and the baby at home."

"And she can handle everything?" asked Sheilah hesitantly.

"Oh, of course," the doctor said, smiling.

CHAPTER SIXTEEN

"Who's That Man?"

August 18, 1956
New Haven, Connecticut

When Sheilah Kapsinow was discharged from the hospital that August Saturday morning, she didn't expect it to be so hot. She also didn't expect to mutter, "Jesus," under her breath when she set eyes on Virginia Jaspers for the first time. Allen had picked Sheilah up from the hospital at 10:00 (it was the best he could do) and drove her back to their place on Brookside Avenue. They still lived in low-rent housing, even though Allen was now a foreman at Armstrong Rubber and Tire Co. Beads of sweat formed as she silently rode in the car. Allen was still waking up.

As their Buick pulled into the driveway, Sheilah got a good look at Virginia standing on the small porch holding Abbe in one hand and a paper fan in the other. The nurse's large hand and arm waved quickly to and fro in a useless effort to make the fan beat the morning heat. She smiled large and mouthed something to the baby that Sheilah could not make out.

"Who the hell is holding my baby?" Sheilah whispered to Allen, who was starting to get out of the car.

"Virginia. Doc told us she was big, didn't he?"

Big was the wrong word. Sheilah thought *enormous* suited her better. *She must be over 200 pounds*, Sheilah thought as she slowly pulled her way to a standing position outside the car.

"Hot day to come home, isn't it?" were Virginia's first words to Sheilah.

"My, it certainly is."

"Here, let me help you up the stairs."

"Oh, I'm okay," said Sheilah as she grabbed the thin metal banister at the base of the first step.

"Nonsense, I can help," said Virginia as she dropped the fan to the ground. "Oops, clumsy me!" she declared.

"Hey, glad it wasn't the baby."

Virginia roared with laughter. "You are a funny one."

"Yes, and slightly invalid."

Virginia roared even more as she slowly pulled Sheilah up the steps. Sheilah felt a bit embarrassed and slightly disgusted as her arm brushed against the nurse's rotund stomach several times. When the goal of the top stair was attained, Sheilah reached for Abbe, who was partly asleep.

"I'll get the door," said Virginia.

Sheilah balanced Abbe in the crook of her right arm and went inside. She kept looking at the little girl. *She's gotten more beautiful*, Sheilah observed.

"I know it's kinda early, but I made you a bologna sandwich. Kosher, as you like."

Sheilah thought the last comment was odd and wondered if Virginia had asked Allen about the things she liked to eat. It was a nice gesture on her part, but she really wasn't hungry.

"How about I put it in the fridge until later. I'd like to spend some time with the baby."

"I'll do it for you," said Virginia, happily walking into the kitchen.

Idiosyncrasies, yes, but maybe she'll work out okay, thought Sheilah as she sat down to be with Abbe.

The soft living room couch became Sheilah's home base all that week. It served every purpose she needed. It was near the Regal desktop radio. In front of the couch was an old cherry coffee table that held a bounty of magazines (many were Virginia's *Photoplay* magazines). A phone was in easy reach. Pillows and a blanket were folded neatly on the floor, and a folding tray was tucked under the couch. Sheilah stayed on the couch day and night, except for a bathroom break, occasional stretch, or short walk around the dining room with Abbe, whose bassinet was kept at the foot of the couch on the floor. She was making the most of Dr. Freeman's orders for rest. There was complete understanding on her part about the necessity of this arrangement. Sheilah was just pleased to be able to spend time with and care for her daughter. The other children were near and dear to her heart, but there was something about Abbe that was very special, something unique that created a matchless place in her heart.

August 22, 1956
New Haven, Connecticut

"What time are the children arriving for their visit today?" asked Virginia, waking Sheilah the next morning.

"Well, Virginia, you woke me, for one thing. Abbe was a bit restless last night. And secondly, to answer your question, I believe Allen is going to leave work early and will bring them here for dinner. I'd like to try and move around a bit today, and I'll make the dinner."

Virginia looked a bit downtrodden. Sheilah had been doing much of the care-giving because she wanted to, so Virginia had done light housework and ran errands. She also gave Abbe some sink baths, changed many diapers, and prepared the bottles. She seemed embarrassed for waking Sheilah.

Sheilah realized this and said, "Look, I wasn't scolding you. I just haven't had my coffee, and you wanted to start a conversation when I had my eyes closed."

"Oh, it's fine," said the nurse as she brought over a bottle of formula.

"I am looking forward to seeing Marcy and Heide tonight. Oh, would you be kind and walk over to the market and buy a few goodies for the children? I'll send money with you."

"Of course, Mrs. Kapsinow," Virginia said as she trotted off to get her bulging purse.

Sheilah often wondered what the contents of her purse were. It was a large white purse with two side straps on the top. Sheilah bet there were several hankies inside (Virginia was always wiping her nose and sometimes blotting her eyes), a hairbrush, a glasses case, a compact (without make-up), pencils, notepad, etc. Virginia's purse was equivalent to the couch for Sheilah—everything she needed was within reach. Sheilah, at times, felt sorry for the large woman. Her job was her life. From the couch, she'd often see the nurse sniffling into one of her hankies and shaking her head from side to side causing her bobbed, curly hairdo to shake in rhythm. Her black horn-rimmed glasses would teeter on the edge of the kitchen table and even sometimes fall to the floor. Sheilah recognized that she was a sad woman who laughed and made small talk just to make her own day brighter. The Kapsinows never entertained, so it was a very quiet household for the baby nurse. She seemed bored, which was why Sheilah wasn't surprised when Virginia raced for the door to go to the market.

"Mommy! Mommy!" the voices filled the air, which pleased Sheilah to no end. The two children raced through the front door and showered their mother with hugs and kisses.

"Oh, how it's great to see you two!" said Sheilah, sitting on the edge of the couch. "I've missed you both terribly."

Marcy and young Heide smiled, giggled, and continued to hug her. Sheilah asked about their time with their grandparents.

"Oh, Mommy, we like it there, but we really want to be with you!" exclaimed Marcy.

"Yes, Mommy wants to be with you too, maybe in a couple days. I'm feeling so much better. I even made your favorite dinner tonight— spaghetti and meatballs!"

"Oh boy!" cried the children.

Allen picked up Abbe from her bassinet and carried her around the living room, cooing lightly in her face. She blinked several times, still having difficulty focusing on anyone who held her. Allen was being careful, and the baby seemed content, so Sheilah paid them no mind and focused her attention on the other children. The two girls talked about the rhymes that Grandma shared with them and how Grandpa made them each a wooden boat.

As Marcy began to recite one of her rhymes, Virginia walked into the living room up close to the children. Marcy heard the footsteps and Virginia saying, "You must be the children." The five-year-old turned around quickly and found herself facing the nurse's blue dress. Her eyes looked up toward Virginia's face, and the girl's mouth dropped open. She felt a warming sensation in her body. She dared not look away. She wanted to say something but couldn't.

"Cat got your tongue, dear?" Virginia kidded.

Marcy immediately turned back to her mother and buried herself in the nape of Sheilah's neck.

"Are you a shy one?" asked Virginia.

Marcy tried to be quiet but whispered aloud, "Mommy, who is that man?" She had never seen a man wearing a dress before or a hairdo like that. He seemed very strange.

Her mother broke the silence. "Marcy, this is Miss Jaspers. Why don't you shake hands?"

Marcy shook her head, which was still buried in Sheilah's neck. Heide's mouth was propped open as well. She stood and stared.

Virginia seemed to take the whole affair personally and said, "Well, I wanted to tell you all that dinner is almost ready." She then turned and walked into the kitchen.

"Marcy, that wasn't nice of you. You usually aren't shy."

"She is scary-looking, Mommy. I don't like her."

Heide then noticed her sister cuddling Sheilah and raced next to her too.

"Oh, you're both being silly. She is helping me take care of baby Abbe. Come on, let's get some dinner after we wash our hands."

What was eaten of the dinner was tasty for the children, but they pushed their food around in a distracted way. It was hard for them to enjoy their meal with someone as intimidating as Virginia sitting across from them talking constantly, shoveling heaps of spaghetti into her mouth, and laughing loudly. Whenever she asked the children questions, Marcy would be the only one to answer, but even she looked away and offered only concise responses.

"Marcy, dear, what's wrong?" asked her mother.

"Nothing, Mommy, I guess I just miss you."

"I know, honey, it'll only be a few more days, and then you kids will be back here. Miss Jaspers will stay another couple of weeks."

Marcy looked over at Virginia, who was lost in her meal. The girl's eyes were sad, and she wondered when things would get back to normal. At her grandparents' house that night, she cried herself to sleep as her younger sister slept. *When?* she wondered. *When?*

CHAPTER SEVENTEEN

"Don't Worry, She'll Be Fine"

5:00 p.m.
Thursday, August 23, 1956
New Haven, Connecticut

"Oh, God, yes! I've never heard of anything so ridiculous. He went on to say that ..." Sheilah's voice trailed off as Virginia walked over to one of the cupboards to get the dinner dishes. Sheilah was on the phone with her good friend Muriel Esposito for the second time that day. Virginia could tell she was bored. She had said some spiteful things to her that morning, or at least Virginia interpreted them to be spiteful. Virginia hummed as she set the table for dinner; her thoughts jumped in her head. She couldn't connect with any one thought, as if her mind were playing hot potato. The humming helped keep the urge to cry away. *Babies ... strollers ... that house ... evil ... don't you cry ... look at the horse ... Virginia, I don't know about that ... What the hell happened?*

The volume of Virginia's humming intensified to the point that Sheilah called out from the living room, "Virginia, please, I'm on the phone!"

"Okay, sorry, Mrs. Kapsinow," the nurse replied. She then tilted her head and silently mouthed in a mocking way, "Virginia, please I'm on the

117

phone." The word *phone* slipped from her mouth and was audible enough for Sheilah to hear.

"Excuse me?"

"Oh … oh nothing, I was just saying that I like the style of your phone."

Sheilah shook her head and said to her friend, "Muriel, I've got to get out of here tonight. I'm really going stir crazy. No, I know what the doctor said, but I feel fine. I made dinner last night and everything. Do you mind if I come over after dinner? Allen should be home to help Virginia watch the baby."

Virginia straightened up a bit when she heard about the plan for Sheilah to leave the house. A smile crept to her face. *Oh good,* she thought, *a chance to show them how well I can care for the baby. Maybe I'll send Mr. K. out to do something, and I can then show them that I took care of Abbe all by myself! They'll be very proud of me and even give me a small raise.* Virginia glowed in the thought of having Abbe all to herself. She'd show them, she would. And she started humming again.

At 5:30, Allen came home and headed for the refrigerator to get a cold Budweiser. He sighed as he dropped into the cushioned chair in the living room.

"You're a little late. Tough day at work?"

"Yeah, some craziness, since we're short-handed with people going on vacation."

"Are you ready for dinner?"

"No, I just want to rest."

Allen closed his eyes, slouched down in the chair, and sucked on his beer.

Sheilah shrugged her shoulders and checked on Abbe in her bassinet.

"Oh, you're awake! Well … how was your baby nap?"

Sheilah picked Abbe up under her tiny arms and noticed that she couldn't feel the baby's bones as easily as she could several days ago. "My, you are getting big. Eating so well! Are you hungry now?"

Abbe stared at Sheilah, who looked at the clock. *She's pretty quiet. I'll have Virginia feed her when I go*, she thought.

They both sat down with Virginia, who was already sitting and waiting patiently at the table for anyone to join her. The two women ate quietly, so as not to disturb Allen, and Abbe rested passively in her mother's left arm. Sheilah physically had felt quite good all day, and she was looking forward to leaving the house. She had some slight pangs of guilt when she thought about leaving, but she reasoned that between Allen and Virginia, Abbe would get at least adequate care for a few hours. Sheilah made eye contact with Abbe during each bite of her food; Virginia concentrated on the morsels on her plate.

"You're a beautiful baby, you are," she whispered to her baby. "I'll miss you."

7:00 p.m.
Thursday, August 23, 1956
New Haven, Connecticut

Sheilah put on her shoes and coat and prepared to leave. She walked over to Allen, who was nearly sleeping, and gave him a kiss on the cheek. He mumbled something, and she turned toward the front door. Virginia held the door open for her and said, "Now, don't you worry about anything. Have fun tonight!"

"Well, Virginia, I don't know how much fun it's going to be, a couple of young ladies sitting around talking for a few hours. But, thank you. Please take good care of Abbe."

"Oh, I will. Yes, I will. You can count on me!"

Something made Sheilah reconsider her decision about going to see Muriel for a second, but she shook off the urge to change her mind and walked out into the dusky evening. Before she did, she looked over at Abbe, who was busy staring at the ceiling.

Virginia decided to make a bit of racket in order to accomplish her plan. She went into the kitchen and grabbed a few dirty dinner pots and pans and turned on the hot water. While she was scrubbing them, she banged them against the side of the metal sink. She hummed loudly as well.

"Christ, Virginia, can you make some more noise?" Allen called from the other room.

"Oh, I'm sorry, Mr. K. Were you still resting?"

"Yes, I *was*. Guess I'll go sit on the porch."

"Well, Mr. K., I'm fine here with the baby. Why don't you go out and have some fun? Take a load off and all that! Maybe at *Kelsey's?*" Virginia emphasized the name of the bar since she knew that Allen was fond of it.

"I guess I could go for a few brews, now that you mention it."

"Goody!" the nurse said aloud.

With that, Allen proceeded outside, and Virginia proceeded into the living room.

7:30 p.m.
Thursday, August 23, 1956
New Haven, Connecticut

Shortly after Allen left, the shaking began. Abbe was slightly fussy, and Virginia suspected she was hungry. After a bottle was made and heated, Virginia made herself comfortable on the living room couch and clicked on the radio.

"See?" she said. "I can be just like Mommy!" She cackled with delight. Abbe turned from the bottle as it was presented to her lips. Virginia scowled and pulled the bottle from her mouth and said, "Okay, baby. Bottle time!"

Abbe began to root for the bottle, but when it was presented to her, she cried.

"No, no, no time for crying. Bottle time!" Virginia said angrily.

Abbe continued to cry. The nurse stood, threw the bottle to the floor, and began to walk in circles while holding the baby.

"Okay, baby, any time you want a bottle."

Sweat began to form on the nurse's brow, and her heart began to race. Virginia knew it was coming. She didn't feel that she could stop herself. She tried, though, and paced more quickly. The walking became harder. Abbe spit out saliva and gagged on Virginia's shoulder.

"No! No! You Jew baby!! No spit up!"

Virginia grabbed the eleven-day-old under her arms, unlike her mother had just hours before. She began to yell nonsense phrases about burping and carriages and mean people. Abbe screamed in response. The nurse's shaking was sudden and brutal as if she were trying to take the baby's head off her shoulders. Abbe's head whipped back and forth, her chin hitting her chest and the crown of her head striking her back. The baby was unconscious within the first five seconds of shaking. The nurse continued to shake for fifteen more seconds and then tossed the baby onto the couch, where she lay in a tiny heap on her side. Remnant tears rolled down the baby's nose. Her breaths were shallow. Virginia towered over her and just glared. She then reached out to the baby and swatted her behind, saying, "I told you bottle!" Abbe did not feel a thing.

CHAPTER EIGHTEEN

"Look at me. Get an autopsy!"

5:50 a.m.

Friday, August 24, 1956

Grace New Haven Community Hospital

New Haven, Connecticut

Dr. Taylor looked at his watch as he stood over the girl laid out on the metal table before him. Dr. Salinger and Dr. Michel stood by looking at her as well. Their faces were sad and tired. It had been a long night.

"Time of death: 5:50 a.m."

Dr. Salinger reached down and pulled the sheet over the baby's body.

12:10 a.m.

Friday, August 24, 1956

Grace New Haven Community Hospital

New Haven, Connecticut

"I need you to get Dr. Salinger please."

"Yes, Doctor," said the nurse running out of the examination room.

Dr. Michel noticed a delicate trickle of blood running down the baby's back from where her lumbar punctures had recently been performed. He was now poking the top of her scalp with a fine-gauge hollow needle. No blood squirted out as he had thought it would, no xanthochromic fluid, no CSF—nothing. Michel moved over to the right frontal lobe of the skull and slowly slid the needle in through the anterior fontanel. He felt the needle hesitate a bit at the juncture of the dural membrane, and he applied more pressure. The needle pierced through and entered the subdural cavity. *I know you're in there*, he thought, *where's the blood?* He watched the tiny hole at the end of the needle to see if anything came out. Again, there was nothing. "What the hell?" he said and withdrew the needle.

While he waited for Salinger to arrive, he rechecked Abbe's vitals and cleaned her back. He held up the test tubes of cerebrospinal fluid and examined them. They were floridly bloody. *Too bad it couldn't be clear colored as it should be*, he pondered. The baby's respirations were becoming shallower, and he asked another nurse to give her oxygen. He looked again at Abbe's body, naked except for a small diaper. He wondered about the origin of the tiny scratch on her abdomen and the roughened area on her left knee, which looked very much to be a sheet burn. There was a two-centimeter pale brown contusion on her right elbow that caught his eye. He looked at it more closely and could not tell how she got it. He reached down and stroked her head. He felt her downy hair and looked at her long eyelashes. He shook his head side to side in despair.

Dr. Salinger walked quickly down the hall of Grace New Haven Community Hospital toward the emergency room. He had been on call that night and had been working on his charting when the nurse knocked on his office door and called his name. She explained that an infant girl was semi-comatose and had been brought in within the last hour. Salinger could not surmise as to what had happened and did not have any names. Larry Michel was a very competent pediatrician, and he really did not need monitoring. Salinger thought that it must be something that was going awry; the nurse didn't elaborate.

He proceeded into the examination room and observed Michel huddling over the infant.

"What's up, Larry?" he asked.

"Oh, hi, Bob. Tough case here. I suspect this girl has an infection or fell or something and sustained a head injury, because her anterior fontanel looks like it's about to pop."

Salinger first looked at her fontanel and then felt its raised ridge. "Yes, it's something. What's her temperature?"

"Really nothing to shake a stick at: 100.8."

"No, you're right. I doubt infection."

"Bob, one of the reasons why I bothered you ..."

"Hey, no bother—it's why I'm on call."

"True, but one of the reasons was that her CSF is bloody. I stuck her three times, because at first, I thought that it was a traumatic tap and that I wasn't hitting the spinal fluid. But, I mean, it's bloody!"

Dr. Salinger looked at the tubes of spinal fluid. The majority of the liquid was blood. He looked at Michel with a concerned expression and said, "Do you suspect head injury?"

"Yes, unfortunately. But the thing is, I tapped for subdural blood twice now and got zero back. I don't know if I'm not hitting it or what. With the blood in her CSF, it looks like subarachnoid bleeding."

"Quite possibly," Salinger said. "Tell me her history."

"Well, the mother calls the operator, who reaches me at home. I get on the line, and this woman is hysterical. I took it with a grain of salt, but I was concerned, so I drove right over. I took one look at the baby and called the ambulance. I've been working on her awhile. We gave her one million units of penicillin, 120 micrograms of Gantracin, and 150 micrograms of Chloromycetin. She is on oxygen and looks like crap."

"Okay, very good. But tell me who was caring for her at home."

"The mother states that she had been over at a friend's house, and when she came home, this is how she found the baby."

"Who was caring for her while the mother was gone?"

"The mother told me it was a baby nurse."

Salinger tilted his head slightly to the right so he could hear Michel's response as he asked his next question. "Do we have the name of this nurse?"

"Yes, the mother said that her name was Jasper, or Jaspers, something like that."

Dr. Salinger's face sunk. He walked over to the wall and pounded the cork bulletin board that was hanging there with his fist and shouted, "Good God! Not again. She keeps killing these babies!"

Dr. Michel was taken aback and calmly waited for an explanation.

Salinger stared down at the floor for a minute and gained his composure. The Jaspers woman had been the biggest challenge of his career, and she was winning. He felt that he was useless in being able to protect defenseless babies in and around New Haven. The Hippocratic oath demanded that he "do no wrong," and this was a pledge that he not only upheld, but also lived by. He was sorry that there wasn't a similar one for the in-home pediatric nurse profession.

"Larry, I'm sorry for my outburst, but the woman is driving me crazy!"

"Well, please clue me in on what the story is," said Michel.

Salinger briefly described the history of Virginia's cases and the mortality that she left in her wake. Michel was stunned and then looked over at Abbe, still gasping for breath under an oxygen mask. "So, this is her latest victim. What are we going to do?"

"If, God forbid, this girl dies, we'll need to get an autopsy and combine the results of that with the nurse's history. And then press Bob Taylor to push for an arrest."

"Well, you know, the baby's mother is Jewish. It'll probably be a feat getting her to agree to an autopsy, since it's a problematic procedure in the Jewish faith."

"I'm sure you will work wonders with her," said Salinger patting the young doctor on the arm. "Now, let's quit talking about her dying and get to work saving her life."

A third tap into the subdural space of Abbe's brain produced no blood. Salinger pursed his lips. He and Michel highly suspected that

Abbe had abnormal bleeding in her brain, but she was too unstable for any kind of surgery. It was a waiting game for the two—all they could do was keep her vital signs stable.

After a half hour, Dr. Salinger asked the nurse to contact Dr. Robert Taylor, who was the acting medical examiner for the county. Salinger said to Michel, "It doesn't look good, so I want to make sure he has all the information, so we can nail down a case for this nurse."

Michel looked down at Abbe again and stroked her head. "Such a waste," he said.

6:15 a.m.
Friday, August 24, 1956
Grace New Haven Community Hospital
New Haven, Connecticut

When Abbe's mother saw Dr. Michel walk towards her in the hallway outside the emergency room, she knew that her baby was dead. She shook her head from side to side and cried into the palms of her hands. Dr. Michel led her slowly to a padded bench and pulled a fresh handkerchief from his lapel. He sat with her in silence and allowed the mother to grieve.

Still sobbing, Sheilah looked at him and said, "It's not fair, you know. The baby and I both go through hell trying to get her born, and then she dies. God, it's not fair!"

Michel felt his own tears begin to well and brushed them away quickly. He was not sure what to say, so he focused on the clinical aspects of Abbe's death. "She didn't suffer. She lapsed into a coma, and her heart stopped."

Sheilah looked up at the doctor. "Oh, but she did suffer. Aren't you aware of that?"

"Mrs. Kapsinow, I meant that she didn't suffer in death. I am aware of the fact that her injuries were most likely not natural."

"Yes, you are absolutely right about that! It was that nurse, that scum nurse," said Sheilah with abhorrence in her voice. She then laughed slightly. "I ... I thought it was my husband who beat her. It would be like him to do that, but he was at some gin mill, instead. Why? Why did I let Dr. Freeman talk me into getting a nurse? Why did I leave Abbe? She needed me," cried Sheilah, burying her head in her hands.

"Mrs. Kapsinow, in order to find out what truly happened to your baby, we are going to need, well, an autopsy. You will need to approve it. It is very important in matters like this."

Sheilah continued to cry with her head bowed. "I don't know. How can I live with this? How?"

"Look at me."

Sheilah slowly raised her head; her face was wet with tears.

"We need to get an autopsy, regardless of what the Jewish faith says. It will tell us what happened."

"Okay. I don't care about what my synagogue or the Jewish faith has to say right now. I want to do what is right. I want to find out what happened."

10:20 a.m.
Friday, August 24, 1956
New Haven, Connecticut

Dr. Steve Downing spoke into the dictating machine just before he pulled the baby's brain from her cranium.

"After opening the dura, the brain tissue bulges. The gyri of the convexity of the brain are flattened and the sulci compressed. Massive fresh subdural bleeding is encountered over the convexities bilaterally. The subdural hematoma can be removed with ease. No rust-brown discoloration of the dura or leptomeninges is observed. The tentorium cerebelli does not reveal any old or new tears ... however, an accumulation of blood is seen in those regions where the meningeal veins converge to enter the superior sagittal sinus. Fresh blood, partially clotted, is seen to cover the falx cerebri … There is subarachnoid bleeding, especially on the median surfaces of the brain, bilaterally, as well as over the convexities of the brain."

"What a mess," he said as he replaced the organ carefully back into its shell. He paused and rubbed the tip of his nose with his gowned forearm to satisfy an itch that had interrupted him. All these perfect organs in a perfectly well-nourished body and a brain that looked like it had been pulverized. He continued his work in thorough, yet expeditious, silence. This baby was one of those hot ones that had been handed to him from the top. Even if he was only the acting ME, when Bob Taylor said, "Jump!" Downing said, "How high?" Taylor gave him the case, because he was one of the best pathologists in the area. Downing didn't miss much. Even with this case, he weighed and measured everything carefully.

"Kidneys—microscopically normal; weight is 15 grams each. Pancreas—pale pink, no evidence of congestion, main duct is patent throughout; length 6 centimeters. Ovaries—one tiny ovary is present on each side of the pelvic cavity; they are grossly unremarkable. Stomach—the surface of the stomach is unremarkable. On opening the stomach, 30-40 cc's of curdled milk is seen. The duodenum contains a small amount of pasty food material."

Dr. Taylor entered the autopsy room as Downing was beginning to suture the body closed.

"What's the verdict?" Taylor asked.

"Homicide. Her brain looks like mash. Yet, we don't have a confession or story indicating what happened. So, it looks like an undetermined manner of death."

Taylor positioned himself above the body and pulled the flap of the dural membrane from over the brain and peered in.

"Hey, good thing I didn't close that yet—you'd have been messing up my art."

Taylor chuckled lightly and continued to examine the skull and scalp as Downing continued to work on suturing the thoracic cavity.

"No fractures?"

"Nope. Some scratches that shouldn't be present, though."

"No bruises?"

"Slight contusion on the right elbow."

"Well, how in the hell did she get the subdurals? There is no evidence of scalp damage, like she was thrown down or hit in the head."

"Like I said, not sure of mode of injury. Remember, my job is to document *what* she has not how she got them," Downing joked.

"Okay then, Steve, as always, I appreciate your fine work. I'll speak with Corrigan, and then let's get the secretary to type up your report pronto and hope for a confession. I really hate to leave the manner of death section on death certificates blank."

"Less paperwork for me, isn't it?" Downing said with a final grin before Taylor hurried out the door.

CHAPTER NINETEEN

"Let's Go Pick Her Up!"

4:15 p.m.
Friday, August 24, 1956
Coroner James Corrigan's office
New Haven, Connecticut

"Yes, Chief, that is my recommendation. She has a history of possible infant homicides and other abuse. Yes, I spoke with Dr. Salinger and Dr. Taylor. Oh, Salinger contacted you directly? Well, that is fine—he called me too. He knows this woman well, unfortunately, I guess. You think you will be able to get something tangible for this gal? Oh, I see. Well, I am having a courier bring the autopsy report over to you now. Fine. Well, you know where to find me. I hope this won't be anything earth-shattering. But, yes, let's put a stop to her, especially if she has a past. Okay. Good-bye."

4:15 p.m.
Friday, August 24, 1956
Police Chief McManus's office
New Haven, Connecticut

Chief Francis V. McManus hung up the phone and turned his small, thin frame to the outside of his desk to stand. He walked quickly into the next room and called, "Eagan!"

Assistant Chief Raymond Eagan popped up from his desk as if he had just heard a fire drill. "Yes, Chief?"

"Just got a call from Corrigan—we got a baby killer on our hands. Guess who?"

Eagan frowned with a questioning expression in response.

"The ex-senator Jaspers' daughter."

"No foolin'?"

"No foolin'. Let's go pick her up."

6:00 p.m.
Friday, August 24, 1956
East Haven, Connecticut

It had been awhile since Chief McManus had been on a stakeout, but he wanted to be a part of this one. Prior to leaving the station, he had asked Lieutenant Mae Gilhuly to phone the Jaspers' home and ask for the nurse. Gilhuly posed as a potential client and spoke with Virginia's mother. "No, I'm sorry. She is at her sister's house right now. We are not sure when to expect her. Maybe you could call back on Monday morning."

So, a stakeout was planned and formed, with schedules set for the whole weekend. McManus was sensitive to the political nature of this case and decided that watching the Jaspers' house would be the best strategy. The first unmarked police car that held McManus and Assistant Chief Eagan sat one block east of the home. The familiar stakeout smell of coffee and cigarettes already permeated the air of the coupe. The two spoke in non sequiturs for the better part of two hours. They saw William Jaspers come home around 7:00 p.m. and look over at the neighbor's yard, but not in their direction. The sun began to set at 8:15.

"This could be a long weekend, Chief. Suppose she doesn't come back 'til Sunday night?"

"Well, I guess we wait then. Hey, what's the rush, anyway? You got my company for a couple of hours tonight, and then we take the Saturday evening shift too."

Eagan grinned and then sipped on his cooled coffee. An uncomfortable stirring in his bladder prompted him to set down his drink and say, "I'm goin' over to Charlie's garage on the next street over to use the head."

McManus chuckled and said, "Rookie! Just don't fall in—I don't want to bring her in alone."

Eagan swiftly went out the driver's side door and ducked down the nearest alley. He knew Charlie Ottman and also knew that the mechanic would not ask too many questions.

Chief McManus leaned against the door of the coupe and tried not to get too comfortable. He peered up and down the street for any signs of people walking or driving toward the Jaspers' house. Stakeout relief would be there in three hours. He took out a *True Crime* magazine that was surreptitiously folded lengthwise in his jacket pocket and thumbed through it. *What a rag*, he thought, *full of broads, guns, and crooks.* He loved it.

8:00 a.m.
Saturday, August 25, 1956
East Haven, Connecticut

Jane Jaspers looked out their second-floor bedroom window after she raised the shade to let in the rays of the morning sun. She noticed the green sedan that was parked down the block with two dark figures inside. *Funny*, she thought, *why are there two people sitting in their car on an early Saturday morning?* She continued to watch for several minutes. She then caught herself feeling like a peeping Tom and turned away to head downstairs.

William Jaspers was in the den reading the morning paper. There was nothing significant going on in the news, and he perused the paper as he did every morning—with casual indifference. He was near retirement, and he was through with the hectic schedule of a civil and state representative. He liked the passive side of life that was of his choosing. Being assistant manager of personnel at the railroad was a very passive position. His monthly duties as treasurer for the county were relaxed. He balanced the books on Thursday evening for a few hours and was paid for his work. He went to monthly meetings for an hour and then came home. Life was not pressing, and he liked it that way.

Jane saying, "Bill, I think there are two men in a car down the block watching our house," interrupted his reading.

"What? Jane, you've watched too many *Perry Masons*."

"No, really. I saw them from the bedroom window. They are just sitting in there."

"How can you tell it's our house?"

"Well, I can't."

"Then don't worry about it."

"Well, Bill, I think it is just strange that two men are sitting in a car on an early Saturday morning. I've never seen it before."

"Well, if it makes you happy, I'm going to be walking Baby soon, so I'll check it out."

"Oh, good. Thank you."

The Jaspers' two-year-old dog, Baby, hurried ahead of its master in a mad frenzy for a hydrant or pole to urinate on. The leash was taut around the little dog's neck, and it coughed and wheezed as it pulled forward.

"Okay, Baby. Calm down for Chrissakes!"

Jaspers decided to go toward the men in the car to see what they were up to. As soon as he was within twenty-five yards of the sedan, one of the men jumped out and walked around to the trunk. He watched Jaspers as he opened it. He then pulled out a briefcase, closed the trunk, and walked back toward the driver's side of the car.

"G'morning," Jaspers said cordially.

The undercover police officer grabbed the tip of his hat and nodded his head. As he reached for the door handle, the ex-senator said, "Do I know you?"

The officer shook his head and said, "Nope, don't think so."

"Anything I can help you with?"

"No thanks, just a business meeting we are preparing for."

"On Saturday?"

"No, we're just meeting today. Good day," said the officer as he hurriedly sat down and started the ignition.

Jaspers bent forward slightly and caught a look at the second man in the car.

As they drove off, the passenger said displeasingly to the driver, "Business meeting?"

The rest of the day was humdrum, for both the Jaspers and the stakeout officers. McManus and Eagan took the fourth shift, which began at 5:00 p.m. The coupe was positioned on the opposite side of the street with somewhat of a new view.

"I'm tellin' ya, she's not going to show until Sunday!" Eagan protested.

"Hold your water, will you?"

The two settled in for their time and waited for something to happen. Little did they know, something would within the hour.

William was the first to see the coupe this time. *Different car, but still two men inside*, he thought. He didn't want to alarm Jane, so he said, "Honey, I'm taking the pooch out for an early stroll."

"Alrighty," came the response.

Jaspers flung open the door to his house with vigor and this time, carried his excitable dog.

As Jaspers approached the car, Eagan looked over at McManus and asked, "Do we take off?"

"No, Ray. I know Jaspers well, and he has recognized me. So, I'm gonna ask where the hell his daughter is."

McManus opened his passenger door and stood to meet Jaspers, who towered over him.

"Good evening, Chief. Here for a *business* meeting?"

"Sort of. Can you tell me where your daughter is?"

"Why do you ask?" Jaspers asked confidently.

"We'd like to ask her some questions about a baby who died under her care."

"What would she have to do with that?"

"Is she home?"

"No, she's at her sister's in Essex for the weekend."

"When do you expect her home?"

"Probably late Sunday evening."

McManus backed up two steps to position himself closer to the car and scratched the back of his head.

"Could you bring her down to the station Monday morning first thing?"

"We can be there. I believe you are wasting your time, as well as taxpayers' dollars, especially after taking most of the weekend to watch my wife changing her undies and watch my dog take a piss."

McManus pushed the button on the handle of his car door and pulled it open to get in. "We'll see you first thing Monday morning."

Jaspers chuckled and said, "First thing."

The stakeout ended. It did not go as McManus had planned; in fact, he never participated in one ever again. As Eagan drove back to New Haven, the police chief looked out on the bay and thought, *We'll see what Monday brings.*

CHAPTER TWENTY

"It Was All Uncontrollable; I Should Be Given the Electric Chair"

10:15 a.m.
Monday, August 27, 1956
New Haven Police Station
New Haven, Connecticut

Chief McManus held the interview room door opened for Virginia and her father. Ray Eagan sat in the corner of the room, steno pad in hand. Lieutenant Mae Gilhuly sat across from him, and County Coroner James Corrigan sat in the room adjacent to the interview room, watching through the new one-way mirror that had been installed last month. Eagan and Gilhuly were to be the primary interviewers, and McManus was to observe.

Minutes before, as Virginia walked down the hall with her father, she passed by several police officers. Mouths dropped as she passed. One officer's lit cigarette dropped from his mouth as he sat typing a report. He jumped up suddenly, brushing off his pants. Virginia was oblivious. Her focus was the door at the end of the hall. It took her back to the principal's office. The hallway was narrow and dimly lit. Her heart pounded, and her mighty hands were profuse with sweat. She wanted

137

to turn and run away but knew that she couldn't with her father close behind her. *It's no use. I just need to answer their questions and then leave and go back to work. I have appointments, you know,* she said to herself in an effort to calm down.

The police officers in the station looked at each other after the interview room door closed. Bernie Lawlor looked at Harold Berg. "Didja see the size of that broad?"

"Bernie, how could anyone miss? She musta been over two hundred pounds and six feet tall."

"I'd hate to meet her in a back alley."

"Yeah. And besides, she was mighty ugly too."

The officer who dropped the cigarette piped up and added, "No, not ugly. She was fugly!"

Several of the officers chuckled. They milled around nervously. They knew why she was at the station and about the importance of this interview. They knew it would have repercussions in town, yet they didn't know to what extent it would affect them and their work. Three of the six officers who witnessed Virginia come into the station had bad dreams that night, something they wouldn't admit to each other.

William Jaspers held a large cushioned chair for his daughter as she sat down. He, in turn, sat and asked, "So, where do we start?"

Gilhuly began, "Miss Jaspers, we are aware that up until last Thursday, you cared for a baby named Abbe Kapsinow and were staying in her parents' home." She paused to look at her notes for names. "Um … the home of Mr. and Mrs. Allen Kapsinow?"

Virginia swallowed hard and grimaced. "Yes," she replied.

"You also know that she was taken to the hospital?"

Virginia nodded.

"Miss, if you would please actually say 'yes' or 'no' that would be very helpful."

"Yes."

"And you know she was critically ill when she arrived at the hospital's emergency room?"

"I guess. She didn't look too well when she left the house, and her mother was panicking terribly." Virginia smiled as if she had made a joke. She quickly panned the room to look at others' facial expressions, including her father's. He wore a deep frown on his forehead. She then lost her smile and looked down at the wooden table in front of her.

"We spoke with the baby's mother this past weekend, and she told us that Abbe was fine when she left her in your care before she went over to her friend's house. Can you tell us what happened?"

"Well ... the baby was awfully hungry, you know, and this was after Mr. Kapsinow left, so I ..."

Gilhuly interrupted. "Mr. Kapsinow was there with you after Mrs. Kapsinow left?"

"Yes, he was in one of his moods that he gets in. You know, angry. So he decided to go out."

"Do you know where?"

"No, I assume some bar. He likes to go to them, you know."

"Anyway, the baby was hungry ..."

"Yes, very. She tried to drink her bottle that I held, but she couldn't do it!"

"What happened when she wouldn't feed?"

"I tried to burp her. She had on such a face, and she was carrying on so. I must have tried for four or five minutes for a burp. Babies get such bubbles in their stomachs even when they don't take feedings, you know?"

"Yes. So, then what happened?"

"I guess I gave up and quit trying. She wasn't going to feed from that darn bottle, so I put her on the couch. And then I put a pillow next to her."

"What did you do then?"

"I went into the kitchen for my snack. Ice cream, my favorite," Virginia said with a smile.

"Was the baby crying?"

"A bit, more like fussing. I just left her be and did some chores. After that, Mrs. K. came home."

"You left her on the couch for almost three hours?"

"Well, she went to sleep."

"Did you check on her?"

"Yes, ma'am, I looked in on her. She looked just fine."

Eagan leaned forward suddenly and blurted out, "She obviously *wasn't* fine."

The nurse was so taken aback that she lurched back in her chair and said, "Well ... I ... I ..."

The elder Jaspers spoke up for his daughter and asked, "Must we be so harsh in tone?"

Eagan did not miss a beat and replied, "Yes, we must. This is a police interview."

Jaspers leaned back in his chair and folded his hands over his lap. His daughter began to look at the table once again. Her mind searched for something to say. She remembered her father telling her to keep her conversation minimal. *Let them do the talking, Virginia.*

Lieutenant Gilhuly broke the awkward silence and recapped Virginia's story for her. She ended by saying, "And from your point of view, the baby Kapsinow was fine and placed on the couch in your care up until Mrs. Kapsinow arrived home, is that true?"

"Why, yes, that is true."

Gilhuly looked over at Eagan, who nodded at her. "Miss Jaspers, the Kapsinow baby died on Friday morning."

"Ohhh," cried Virginia as she covered her mouth and began to cry. William Jaspers looked shocked and sat without moving as if stunned.

"In fact, Miss Jaspers, we have the autopsy report right here, and it says that she died of a cerebral hemorrhage. In laymen's terms, that meant she had bleeding on her brain, and the doctors believe it was from a head injury."

"Virginia!" William Jaspers said as he turned to his daughter.

"No, Daddy, I didn't do a thing. It ... it was hungry. It wouldn't feed. Really, that's what happened."

"It? You mean Abbe? She didn't happen to fall off the couch? Or maybe you dropped her?" Gilhuly asked the nurse.

"Well, it might have fallen, I mean she ... the baby ... Ab ... oh, you know what I mean. I really can't remember; it's all a blur."

Gilhuly turned to one of the uniformed officers seated in the corner and asked for some water for the nurse.

When the officer returned with the glass of water, Virginia gulped it down at once. A thin line of water and saliva trickled down her chin and dripped on the table. She seemed oblivious and held out the glass to the officer as if she were a toddler motioning for more. The officer grasped the glass, left the interview room, and soon came back with the glass and a pitcher full of water. Eagan smiled slightly and thought to himself, *Hmm, a bargaining tool.*

Gilhuly continued with her interview. "Now that we've had a break, Miss Jaspers, is there anything else that you'd like to say about the Kapsinow baby?"

"No, ma'am, I can't think of anything."

Eagan then spoke up. "Ginny … May I call you Ginny?"

"Well …" was all Virginia got out before Eagan interrupted her.

"Ginny, I'd like to bring up some other cases with you, since you have this mental block about the Kapsinow baby. If this is okay with Lieutenant Gilhuly?"

Mae Gilhuly nodded affirmatively.

"Maybe I should just read some names to you. I'll do it *slowly*, so you can follow along, okay?"

"I don't like …" William Jaspers began to protest.

"Mr. Jaspers, please remember this is a police interview. You are welcome to sit in as long as you do not speak. This is your final warning, or Officer Brantley will escort you out," said Eagan.

"Fine," Jaspers answered.

"Here we go, Ginny. Ready? Bruce Schaefer, Jennifer Malkan, Cynthia Hubbard, any of these names ring a bell, Ginny?"

"Well, of course. They were all infants that I … I cared for," said Virginia semi-confidently.

"You 'cared for,'" repeated Eagan.

"Yes, why do you ask?"

"Well, because two of the three names that I just read are infants who have died under your care in the past eight years, that's why. You want to tell us what the hell happened to 'em?" Eagan barked at the nurse.

She shied back in response and began to cry.

"What is going on here?" asked William Jaspers.

"Thanks for being here, Mr. Jaspers. Officer, please escort him out of the room."

As the elder Jaspers left the room, he stared at his daughter who sat and cried. He was dumbfounded as to the allegations. *They can't mean what they're accusing her of,* he thought as he was shown into the room next door with the one-way view.

Two hours into the interview, Virginia began to confess her crimes. It was partly due to the aggressive "bad cop" style of Eagan and partly due to her full bladder.

"Come on, Ginny. Give us something. We know you hurt those babies. Give us a proper story," Eagan pressed.

"Okay!" she finally blurted out. "I didn't want to hurt her. She was just crying so much."

"Who, Ginny? We need a name."

"All of them!" she shouted.

Silence took over the room. All the officers looked stunned. William Jaspers hung his head in the next room, while Coroner Corrigan took notes.

Gilhuly broke the silence. "You killed all three babies?"

"Yes."

"We need to know how you did it."

Virginia cried loudly and called out, "Ohhh."

"Miss Jaspers, it is important that we know what happened. Go ahead and take a deep breath and tell us."

Virginia swallowed, looked at Mae Gilhuly, and asked, "May I go to the bathroom first?"

Gilhuly's eyes narrowed, and she said, "Maybe after you make your statement."

"I shook them," Virginia said under her breath.

Everyone in the room craned their heads forward in order to hear. Gilhuly asked, "Could you please repeat what you just said more loudly?"

"I *shook* them."

Eagan looked at her questioningly and said, "Whaddya mean 'shook'?"

"You know," said Virginia has she held up her hands and pretended to shake an infant violently back and forth.

The onlookers' eyes widened even more. Officer Brantley muttered what the others in the room were thinking, "Shit!"

Virginia sat back in her chair, seemingly at ease with her confession.

"So, you picked up … Let's begin with the Kapsinow baby. You picked her up as you've shown, and it looked like you had two thumbs on the infant's chest, and you put the tips of your fingers around the baby's sides and back and would then vigorously shake? Is that correct?"

"Yes. Oh—and I squeezed too."

Eagan looked at the floor and shook his head side to side.

"Why did you do this, Miss Jaspers?"

"Because she would not take her formula and go to sleep."

"No, I mean, did you do this to all the babies?"

"No, just the three that died."

"So, if you are a pediatric nurse, aren't you supposed to care for these babies in a kind, loving fashion?"

"Oh, ma'am, I did. I am a very kind woman."

Eagan couldn't take it any longer and said, "You weren't kind and loving. You killed three babies, for Chrissakes!"

"Yes, I know, I'm sorry," Virginia cried.

"Tell that to the parents, lady."

"Oh my God. It was all uncontrollable. I don't know why I did it. Children sometimes get on my nerves."

"You are in the wrong business to be saying that," Eagan said disgustedly.

"All my life I wanted to take … take good care of little ones," Virginia said in between sobs. "I wanted to be a good nurse in people's houses and have them love me like I loved them. I just get these urges that I can't control. I really can't stop myself. They take me over. I know I'm evil. I should be given the electric chair."

Virginia laid her head down on the table and cried. There was another brief moment of silence as the group in the room gathered their thoughts and reconnected to their feelings, made raw by what was just disclosed to them.

"Who else have you injured, Miss Jaspers?" asked Gilhuly.

"Nobody. Now may I please use the bathroom?"

Gilhuly motioned to Officer Brantley, who opened the interview room door. Gilhuly pulled out Virginia's chair for her and led her to the bathroom down the hall. She went into the bathroom with the nurse and allowed her to privately use the stall. After two minutes of urine splashing into the toilet water, Gilhuly asked, "Almost done, Miss Jaspers?"

"Almost," came the soft reply.

What a bladder! the policewoman thought.

Virginia exited the stall. She poofed her hair in the mirror and dabbed her swollen eyes with the hanky that had been stuffed underneath her watch. Gilhuly opened the bathroom door and upon leaving, bumped into Lonnie Renwald.

"Oops! Hey, sorry, Lieutenant!"

"No problem, Lon."

"Hey, Lieutenant, got anything for me today?"

"Nope, sorry, Lon. Let's go, Miss Jaspers ..." When Mae Gilhuly said Virginia's last name, she knew she had made a drastic mistake.

"Jaspers? Whoa, you're a big gal, ain't ya?" said the undersized newspaperman as he grabbed for his memo pad that he held stowed in his hatband. "Would you be any relation to Senator Jaspers?"

"Move along, Lon. Nothing for you today," Gilhuly said as she and Virginia moved back toward the interview room.

"Hey, Mae! What she bein' questioned for? Hey! Are we talkin' some headlines here? I got a deadline for some juice for tonight's edition. Come on!"

Gilhuly closed the interview room door in Renwald's face. Officer Berg lumbered down the hallway to usher the newspaperman to the station lobby.

"Hal, what's the buzz?"

"Can't talk about it, Lonnie."

"Sure ya can, old chum."

"No, I can't. Now get along, will ya?"

"Okay," said Renwald whistling as he strode toward the front entrance. "The headlines are gonna look great! 'Ex-Senator's daughter questioned at the detective bureau today.' Yep, will look great!"

"Lonnie, ya wouldn't!"

"Give me somethin' then."

"Okay, let me talk with the lieutenant."

Gilhuly and Eagan conferred with Chief McManus and Coroner Corrigan in the coffee room for twenty minutes. They decided that since Virginia had confessed and was now in the middle of writing what she had told, they could make a statement to the press. It was decided that Gilhuly and Eagan would both write the statement and have Corrigan check it before it was given out.

"Look, we probably have a few more hours of interviewing left, the pace she's moving," said McManus. "So, this will quiet the press for a little while, and then tomorrow, we can give them more details."

Gilhuly looked at McManus and the others and said, "This is going to be big, you know."

"Sure, around this area, everybody knows Bill Jaspers," said Eagan.

Gilhuly shook her head slightly from side to side and said, "No. It's going to be big *nationally*."

The others looked at her and contemplated what she had said.

4:15 p.m.
Monday, August 27, 1956
New Haven Police Station
New Haven, Connecticut

Mae Gilhuly arranged her papers in a neat stack as she gathered them for her briefcase. She was the sole person remaining in the interview. She was physically and emotionally exhausted. This had been her toughest interview yet, and she still wasn't through.

That afternoon, Virginia Jaspers confessed to breaking Bruce Schaefer's leg and shaking six-week-old Robert Saidel in February 1955. William Jaspers had some choice words for Assistant Chief Ray Eagan as he left the police station and said he would be hiring family friend and probate court judge Edward L. Reynolds Jr. to represent his daughter. Coroner James Corrigan told Chief McManus that a formal inquest would be held the following day to determine what formal charges would be brought. Tomorrow's early morning gathering of the parents of the dead infants and the Schaefer baby would prepare those involved in the Jaspers' investigation for other parents that would come forward.

Mae Gilhuly would start on her phone calls to the parents this evening. *Tomorrow,* she thought, *is going to be pandemonium.* She was right.

6:00 p.m.
Monday, August 27, 1956
New Haven, Connecticut

John Flanagan and his wife sat down together in their living room to read the evening edition of the *New Haven Register.* The couple was stunned as they read the headlines:

"Nurse Arrested in Death of Baby"

"My God, Sophie! This is about Virginia!"

The two had used Virginia for their baby, Emily, two years earlier. They read the official statement within the body of the article:

A 33-year-old East Haven woman, Virginia B. Jaspers, of 132 Prospect Road, is being questioned by police today in connection with the violent death of the 11-day-old daughter of Mr. and Mrs. Allen Kapsinow of 65-H Brookside Avenue.

Chief Francis V. McManus, who, with Assistant Chief Raymond J. Eagan, has taken full charge of the investigation, revealed that the child died last Thursday night of injuries to her head and body.

The police investigation was ordered Friday afternoon at 4:15 p.m. by Coroner James J. Corrigan, who had been notified by Dr. Sterling P. Taylor, acting medical examiner.

Miss Jaspers is also being questioned in connection with the sudden deaths of several other infants who have been in her care over the past seven years. The investigation and questioning of the woman is continuing and all other avenues of the investigation will be pursued. The New Haven Police Department is working in close cooperation with the office of the County Coroner and the State's Attorney's office.

All records of babies who have been under the care of this woman are being checked back to the time when she was qualified as a pediatric nurse.

After reading the statement, the Flanagans, both with tears in their eyes, went into the den, where their little girl was happily playing to give her a long hug.

6:10 p.m.
Monday, August 27, 1956
New Haven Police Station
New Haven, Connecticut

Officer Brantley picked up the phone at the front desk of the police station after it rang three times. "New Haven Police Department. Brantley. Yes, she was arrested. Just like the papers said. Oh, you have a complaint? Hold, please. Widmann! Phone!"

Woman Accused In Baby Deaths Leaves For City Court

August 28, 1956

Miss Virginia B. Jaspers, private pediatric nurse who has admitted fatally injuring three infants and harming two others, is shown leaving the New Haven Police Academy en route to City Court. With the six-foot-tall, 320-pound defendant are Police Chief Francis V. McManus, Detective Thomas Murphy and Detective Lt. Mae Gillhuly. Miss Jaspers, given a continuance to Sept. 15 in court, will appear examined at the coroner's request this afternoon. Her attorney Edward L. Reynolds Jr., said he will have her examined by pshychiatrists as soon as possible.

CHAPTER TWENTY-ONE

"Nurse Kills Three Babies"

8:15 a.m.
Tuesday, August 28, 1956
New Canaan, Connecticut

Judy Sinowitz, the Malkans' former next-door neighbor in Hampton, called Joan Brainerd in New Canaan after she read the *New Haven Register* headlines.

"Hi, Joan, Judy S. here."

Joan immediately tensed as if a bad dream had recurred. She breathed in and said, "Oh, hi, Judy, what can I do for you?"

"No, Joan, it's not what you *can* do for me, but what you *have* done for me and my family. I'm holding baby Stephen on my lap, and I can thank you for that."

"What on earth are you talking about?" Joan asked.

"Haven't you seen the papers?"

"Well, no, why?"

Judy then said, "They've finally caught her. And she did do it. It's so unbelievable."

"I'm sorry, Judy. I still haven't had my morning coffee. Who did what?"

"Virginia, Virginia! That's who. She confessed to killing three babies, including yours. Supposedly, she shook them or something dreadful like that."

149

Joan's knees were weak, and they buckled under her. She grabbed a nearby chair and pulled it toward her in order not to fall down on the floor. Her heart raced, and she felt ill. Her hand that held the phone dropped down to her lap with a soft thud. She stared at the wallpaper for what seemed like several minutes. Judy Sinowitz's distant voice brought her back to reality.

"Hello? Hello? Joan, are you there? Joan?"

"Yes … Judy," Joan mumbled. "I'm a bit in shock. I haven't heard from anyone. Why hasn't anyone called me?"

"Well, Joan, I don't know. I'm calling you, though," Judy said, sounding disappointed.

"Well, I meant somebody in authority, who might need some information or something."

"I bet they'll call you this morning yet," said Judy.

"Shaken, you said?"

"Yes, I'm afraid. Another baby died on Friday … which is how they got her. Oh, Joan, I feel so fortunate that I have my whole family. Thank you, dear. Thank you so much."

"That's fine, Judy," said Joan, still stunned by the news. "I need to go now. I need to speak with Willard."

"Oh, all right. Take care and thanks again!"

Joan laid the phone down in its cradle without saying anything. She covered her eyes with her hands and began to cry. The monster had come back to her once again. It was all a waking nightmare. *Oh, my poor Jennifer.*

Five minutes later, the Malkans' phone rang. It was the New Haven police.

10:15 a.m.
Tuesday, August 28, 1956
New Haven City Courthouse
New Haven, Connecticut

"We definitely intend to have her examined by a psychiatrist," Edward L. Reynolds Jr. said to a torrent of newspaper reporters from across the country, who had converged on the city of New Haven on Tuesday.

"In all probability, there will be more than one psychiatrist," he said confidently standing next to the blindfolded justice statue outside the city courthouse.

One reporter asked, "Well, what can you say about her confession, Mr. Reynolds?"

"Well, that there is no confession. She was under duress and typical police tactics that are so prevalent in this town. I have had virtually no opportunity to privately confer with Miss Jaspers. I feel that the police have been cooperative to a limited extent."

A shout from a reporter in the back of the crowd then asked what was on everyone's mind, "Why'd she do it?"

"She didn't know why she did it," Reynolds said, "and I didn't say much to her when I met with her, because her father was with me and she was paying more attention to him than to me. There was also the presence of police officials. She was distraught, crying, and very remorseful. She was almost incoherent. I told her not to worry."

"Mr. Reynolds …"

"I am a judge, you know."

"Oh, sorry, Judge Reynolds, how are you going to defend Miss Jaspers?"

"Well, very carefully, I'm sure."

This brought a quiet chuckle from the crowd.

"Look, based on the information currently in my possession, the only defense I *can* go on, from the little I know right now, is an insanity defense, if what police say is truly what happened to these babies."

"What about the fact that she is an ex-senator's daughter?" another reported asked.

"What about it? She has had a great track record as a competent, hard-working nurse whose work was well sought after in and around this community. I have known the Jaspers family all my life. They are a wonderful family. My client was one grade behind me in the East Haven schools. Though she is somewhat ungainly, she joined right in with the other kids. Her reputation before her arrest was unblemished. She was very much in demand as a pediatric nurse. I know people who have praised her to the skies for her work with children. This is not just a case as far as I'm concerned; rather, it's a matter of family friendship that goes back to my father's time."

Reynolds looked down at his wristwatch and said, "Okay, folks, one final question," he said confidently.

"Is she going to have trouble making bail?"

"Miss Jaspers is being held under $50,000 bond, but I expect no difficulty in raising bail and freeing her this afternoon after the inquest by Coroner Corrigan, scheduled to get underway in his office at two o'clock. Thank you all," said Reynolds, waving as he turned and trotted up the courthouse stairs, his briefcase bouncing next to him.

Edward L. Reynolds leaned up against the cold tiled wall outside the men's washroom in the city courtroom. He closed his tired eyes and did his best to breathe deeply to counter the staccato beating of his heart. Facing reporters was never easy, but this group almost broke him. This was a terrible case, never in his brief career had he had such a case. It was going to be the one that he'd look back on with a sense of relief. It would be relief in final terms—he'd be happy when it was all over. Two years before, when he successfully secured the position of first judge of probate for the newly established Probate District of East Haven, he had also felt a sense of relief. He was only thirty-one years of age when the appointment was made. The title of judge was something he had aspired to when he was at Northeastern University Law School in Boston. He had made some savvy political connections in East Haven. In fact, he was a member of the East Haven Republican Committee. He also had membership in the local Elks Lodge, Knights of Columbus, and American Legion, which added to his civic organization commitment, thus helping secure the judge position. His wife, Josephine, rarely saw him during the week. She shrugged off his minimal time at home, since she knew full well that a busy attorney's life was his destination. Reynolds' father had been a much-revered judge in New Haven, so she had mentally prepared for this when she married him. She spent quality time with the youngsters, Callista and Edward III, at home. Their father was a weekend father, and it was something that became natural.

Because of having such a busy life, Reynolds put much pressure on himself to do a thorough, no-nonsense job, which was why he leaned against that cold wall in the courthouse on that warm August day in 1956. The case was very heavy-laden in a political sense, and he knew that working with a somewhat dim-witted client was going to be an incredible challenge.

"Coroner Corrigan, can we get a statement, please," asked a reporter from the *New York Times*.

"That is why I'm here, gentlemen," said Corrigan, standing outside the courtroom building. He paused to wipe his brow with his embroidered handkerchief. "Now then, let me read this prepared statement," he said awkwardly as he extracted a group of folded papers from the breast pocket of his vest.

"Miss Virginia Jaspers is being held on a technical count of idleness while New Haven police investigate the deaths and injuries of several infants who had been in her care over the past eight years. The suspicious death of the eleven-day-old daughter of Mr. and Mrs. Allen Kapsinow, of 65-H Brookside Avenue, triggered a four-day investigation. The Kapsinow child was taken to Grace New Haven Hospital early Friday and died at 5:50 a.m., two hours after she was admitted. The nature of the injuries attracted the attention of certain physicians and Dr. Robert Taylor, acting New Haven medical examiner, who relayed the information to myself. I, in turn, called police into the case. Miss Jaspers was out of the area for the weekend, preventing police from picking her up for questioning. Her home, at 132 Prospect Road, East Haven, was closely watched, on the possibility that she might return, but she did not appear Saturday or Sunday. Her father, former State Senator William Jaspers, with whom she lives, was informed that police wanted to talk with his daughter. He brought her to headquarters at mid-morning yesterday and questioning, directed by Chief Francis V. McManus and Assistant Chief Raymond J. Eagan, got underway immediately. After a lengthy interview, Miss Jaspers confessed to shaking the Kapsinow child violently because it would not take its formula and go to sleep. She also

confessed to shaking two other infants, Jennifer Malkan, aged three
months, and Cynthia Hubbard, aged thirteen days. The Malkan child,
the daughter of Willard and Joan Malkan died in 1951. The Hubbard
infant died in 1948. Hubbard is the daughter of Allen and Eleanor
Hubbard. The children injured, but not fatally, by Miss Jaspers were
Robert Saidel, eight-week-old boy of Mr. and Mrs. Harry L. Saidel, who
suffered a head injury in February 1955, and the son of Mr. and Mrs.
Marvin H. Schaefer, who suffered a fractured leg last year when he was
three weeks old. The deaths and non-fatal injuries occurred in homes
of the families. In all but one case, the parents were out of their homes
when Miss Jaspers admittedly became 'uncontrollable,' shook the various
children 'strenuously,' and then placed the injured infant in its crib or
carriage. As for the explanation for the deaths, Miss Jaspers only said,
'I didn't know why I did it. Children sometimes get on my nerves.' Miss
Jaspers stated, 'I ought to be put in the electric chair,' in an expression
of remorse at the mass deaths. Miss Jaspers is an exceptionally large
woman. When measured by police prior to being photographed Monday,
she was found to be exactly six feet tall and weighed an even two hundred
twenty pounds. An inquest, led by myself, is scheduled to get underway
in my office at two o'clock this afternoon."

As the coroner finished, he folded his statement papers back to their
original form and re-tucked them into his vest pocket. He said, "Thank
you, gentlemen."

Questioning hands flew into the air with shouts of "Coroner
Corrigan, can you comment ..."

Corrigan looked about and picked out a reporter at random, pointing
in his direction. It was Saul Pett, from the Associated Press.

"Thank you, Coroner. What can you tell us about the parents of these
dead infants? Did they know what was happening before yesterday?"

"No, not until Monday, when police announced that Miss Jaspers had
admitted fatally injuring one child and that she probably was responsible
for the deaths of two others, did parents have any inkling that the deaths
of their babies were not due to natural causes."

"A follow-up question, please. Were any of the parents questioned by the police over the weekend to help build a case against Miss Jaspers?"

"No, none except for Mrs. Kapsinow. The police did a thorough investigation of the Kapsinow home to build their case, as you said. The other parents will be interviewed throughout this week, as well as any others who may have had problems with Miss Jaspers professionally."

Another reporter blurted out, "Coroner Corrigan, how many families has Miss Jaspers helped out over the years?"

"Well, she supposedly has been working as a pediatric nurse for the past twelve years since she finished an eighteen-month course at the St. Agnes Home in West Hartford in 1944. So, your guess is as good as mine as to how many families she's worked with. My guess would be hundreds. Okay, that's all for now—I need to prepare for the inquest this afternoon. Thanks, gentlemen."

Some reporters tried to pose further questions to the coroner, but he calmly walked to his car, got in, and drove away.

9:30 a.m.
Tuesday, August 28, 1956
New Haven Police Department
New Haven, Connecticut

As Virginia Jaspers' case was being presented to Judge Henchel in the courthouse building, Allen and Eleanor Hubbard sat in the small office of Detective John Widmann. The couple wore dark clothes, which contrasted with the policeman's white wall. They sensed some urgency in his voice as he spoke. What they were not aware of, however, was the fact that Widmann was working on three hours of sleep. When the initial calls came in to his office last night, he and Bernie Lawlor were the only ones in the office that had been assigned to the case. He fielded at least twenty calls and scheduled seven of those callers to come in today to be interviewed. As he stood to pour his sixth cup of coffee that morning, he talked to the couple. "Now, as I understand it, your baby died in 1948 and died in the care of the Jaspers woman, is that correct?"

"Yes," Allen spoke up. "She, Miss Jaspers, came and woke us up. She found Cynthia, so I guess that would be considered under her care."

"Yes, it would. Now, folks, tell me how she was with the baby?"

The Hubbards both relayed how Virginia was "heavy-handed" and imposing but generally good-natured and talkative. Eleanor expressed to Widmann that Virginia was very sorry for not doing more to save Cynthia's life and expressed much regret. The Hubbards took pity on her and used her for their son, Stephen.

"You used her *again*? Why?"

Eleanor addressed the detective. "Because we felt badly about what she went through. Cynthia's death was a loss for her as well. And we used her again because no one had given us a reason to suspect her, Detective."

"Okay, Mrs. Hubbard, it was just a question. No need for you to become irritated."

"The only reason that I'd be irritated, Detective, was the fact that it seemed like you were accusing us of hiring back a criminal."

"Eleanor," Allen started.

"No, dear, I won't be accused of something."

"All right, I'm sorry for upsetting you, Mrs. Hubbard. I've had a long night."

"Fine. Just don't take it out on us, please."

Widmann ignored the final comment and went on with his questions. "Okay, folks, a couple more questions for you. First, did you ever see Miss Jaspers get upset with your daughter?"

Allen answered, "No."

"Did she have a problem with anger at all?"

"No, but she was moody. Like she'd cry at the drop of a hat, you know, for no reason at all. That surprised us, since she could be so happy and all."

"All right. Well, that should do it for now. We'll call you if we need anything more from you. I have five or six more people to see yet this morning," said Widmann as he stood to show them out.

The Hubbards stood and filed out the detective's door. There was silence during the ride home. They both felt alone. Their world had been turned upside down overnight, and they had no one to talk to about the whole tragedy. Eleanor cried herself to sleep that night as Allen paced in the den. Old scars were freshly opened, and it affected them more than they could say.

"Catfish in a barrel," Lonnie Renwald said to himself as he approached the next person coming out of the police station. He'd been there since early that morning, just waiting to talk with people who had been interviewed about their involvement with the Jaspers case. He grinned widely as he thought about his strategy. *Brilliant, boy, brilliant!* He had cornered the market on interviews and great storylines. All the rest of the schmucks would be using his stuff. One thing Lonnie didn't know was how long his luck would hold out. Some other reporter might figure out such great thinking too and come along. But, hell, for now, they were all his!

"Ma'am, may I have a word with you?" he said as he approached a matronly looking woman in a very sharp-looking suit.

"And who are you?"

"The name is Lon Renwald. I work for the distinguished *New Haven Register* newspaper. In fact, I am their top reporter sent out to cover this important story of the very tragic Virginia Jaspers case that is making headlines across America as we speak."

"My, then today is my lucky day."

"Ah, glad that you recognized it. And who might you be?"

"I am Miss Lillian Riley, assistant chief examiner for the Connecticut State Board of Examiners for Nursing."

"Wow, that is a mouthful, miss!" replied Renwald.

"Yes, well I'm from Hartford, and I read about the unfortunate situation, and I drove right down here early this morning to talk with detectives."

"Well, miss, what connection do you have to Miss Jaspers?"

"I am in charge of licensing nurses in the State of Connecticut, and I wanted to point out today that Miss Virginia Jaspers, held in connection with the deaths of several babies in her care, was a graduate of a nursing program *not* approved by the state board."

"Oh, I see. That is very interesting, ma'am, and I'm sure very helpful to the police's case."

"I thought so."

"Well, so you are questioning Miss Jaspers' competency as a nurse?"

"Yes, I am. She could not be considered a licensed nurse of any type and has never been."

"Well then, what did she do in these people's homes?"

"The St. Agnes Home in West Hartford teaches a private pediatric nurse course. Upon completion, the graduates go to the homes of babies who are ill or otherwise in need of nursing care. These nurses, if you can call them that, also are there to help new parents."

The two noticed another woman coming toward them.

"How was it for you?" the woman asked.

Lonnie was curious if she was talking to him and began to answer, "Well, that depends on what you mean. I never refuse ..."

"Mr. Renwald, she is talking to *me*, thank you. I'd like to introduce you to Mrs. Helen Cullen, executive secretary of the Connecticut State Nurses' Association. She is also from Hartford."

"Oh, another dame with, I mean, another lady with a long moniker. Pleased to meet ya. Lonnie Renwald, special reporter from the *New Haven Register.*"

Lillian Riley smirked and said, "Mrs. Cullen rode with me. We are close friends and have been for thirty-plus years."

Helen Cullen looked at the reporter skeptically. Lillian said, "Oh, he's all right, a tad queer, but all right just the same."

"Yep, that's me—queer as an ostrich in army boots!"

The two women laughed. Lonnie beamed, as he had now found an audience for his fodder. He turned to Helen and briefed her on what Lillian had told him and asked if she could add anything for the story.

"Well," she began, "I guess I could add that because the pediatric courses at St. Agnes did not cover all clinical fields of nursing, those who attended the courses are not qualified for licensing."

"So, Miss Jaspers should have gone to nursing school to be considered a nurse."

"Yes, an accredited one."

"Great, well, I think that's all the questions I got for you two fine ladies. I see a few more people coming out of the station. Heck, there must be four or five interviews going on at the same time. Anyway, here's my card. Maybe I'll look you up next time I get a hot lead in Hartford," he said as he looked directly at Lillian.

Both the women smiled, took his card, and walked to their car. Lonnie smiled too and said, "When ya got it, Lon, ya got it!" He then hurried over to get a scoop from his next victim.

9:00 a.m.
Tuesday, August 28, 1956
New Haven Jail/Police Academy
New Haven, Connecticut

"Let's go, miss," the jail matron in Station Two said to the nurse. "Can't keep Judge Henchel waiting, now."

Virginia looked up toward the matron with puffy eyes as she sat on the edge of her cot. Her countenance held a sad, forlorn expression. She felt weak, though she had enough strength to get dressed and comb her hair. She wore a blue skirt with white polka dots, a white blouse with a Peter Pan collar, and a light white sweater. On her feet, she wore her favorite white summer shoes with dual straps on top. This was the same outfit that she wore to the police interview yesterday. It was slightly wrinkled, but it had been hung up during the night as she slept in the gray jail dress that the jail provided. Virginia slept fitfully. The cot was uncomfortable and cold, and she kept replaying moments of the interview in her mind. *Maybe I shouldn't have told them what I did*, she thought. She couldn't remember the last time that she cried so. She woke three times during the night. She asked the matron for water each time. Virginia drank insatiably until the matron said, "Hold on, girl, you're gonna be pissin' all night like that!"

Virginia turned her back on the matron and began to mumble. The matron walked up to the cell and eavesdropped.

Virginia repeatedly said to herself, "How will I ever face people again?"

As the matron led Virginia through the door of her cell, she asked, "You sure you don't want nothin' ta eat?"

"I'm sure."

"Well, they told me that you didn't take no food yesterday, only coffee. That right?"

Virginia nodded and stared ahead blankly as she walked. She then felt the matron place her hand inside the left pocket of her sweater. Virginia tensed slightly but didn't look down. The matron's right hand brushed Virginia's hip as she withdrew her hand from her pocket. A sudden rush of warmth caused Virginia's heart to suddenly race and her groin to vaguely ache. It was a feeling that she hadn't felt in a long time. Still, she dared not look at the matron or the secret gift that she had placed in her sweater.

In the hallway of the jail, which led to the main section of the police academy, the two were met by Chief McManus, Detective Thomas Murphy, and Lieutenant Gilhuly. The three of them would be escorting Virginia to the courthouse, which was across the street.

"Mornin', Virginia," Mae Gilhuly said.

"G'morning," came the feeble response.

"Was she a good girl last night?" asked Chief McManus to the matron.

"Sho was, Chief. Talked to herself a bit, but she was good."

"Great. Thanks, Bessie."

The matron smiled and winked at Virginia as she walked to the door that led to the street. Virginia blushed.

Lonnie Renwald jogged up to the quartet from across the street. "Hey, Chief! How 'bouts a picture for the evenin' edition?"

"Going to court, Lon. Stay back, please," answered the chief.

Renwald stood in the street at a 45-degree angle to compose his picture. McManus turned to Virginia and told her to keep looking forward. Murphy scowled at the reporter as he snapped a series of pictures. Renwald followed the small group as they proceeded to the courthouse two blocks away. It was a bright, sunny day and a perfect one for great pictures. Renwald didn't know it, but the pictures that would be taken that day would be used in most of the syndicates throughout the United States and would even be edited for a *Newsweek* article.

"Okay, Lon, enough," Murphy barked as they all entered the courthouse.

"All right, all right, thanks anyway ... putz," Renwald muttered as he hurried away from the police academy toward the police station to talk with the victims' parents.

Once inside the courthouse, Chief McManus directed Virginia toward the detainee room. Edward Reynolds had been waiting for her. "Thanks, Chief," he said cordially.

He turned toward his client and smiled at her. "Okay, Virginia. They were a bit late in getting you over here, but I think we're going to be okay. Let me explain a few things to you before you go in front of the judge. Number one, I do the talking, okay? If I nod at you, then, and only then, may you answer the judge. Agreed?"

"Yes."

"Good. Secondly, I will be asking for remand, which means I hope the judge will let you go home with your parents today."

Virginia looked at him and beamed. "Oh, that would be nice," she said.

"Yes, it would be, but I don't know what is going to happen. The coroner still hasn't had an inquest yet."

"What's that?"

"It doesn't matter to you. It's just a meeting. Anyway, the third thing I want from you is trust. You are to trust my judgment, even if you don't agree with me one hundred percent, okay?"

"I guess so."

"No, 'I guess so,' Virginia. If I am to represent you, you are to trust me."

"Okay."

"Fine, then. We'll be called shortly. Judge Henchel is a prompt man," Reynolds said as he sat down in the chair next to his client.

At 9:35, Virginia Jaspers stood with Edward Reynolds in front of the judge. Vincent Villano, the city attorney, stood on the prosecution side of the courtroom. The court clerk read the charge, "In the people of Connecticut against Virginia B. Jaspers—having fatally injured and doing harm to several infants in her care—there is a technical charge of idleness presented to the court."

Judge Henchel looked at the briefing before him. The police and Coroner Corrigan, who stood on the prosecutor's side of the courtroom, had prepared it. "Hmmm," emitted the judge.

"Ma'am, how do you plead?"

"Not guilty, Your Honor," answered Reynolds for her. "Your Honor, we are asking for remand while the people are putting together a case. There is to be an inquest this afternoon, so really nothing is solid yet."

Judge Henchel looked slyly at Reynolds. "Well, don't you think there is sufficient evidence to hold her? I mean, we have a statement that your client made to the police—it sure sounds like a confession."

Villano then spoke. "Judge Henchel, the people believe that Miss Jaspers should be held without any bond as a matter of community concern and public interest."

"Well, Mr. Villano, all you have is a technical charge of idleness."

"Yes, which is standard while we wait for the coroner's inquest."

"Judge, if I may," began Coroner Corrigan as he stood.

Judge Henchel nodded.

"There are several key people that we need to draw together to figure out what charges should be filed on Miss Jaspers. There is the possibility of murder charges."

Virginia blurted out, "Ohhh."

Reynolds did not look toward her but instead, placed his left hand on her shoulder and whispered, "Shhh," to her.

Virginia swallowed hard and looked at the judge. Her eyes were blurry.

"Judge, this is a girl from a well-known and respected family. She can stay with them while the inquest occurs and while the state makes its case."

"Yes, Judge Reynolds, I know her family too, but these are very serious charges," said Henchel as he looked down his bifocal lens glasses at the attorney. "I'm going to continue this case until September 15th, whereby the state's attorney and Coroner Corrigan will be able to come up with appropriate charges. In the meantime, the technical charge of idleness stands, and I impose a bond of $50,000."

Virginia looked up at Reynolds and said, "$50,000? I don't have that kind of money."

"Quiet!" came the response.

As she was being led out of the courtroom, Virginia freely sobbed. She knew that she'd probably have to stay in jail now. She felt sick. Her father could likely afford that money. She didn't know how it all led to this. The thoughts swam in her head. It wasn't until five minutes later when Edward Reynolds explained to her about the 10 percent rule of bond that she felt calmer and stopped crying.

Right before the police took her back to the jail, she remembered the gift from the kind jail matron. She reached carefully into her sweater pocket and pulled out the lump that was tucked inside a white handkerchief. It was like opening a birthday present. She threw back the folds hurriedly and discovered a flaky crumb bun. The saliva flowed freely in her mouth. She looked about; the others were busy talking. She hungrily bit into the bun. It was sweet and fresh and melted in her mouth. After four hefty bites, it was gone.

Jaspers Mug Shot

–AP Wirephoto

VIRGINIA B. JASPERS
Held in Slayings

CHAPTER TWENTY-TWO

"Well, My Son Got His Head Hurt Last Year—Was It Because of Her?"

2:00 p.m.
Tuesday, August 28, 1956
Office of County Coroner
New Haven, Connecticut

County Coroner James J. Corrigan's office was not an expansive one, so the chairs in which the participants of Virginia Jaspers' inquest sat were placed closely together. This made for discomfort, not only because of the room temperature, but because of the elevated levels of anxiety as prosecution and defense sat side by side. Corrigan made his way around the chairs and passed out copies of Virginia's signed confession and the initial police report. He then sat down and said, "Let's review these papers for a few minutes while we wait."

City Prosecutor Vincent Villano asked, "Wait for what?"

Corrigan looked at Edward Reynolds and his assistant Francis J. Moran, whom he had brought on the night before, and said, "Well, the guest of honor, of course."

"She won't be joining us, I'm afraid," came the response from Reynolds.

Corrigan's brows furrowed, as if someone had just cancelled a birthday party that he had planned. He took a slow breath and said, "Well, Mr. Reynolds, isn't it standard practice for the accused to have a say when it comes to an inquest that has gathered, which may ultimately decide her fate? She is scheduled to be the first to testify on her own behalf."

"Not at this inquest, Mr. Corrigan. Miss Jaspers has declined to testify, on the advice of her attorneys, since we do not want her to take *any* stand without first undergoing a psychiatric examination. Mr. Moran and I have decided to meet with Judge Henchel in order to have her released on a reduced bond. We would then take her to at least one psychiatrist for an examination."

"Interesting," remarked Corrigan. "Then I guess we have nothing further to discuss. This hearing is then recessed indefinitely. Good day, gentlemen."

With that, the entourage all stood and departed the coroner's office.

Villano cornered Reynolds and Moran out in the hall. "You could have given me a little warning about going to the judge."

Reynolds smiled and said, "Consider yourself warned—see you over at the courthouse."

City Court Judge Charles Henchel's secretary lightly knocked on his door at 2:15. He was staring out his window having just reviewed several court documents for upcoming trials. His eyes were tired and staring out at the blue sky was therapeutic for him. It was as though he were focusing on something beautiful for a brief moment in time, rather than words on a paper that signified death, hatred, and wicked deeds. The knock startled him somewhat, but he remained calm and answered, "Come."

His secretary, Gina, entered and said, "Miss Virginia Jaspers' attorneys are here for a special request meeting. Can you see them?"

"Is Mr. Villano with them?"

"Not yet, though he is on his way."

"When he shows up, have them all come in."

Five minutes later, the attorneys filed into Judge Henchel's chambers.

"Gentlemen, please have a seat."

The attorneys took their places, this time having ample space to avoid physical contact.

"How may I help you with your 'special request'?"

Reynolds spoke up. "Thank you for seeing us, Judge. Mr. Moran and I would like to ask for a reduction of Miss Jaspers' $50,000 bond."

"For what reasons?"

"We believe it is excessive, so we are asking that her bond be reduced to $15,000. At this level, her father can then pay to get her out of the county jail, and we can take her to an appropriate psychiatrist for examination."

"Nice try, Mr. Reynolds," said the judge, swiftly knocking down their appeal. "As I've thought more about it, I'm surprised at myself that I set *any* bond—I don't feel that $50,000 was excessive at all."

Villano also opposed Reynolds' request, saying, "Judge Henchel, here's a woman who may be eventually charged with three murders."

Moran piped in and protested, "The prosecutor has no right to say that." He added, "The police haven't used the word 'murder.'"

Henchel looked at his watch and asked, "How was the coroner's inquest, gentlemen?"

Villano spoke up and said, "Well, Judge, it was cancelled because Miss Jaspers was counseled not to attend."

"Look," remarked Reynolds, "we just want it so she can be examined *outside* the jail, by a psychiatrist selected by myself and Mr. Moran. The atmosphere at the jail is not conducive to such an examination."

"Sorry," said the judge, "bond stays at $50,000."

4:00 p.m.
Tuesday, August 28, 1956
New Haven Police Department, New Haven, Connecticut

Police Appeal to Parents to Tell of Cases Under Miss Jaspers' Care

The New Haven Police Department today issued an appeal to all parents who have had Miss Virginia Jaspers as a nurse for their children and who may have had unusual happenings occur during the period of her employment to come forward and provide any information they may possess.

Chief Francis V. McManus said, "Already reports have reached us unofficially that there are several cases where children in Miss Jaspers' care were mysteriously injured and in at least one instance required extensive hospitalization. These reports are now being investigated to ascertain their veracity. We are anxious to obtain all additional information so that we may present a complete picture in our report to the state's attorney. Any person having any information, which will be helpful in any way in this case, is requested to get in touch immediately with Assistant Chief Raymond J. Eagan, who is in complete charge of the investigation. Every available man in the Detective Bureau has been assigned to this case. The parents of all of the five children who were mishandled are being interviewed and complete statements taken. Every available step is being taken to clear up this case." Police this afternoon said that five additional complaints have been received from parents who say their children were injured while being "cared for" by Miss Jaspers. Most of the new complaints were made by telephone.

Even before the newspaper headline reached people's hands, there was plenty of business at the New Haven Police Department on the day after the big news broke across the nation. The steady stream of people dwindled in the afternoon, but the phone calls kept the five detectives assigned to the case busy throughout the entire day.

The last parent who had been tied to Virginia's confession the day before was interviewed after he was done with work at 3:00 p.m. Harry Saidel was a no-nonsense person and chose to attend to his responsibilities at his place of employment instead of hurrying to the station first thing in the morning as other parents had done.

"Hell, I gotta work for a living. I knew you guys would be open after work, right?"

Detective Lieutenant Robert Mulhern smiled slightly but thought to himself, *I think you got your priorities mixed up, pal.* He continued to shuffle some papers while he collected his thoughts. "So, Mr. Saidel, your son was injured in February of last year, is that right?"

"Yep."

"Umm, could you tell me what happened?"

"Sure. Little Bobby had to go to the hospital on account he got his head hurt."

"Okay—how did he get hurt?"

"I really can't say for sure, but I bet my money on that Jaspers girl."

"Well, Mr. Saidel, how 'bout telling me exactly what happened, like I asked?"

"Sure. She started working for us in late January, and she ended up staying just about two weeks."

"Okay," prompted Mulhern. "Please continue."

"Well, she was kinda looney, if you know what I mean. The wife made all the arrangements to hire her, so we didn't know what we were gettin'. She'd cry at the drop of a milk bucket. But she did okay with Bobby. Seemed to know what she was doin' and came recommended by the wife's doc."

"Tell me about the day your son was injured."

"Jesus—still gives me shudders just thinkin' about it. I was downstairs tinkerin' with somethin' or other in the kitchen. Jaspers is upstairs with Bobby, and the wife is out hangin' laundry. I hear Bobby cryin', and I think he is just tired or hungry or somethin'. Then, I hear some feet shufflin' around in his room and then this God-awful crack ... like somebody broke a bat hittin' a line drive. You know what I'm talkin' about?"

"Yeah," said Mulhern.

"So I race upstairs, and I yell, 'Jesus, Mary, and Joseph, what the hell happened?' I look at Bobby, and he looks like he's sleepin'. Jaspers is lookin' at me with these wide eyes, you know, and she blabs out, 'Nothing. No nothing!'"

"What do you think she meant by that?"

"I don't know! So I asked her what the hell she is talkin' about? She tells me that she was changing Bobby's diaper, and he fell off the table onto the floor. We got hardwoods throughout the house. She started cryin' and sputterin' and carryin' on. And I grab Bobby and run to the car callin' the wife's name. We get to the hospital, and he still hasn't come out of it." Saidel then paused to take out an old handkerchief from his back pocket. He dabbed his eyes and honked his nose quickly and stuffed it back into his jeans. "I'm sorry, Detective, it still kinda upsets me."

"No, that's fine. Take your time." Mulhern felt sorry for him now.

"Anyways, the doctor at the emergency room finds that Bobby has a skull fracture on the back of his head, and they keep him. Over the next few days, his head swells, and he still ain't out of it."

"You mean, like a coma?"

"Yeah! Exactly. I was peeved as all heck that Jaspers allows this fall to happen in the first place. She comes to the hospital to visit, and I tell her to not come back—to the hospital or our house. The wife scolded me 'cause she felt sorry for this nurse, but, like I said, I was peeved."

"Well, what happened to your son?"

"He ain't been right since. For Chrissakes, he's almost two, and he's still scootin' around on his butt. He doesn't know what walking is!" Saidel began to tear up and hid his face in his right hand as he leaned forward.

"My God, Mr. Saidel, I'm sorry about what happened," the detective said comfortingly.

"Oh, it's all right. I try not to hold a grudge."

"Well, I wanted to let you know that Miss Jaspers confessed to deliberately hurting your son when we brought her in on Monday."

Harry Saidel's grief hastily turned to anger. "Tell me you're kiddin' me."

"No, sir."

Saidel didn't utter a word. He sat and stewed, clenching and unclenching his fists. After a few moments of silence, he looked at the detective and asked, "Is there anything else? Can I leave?"

"No, nothing more. You can go. Thanks for coming down."

Saidel stood slowly, grabbed his hat off the table, and headed toward the door.

"Mr. Saidel?" said Mulhern. "I'm really sorry about your boy."

Without looking back, Saidel pursed his lips, nodded, and went out the door.

The detectives who had been assigned to the Jaspers case, which was almost the complete unit, were kept busy on Tuesday, August 28. Fielding phone calls and making visits to parents' homes helped encapsulate and clarify the breadth of Virginia Jaspers' path of destruction.

At approximately 11:00 a.m., Detective Harold Berg received a telephone call from a Detroit man, who was in Massachusetts on business. The man said he recalled, after reading newspaper accounts of the Jaspers case, that his three-week-old child was injured while the nurse was in attendance. The family had lived on Mather Street in Hamden, Connecticut, at the time. The man said his son was now mentally retarded but stated that he did not know whether there was any connection between his child's present condition and the injury. The Detroit man said he planned to stop in New Haven to give police a formal statement.

At noon, Detective Bernie Lawlor interviewed a woman who had hired Virginia two years ago to care for her child. She told Lawlor that she surprised the nurse while she was reportedly "roughly handling" the infant. The mother fired Jaspers on the spot and ordered her to "take a walk." Virginia packed her bags and left the home, but no complaint about the incident was ever made to authorities.

At 12:45 p.m., Detective William Holohan started out to visit various parents in his unmarked sedan. He had received numerous calls that morning from people saying they recalled that their children were bruised, cut, and even punched by Virginia. Before leaving, he updated Ray Eagan, who exclaimed, "Why the hell are we just now hearing about these cases?!"

Detective Thomas Murphy went to the home of a West Haven father at 1:30 p.m. The man claimed on the phone to the detective that his child, who had been under Virginia's care the year before, was mentally retarded but not born that way. The man posed to Murphy, "Well, my son got his head hurt last year—was it because of her?" The man stated that he didn't know whether there was any possible connection between the handling of his child and the boy's mental condition. Doctors never told him.

At 3:30, as he was about to leave the police station, Robert Mulhern spoke with another caller who alleged that Virginia fed his child whiskey while she was caring for the boy. When he hung up the phone, Mulhern shook his head. It had been a rotten day. A numb feeling still lingered from the Saidel interview. He wanted to go home and have a few hits of his own whiskey, so he decided to give this final call to Berg. Later that night, it would be up to Berg to question Virginia at the jail about this and several of the other complaints. *What has this world come to?* Mulhern wondered as he walked alone out to his car.

At 4:00, in his office, Chief Francis McManus met with a handful of reporters from several newspapers. He knew that the late edition of the *Register* would be delayed because of him, but he did not want to speak prematurely, so he waited until he had the latest information that could be shared with the media. He began by giving synopses of what he decided to be "significant complaints" that were being investigated. The eyes of the reporters were wide during his entire statement; it was as if he were reading a bedtime book to a group of children. They were stunned by the wrath that was finally being uncovered.

Finally, Saul Pett from the Associated Press asked, "How could you have someone who killed three infants and maimed countless other children over an eight-year period?"

McManus felt hot. He knew he did not have an explanation for the mess that was in his hands. He just knew that this crazy woman slipped through the cracks, though he wouldn't say that to the press. Instead, he adjusted his chair, stroked the front of his face, leaned forward on his elbows, and said, "Gentlemen, the deaths of the Hubbard and Malkan infants passed without suspicion and were not linked to Miss Jaspers until yesterday. They were written off as due to natural causes. We have proof of this and doctors' signatures to go along. Not until the death of the Kapsinow child, who suffered head and body injuries last Thursday night, did Miss Jaspers' treatment of infants come under suspicion."

"Yes, but didn't anyone make a complaint before this?"

"Apparently, parents either dismissed the rough handling as accidental or had no desire to make an issue of the treatment. It turns out that the Schaefer boy, whose leg was broken by Miss Jaspers last year, was the only one in which a parent made a formal complaint."

"How did that one get by?" Pett said cynically.

"The state police ruled that it was an accident. The New Haven police were not involved in that investigation."

Pett and the other reporters nodded and continued to take notes. McManus felt slightly nervous but knew that he was doing everything that he could at the present time. He filled in the silence with, "Look, we have learned that her services were greatly in demand and she was constantly busy. Heck, even Mrs. Hubbard hired Jaspers again for her second child. Beyond that, who knows how many children she harmed? We are now reaching out to those parents who have made complaints. I do ask that a formal call go out in the papers to other parents who have hired Miss Jaspers to see if any other child has been injured. The complaints that we received today are from parents who recalled mistreatment by Miss Jaspers after reading accounts of her arrest in yesterday's newspaper. So far, gentlemen, these cases are being classified as 'unofficial' until they have been thoroughly checked out by my detectives."

Lonnie Renwald held his pen in the air.

"Yeah, Lonnie, what's your question?"

"Chief, uh, what's the final tally for today?"

"Well, Lon, the day's not yet over, but we have about fifteen complaints that we are following, and it appears that Miss Jaspers may have mistreated as many as twenty infants. We just can't say yet, for sure."

The room seethed with activity. A *New York Times* reporter hurried out of the room. McManus silently wondered if he was headed for the phone to call in his story or to the bathroom to vomit.

A thought came to him, and he shared it with the reporters. "I wanted to let you all know that one of my officers is responsible for checking the death records of other children in the New Haven area for the past eight years. Coroner Corrigan let me know that he will investigate the sudden deaths of other infants in New Haven County since 1953. There are five communities that will be involved: New Haven, West Haven, East Haven, Woodbridge, and Hamden. All these surrounding towns were selected because almost all of Miss Jaspers' calls were in these communities. We are trying to connect Miss Jaspers with other infant deaths, which may have been improperly labeled as natural deaths."

The meeting ended abruptly as a police dispatcher came in to inform the chief of a bank robbery in progress at the County Trust Bank. The reporters filed out, and McManus grabbed his chief's jacket. He didn't feel well.

Lonnie Renwald called Sheilah Kapsinow at home before he called in his story to the *Register*. Sheilah was asked how she felt about the Jaspers case and about all the reports that were starting to surface. Lonnie wanted to get a human touch in his story. Sheilah answered him succinctly, "Write what you will, but I can't put how I'm feeling into nice words. If you want honesty, I'll give it to you. If she were standing in front of me right now, I'd probably rip out her heart and feed it to her."

In the *Register* that evening, readers learned that "Mrs. Kapsinow, still grief-stricken at the death of her baby last Friday, said she had what she described as 'very strong and intense feelings toward Miss Jaspers.'"

Saul Pett called Sister Bertrand at St. Agnes Home in West Hartford. He had some questions that were plaguing him that he needed to have resolved. The nun was courteous but reserved. She told Pett a few other reporters had been in touch with St. Agnes that day and that some were "so brazen as to try and set foot in my office!" He kept a singsong tone in his voice, which seemed to make her amiable to talking about Virginia. Pett wanted to get to the heart of what went wrong and decided to go to the hub of where Virginia's training took place in 1942 and 1943. Sister Bertrand stood while she spoke to the reporter on the phone—she felt it helped convey more authority, as well as giving her a sense of inner strength. Pett was not frustrated but persisted in his questioning of the nun. Bertrand politely ended the conversation within minutes of it beginning, stating, "Mr. Pett, I am sorry that I'm not giving you what you are looking for. All day, reporters have been trying to see how St. Agnes created a monster. Well, I'm telling you what I told the others—we did our best with her, just as we do with anyone who comes through our doors for training. Miss Jaspers showed no indication that she was disturbed as far as her relationship with children was concerned."

Behind her back, Sister Bertrand had her fingers crossed. She prayed that God wasn't listening to her conversation.

9:00 p.m.
Tuesday, August 28, 1956
New Haven County Jail
New Haven, Connecticut

"Lights out, sweetie!"

Deputy Jailer Philip Mancini looked in at Virginia in her cell as he passed by while making his rounds in the women's section of the county jail. The newcomer inmate sat on the edge of her cot, smiled at him gleefully, and said, "Okay."

Mancini smiled back and proceeded forward down the hall to check the other three women who were housed at the jail. As he walked, he ran his wrinkled fingers along the cold steel bars of the cells. He had walked this path several times a night for the past thirty-seven years. Other people who worked at the jail swore they could see a dip in the concrete from the path that Phil Mancini had walked over the years. The jailer took the kidding well and laughed off the comments of these young folks that came and went over the years. He was a kind man, who respected the women who had graced the six-by-eight-foot "cubicles," as he was fond of calling them. Sure, he'd had his share of rough ones. He remembered one in particular, Sadie Burns, who had killed her husband in 1938 by breaking his back in a fight. She was nearly as tall as Virginia and mighty strong. Mancini had put a chokehold on her with his wooden baton after she went ornery while being searched for contraband. Stan Clemens helped him out, and they still both ended up on the floor with Sadie. Two other deputy jailers finally jumped in and helped restrain her. During the whole incident, Mancini spoke calmly in her ear and said, "Now, miss, we can do this the easy way or the hard way. It is entirely up to you." Sadie chose the hard way and was restricted to her cell the entire time that she stayed at the county jail.

Mancini thought about Virginia as he hummed and walked down the corridor. He had never seen a woman quite like her. She was an odd duck, and, boy, she could pack away a meal. That evening, she'd had double portions of meatballs, fresh tomatoes, potatoes, and applesauce. She washed it all down with a pot of coffee. She then topped it off with a big double ice cream sundae. Mancini had heard that she hardly ate anything the day before while she was housed at the police academy. He wondered if Virginia was going to eat this way the whole time she would stay at the jail. *Hell, it doesn't matter*, thought Mancini. *Guess she needed all that fuel for her size.* He had been in the next room when Doc Mongillo, the jail physician, gave the new prisoner her routine physical at 4:30 that afternoon. He heard Mongillo's nurse say aloud the numbers as she weighed and measured Virginia.

"Two hundred twenty pounds," announced the nurse.

He then heard Virginia say, "Oh really? I must have gained some weight in the last few days."

Mancini nodded his head sarcastically.

"Exactly six feet tall," the next number was announced.

"I've always been a big girl," Virginia said to the nurse.

"Have you now?" came the reply.

The examination was insignificant, the findings normal.

Dr. Mongillo told Virginia, "You're healthy ... big, but healthy."

"Thank you, Doctor."

Mancini stood in anticipation of the opening of the doctor's office door.

"Oh, Miss Jaspers, one more question," he heard instead.

"Yes?"

"How have you been sleeping? I always like to ask the new women who come to this facility. Sometimes, things can get pretty stressful. I didn't know if you might need something to help you sleep."

"Well, isn't that kind of you, Dr. Mongoli! No, I'm just fine, thank you. I've been sleeping like a ... well ... just fine."

Mongoli? Mancini thought about the faux pas and snickered aloud. It would be fodder for later teasing.

As he headed back toward Virginia's cell, the deputy jailer remembered what she said to the police officer who dropped her off that afternoon. It was a sad statement, thought Mancini when he heard it. He knew all about the case from the newspaper and from others who worked at the jail. He had anticipated Virginia's arrival since the story broke last night. When she did arrive, the young officer who escorted her showed her to the holding room by the entrance. Mancini was overseeing the transfer. As the officer took the handcuffs off Virginia, she looked at him and said, "I've always loved children."

The officer nodded and folded the cuffs in his hands nervously.

"I've always wanted children of my own."

He didn't know what to say and just looked at Virginia.

"You know, I was at my sister's place in Essex all weekend and cared for my nephew. I did a superb job with him. He's not yet one."

"I'm going to go now, ma'am. The jailer will help you and show you to your cell."

Virginia seemed to not hear what the officer said to her. She looked at the floor for a brief time, contemplating intensely.

As he was stepping out of the room, she looked up quickly with an appearance of urgency on her face.

"Mr. Policeman!"

The young officer almost dropped the handcuffs he had been toying with the entire time.

"What?" he answered.

Mancini poked his head in the door. Virginia looked at both men and smiled.

"You've never had a case quite like this, have you?"

They didn't know if she was testing them or boasting about her growing celebrity status. She'd seen the lines of traffic that had been formed by the media alone—wherever she went.

The young officer looked at Mancini and then looked at Virginia.

"No, ma'am, I haven't."

He hurried out of the jail and went right to Assistant Police Chief Ray Eagan to tell him what the nurse had shared.

CHAPTER TWENTY-THREE

"Doctors Don't Have the Power to Protect Children"

3:00 p.m.
Wednesday, August 29, 1956
New Haven, Connecticut

Dr. Robert Salinger tapped his fingers rhythmically on his desk. He used different combinations as he strummed. He watched his fingers dance and concentrated to make sure he perfected one combination before he moved on to the next. He liked this custom. He felt it helped keep his mind sharp, while at the same time, helped him pass time. Salinger was waiting for John Steffan, a reporter from the *New Haven Register*, who was almost late for their appointment. Salinger knew that reporters were notorious for being late. He had met with Steffan on several other occasions and was usually very comfortable with his style of questioning. Today, though, Salinger felt edgy. He knew his reluctance and anxiety was because of the topic of the interview: Virginia Jaspers.

His nurse's voice coming from the intercom that sat between medical charts on his desk startled the doctor. He had just been formulating his thoughts about what he wanted to say to Steffan, when the nurse called. "Doctor, Mr. Steffan from the *Register* is here. Shall I send him in?"

"Go right ahead, Myrna," said Salinger. He stood up from his chair in preparation for shaking hands with the reporter. He quickly brushed his perspiring hands on his pant legs; he didn't know why he was nervous.

"Dr. Salinger, it is very nice to see you again," said John Steffan as he pumped the hand of the man whom he considered to be New Haven's most formidable pediatrician. Steffan smiled as Salinger motioned for him to sit in the chair opposite his desk. The two men made themselves comfortable, and Salinger buzzed Myrna to bring in a pot of coffee.

"Thanks, Doc! You sure know how to host!" exclaimed Steffan.

"Well, John, you bet. Anything I can do to make this time a little nicer."

"Why, that's awfully grand."

Steffan opened up his notepad and withdrew a pen from his front pocket. He flipped through some pages and then looked up at the doctor. He began, "Well ... One hell of a week we are having in New Haven, wouldn't you say?"

"Long time coming," Salinger replied.

"Yep, she's been at this for awhile. It is all so tragic, isn't it?"

Dr. Salinger looked over at his credentials hanging on the wall to his left. He sighed and then looked back at the reporter and smiled. He then said, "It is tragic, yes, but at least two deaths and many more injuries could have been prevented had people listened."

"Like who?"

"Like the police, like the coroner, like pediatricians, myself included."

"What do you mean, Doc?"

"Well, let's look backward, shall we? I first learned of Miss Jaspers in 1948 when I was called in on the death of the Hubbard baby. Her case was discussed among several of us at the time," he recalled. "We did not know whether it could be blamed on intent, awkwardness, or just chance. But an autopsy was performed, and we did feel that the baby had been dropped or thrown."

"How could you tell that?" asked Steffan.

"When the autopsy was performed, the Hubbard girl was found to have died of a subarachnoid hemorrhage. Basically, the word *arachnoid* refers to the thin covering over the brain and spinal cord. An infant does not spontaneously get such bleeding in her brain, so this led several of us to consider trauma as the culprit."

Salinger's nurse bringing in a tray with coffee, cups, creamer, and sugar interrupted the two.

Salinger smiled and said, "Myrna, what would I do without you?"

"Be lost forever, Doctor," she teased.

Steffan chuckled and thanked the nurse as she headed back out the door.

Salinger poured two coffees, and Steffan helped himself to the creamer and sugar.

"Now, as I was saying, there are awkward nurses and competent nurses. The line between ineptness and actual intent is very difficult to define. It's just the same as if I know a doctor has performed a dumb operation. I can't say anything about it."

"You mean to the doctor?" Steffan asked, setting his cup down to take some notes.

"Sure, the doctor, the patient, the medical association, you name it."

"Wow, I had never thought about it like that."

Salinger then stood and walked over to his window that looked out over Whalley Avenue. He did not focus on anything in particular, yet he gazed fervently at the passersby, the vehicles, the trees, and the wind that blew scraps of newspaper in swirling eddies. "I've held on to this struggle for eight years," he finally said to Steffan. "I shared my concerns with many people, but few listened. I feel that if this same thing happened again, I would be equally powerless to get action before another series of tragedies befell this city."

Salinger closed his eyes and rubbed them with his thumb and forefinger. His eyes were damp with tears, and they burned. He put his hand down at his side and stared out the window again. "Damn it!" he exclaimed. "Lawyers, psychiatrists, *and* police that I approached informally on several occasions about Jaspers said that I could do nothing."

"But, Doctor, you were the one that put her away this time."

"Yes, somebody listened this time, but ... look at the lives that could have been saved if I had been listened to before. Look at the heartache that could have been spared in the parents of the children who were injured by this madwoman!"

"I know. There are a lot of people who need to answer for their actions in this case. No one seems to be taking responsibility either. I hear the commissioner of the state police and the New Haven police chief are going to be addressing that issue this afternoon."

Salinger failed to hear the last part of what the reporter was saying. Instead, he was lost in his own thoughts. So he continued, "And, you know, by the merest chance, I was assigned this month to help supervise the pediatric section at the hospital. I was told of the Kapsinow baby's death, and I immediately asked the name of the child's nurse when I heard she had a nurse. When I heard the name 'Virginia Jaspers,' I told hospital authorities of her past history. What if I hadn't been there that night, John?"

"You were."

"Sheer luck, it was."

"I'd call it fate."

"Hell, I even convinced four or five other pediatricians to cross Jaspers' name off their recommended lists of practical baby nurses that we share with parents. And even beyond that, one mother asked me about Jaspers last year, and I told her to hire someone else."

Salinger walked back to his desk chair and sat down. He reached for the coffee pot and poured himself some. He held the pot out to Steffan, who declined.

"Doctor, one more question for you."

"Sure."

"What can be done to ensure that tragedies similar to the baby deaths will not recur?"

Salinger looked at Steffan and smiled briefly. He then said, "I know of no answer. I don't know how you can screen these practical nurses. No licensing board or examination paper could have weeded out a psychopath like Jaspers. The only way to tell a good baby nurse from a bad one is to watch her handling the infant. If she has the right touch and the right personality, you can be 99 percent sure she's a good nurse. I guess that an individual mother can protect herself by getting a nurse recommended by her doctor, but that doesn't always work, as we've seen with Jaspers."

"True," replied Steffan contemplatively. He reviewed his notes and then said, "I can't think of anything else I need to ask. I do want to thank you for your time and your service to our community."

"Service?"

"Heck, Dr. Salinger, you're a hero to a lot of people."

The doctor blushed slightly and said, "Thank you," to the reporter.

As the two walked toward the office door, Salinger said, "You know, John, hero or not, I'd like to keep my name out of the paper on this one, okay?"

Steffan didn't argue. He knew that the Jaspers case was a very precarious subject for the doctor. "You bet, Doc," he said and walked toward the waiting room exit.

In his article that he wrote that day for the *Register*, John Steffan included a quote that a Grace New Haven Community Hospital official relayed to him: "The link between one odd case and a series of traumatic deaths was provided by the pediatrician. The case could possibly have gone down as one of death by 'trauma of unknown origin.'" Steffan knew that using this quote would be a way to immortalize a man he looked up to more than he could say.

4:00 p.m.
Wednesday, August 29, 1956
New Haven Police Station
New Haven, Connecticut

"The number of infants killed by children's nurse Virginia Jaspers probably will not go above the present figure of three," said Assistant Police Chief Ray Eagan to a crowd of media representatives outside the front of the New Haven Police Station. "I am basing my opinion on the fact that the investigation, to date, has not turned up any indication of additional deaths and that there have been no complaints of fatal injuries from parents who hired the nurse."

Standing in back of Eagan were State Police Commissioner John C. Kelly and New Haven Police Chief Francis McManus, both of whom exhibited guarded body language with their arms folded in front of them.

"Why'd it take so long to stop the woman?" a reporter called out. "There've been reports that laxity by investigators permitted Miss Jaspers to continue her rough handling of babies up until last week."

Eagan coughed out, "Well, hold on now!" while Kelly and McManus stepped up to the podium at the same time.

McManus gestured to Kelly to speak first.

"I am disheartened to hear reports of laxity by the state police. I—"

Another reporter interrupted the commissioner. "Well, many of us are talking about the case where the Jaspers lady fractured the leg of a Woodbridge child last year. It was discovered that the investigation on that case was stopped. Any comment on that?"

Kelly remained calm and stoic and said, "That investigation was stopped only because it was complete and concluded. State's Attorney Ullman requested the Woodbridge child's investigation. Sergeant John Doyle and a policewoman made a thorough investigation; the full report of which was turned over to Ullman, who found no basis for prosecution."

Chief McManus then spoke up and said, "Gentlemen, it was not until last Friday that anyone formally complained to city police about Miss Jaspers' handling of infants in her care. Pediatricians here have said that they privately discussed Miss Jaspers' rough handling of youngsters, but no complaint was made to the New Haven Police Department until last week, period."

Eagan seemed genuinely riled by the accusatory questions about the police investigation. He said, "You know, folks, it's very easy to blame police after all is said and done. I ask that you print or report accurate information and let us do our job."

Someone in back muttered, "Now they do their job."

The three police officials and most of the reporters heard the comment, but it was ignored as if a child had made an offhand comment in public.

Kelly again spoke freely. "One final thing that I'd like to say is that I spoke with State's Attorney Ullman earlier today, and he told me that his office looked into the Jaspers woman's background when the injury of the Schaefer baby came to light. He said that they became aware that Miss Jaspers was the pediatric nurse in the two other deaths of the Hubbard and Malkan infants. A check of these deaths showed that they were attributed to a 'subdural hemorrhage' and 'aspiration of vomitus.' These diagnoses, on their own, showed that there was nothing to indicate any criminality. I think that is enough of the questions. Thank you."

Eagan concluded the brief meeting with reporters by saying, "Any parent or physician who suspected that there might be some connection between a past death and Miss Jaspers would have contacted police by now."

It was an awkward ending. The three turned and headed toward the police station's front door. The reporters closed their notebooks and quickly abandoned the neat collection, like bees flying off from a hive.

Eagan muttered loudly to his companions, "I wonder which asshole asked if we do our jobs?"

Most of the reporters heard him say this.

Wednesday, August 29, 1956
New Haven, Connecticut

New Haven Register

Miss Jaspers Called Lonely Woman with Child's Passion for Ice Cream

By Saul Pett
Associated Press

She laughed a lot. She talked a great deal. She ate "constantly"
and displayed a child's passion for ice cream and soda pop. But
beneath the pretense of chatty cheerfulness, there were telltale

signs of a woman acutely embarrassed by her inordinate size, a lonely woman who seemed to have no life of her own and tried to enjoy vicariously the lives of her temporary employers.

This was the picture slowly emerging today of Virginia Jaspers, the six-foot, 220 pound baby nurse, who told police she shook three infants to death and injured two others in fits of "uncontrollable" temper.

Parents whose children were once cared for by Miss Jaspers said they had no reason to suspect her ability or motives at the time. One was Mrs. Allen Hubbard, whose thirteen-day-old daughter died in 1948 while under Miss Jaspers' care.

Until Monday, Mrs. Hubbard knew only what her doctor had told her then—that the child died of a cerebral hemorrhage apparently caused by a congenital weakness. Monday, she learned of Miss Jaspers' statement to police—that the Hubbard child was one of three she shook with fatal results.

"Now I don't know what to think," Mrs. Hubbard said. "I have to admit that at the time, she handled the baby well. We even had her for our second child.

"True, she was heavy-handed. When she burped the baby, she seemed a little strong. I remember we kidded her about it a few times but thought nothing serious about it.

"Apart from her handling of the baby, she seemed immature. She had this childish delight in eating, especially ice cream and soda. She was always, it seemed, taking pictures of the baby. Poor thing, she seemed to think she would never have a child of her own and lavished all her attention on ours."

Mrs. Hubbard, like other mothers who once employed the nurse, said that long after she left their homes, Miss Jaspers frequently sent birthday gifts or cards to her child.

The wife of a New Haven attorney said they were so pleased with Miss Jaspers' care of their child last year they recommended her to friends. She and Mrs. Hubbard agreed in their version of the nurse's continual chatter and cheerfulness.

"She was laughing and talking all the time," said Mrs. Hubbard. "She tried to pretend she was happy, but she wasn't."

Both mothers said that the nurse spent virtually all her off-duty hours either eating or conversing with their guests.

"She seemed to have no life of her own," said the lawyer's wife. "She got very sociable with us and our friends."

The lawyer's wife said that last year, Miss Jaspers charged $63 a week for her services but was planning to raise her rates "because others were."

Size and Strength

The brutal and tragic career of nurse Virginia Jaspers is tied to her massive physical traits. Now 33, she is an ungainly 6 feet, weighs 220 pounds, has a 52-inch waist. Police concluded that she probably had no idea of her strength in her cruelly big arms and hands.

CHAPTER TWENTY-FOUR

"I Want to Teach Her a Lesson"

9:30 a.m.
Thursday, August 30, 1956
New Haven Country Club
New Haven, Connecticut

"I'll be honest with you and say that I am sort of surprised to meet you here at the club."

"You know something, Edward? I don't give a good Goddamn what anybody thinks. If I want to play a few rounds of golf and get on with my life, I sure as Christ am going to do it!"

"All right, calm down, Bill. It was just an observation on my part."

William Jaspers looked down at his feet. He studied his white golf shoes and honed in on the crisscross pattern of the laces. After taking a few breaths, he said, "Sorry—I've been justifiably tense this week."

"I bet."

Edward Reynolds and Jaspers sat in the clubhouse at the New Haven Country Club. It was another warm day; the sun beamed brightly, the sky devoid of clouds—a perfect golfing day. Jaspers' rounds were frustrating ones, with bogey after bogey. He even used the self-talk that Sam Snead had written about in his book, *How I Play Golf*. The tricks didn't help today, though. His mind wasn't on the game. He was just going through the motions.

"Bill, we need help with Virginia's case."

"Meaning what?"

"Meaning $5,000 cash to bond her out of the county jail."

Jaspers looked away toward the large picture window that oversaw the first tee. He then looked back at Virginia's lawyer and said, "I don't have it."

"Bill, this is your daughter."

"No shit! Don't you think I know that?" Jaspers retorted in a hostile manner. "I am very aware of the circumstances and how much 10 percent of $50,000 is."

"Okay," Reynolds said as he backed down in the conversation. "I didn't mean to offend."

"Do you know the heartache that my daughter caused my family since Monday? My God, man, my wife hears the doorbell ring, and she races around the living room to gather the local newspapers so she can stuff them under the sofa before she answers the door! She thinks there are neighbors or reporters or politicians, for God's sake, standing at the door. But do you know who is there? The Goddamn eight-year-old from next door selling candy for her school. My wife cries after she closes the door on the girl. Shame! That's what my daughter has brought."

"I am sorry. I really didn't think about how it was affecting you and Jane."

"My reputation is ruined. I wake up in the night ..."

William Jaspers' voice cracked, and tears formed in his eyes. He swallowed hard as if he were pushing a piece of granite down his throat. He then continued, "I wake up, and my heart is pounding—I feel like it's going to explode some nights."

"My God, Bill, maybe you should have it checked by your doctor."

Jaspers blotted his eyes with his handkerchief and said, "No, I'll be all right. Just something I need to work on myself. Anyway, I've taken this whole week off of work and am just trying to relax. But it's damn hard."

Reynolds adjusted his seating position and cleared his throat. He breathed in slowly and said, "Bill, I understand that you are under pressure, but I was wondering ... well I was wondering that since you are the county treasurer, maybe ..."

"Don't," came the response. "Don't even think about it, Edward. That's all I need—scandal on top of scandal!"

"Bill, I didn't mean anything scandalous. I was talking about borrowing some money from acquaintances that you have connections with politically."

"Not a chance! I will not suck up to my 'connections,' as you call them, in order to get my daughter out of the bind she got herself in."

"Bill, you can't blame her. I truly believe she wasn't in her right mind. She couldn't have been and do what she did to those babies. I want to have her meet with a few psychiatrists that I know in order to prove this fact. I can't do it while she's in jail."

"Edward, you're a good man. I've known you since you were a young lad, and I wouldn't want anyone else in the world to represent Virginia— but ... I am not going to pay to bond her out. I want to teach her a lesson. It's the best thing for her and for my family."

"But ..."

"Save your breath. I'm done talking," said Jaspers as he stood from the large oak table. "I have another round of golf to play. Maybe I'll get lucky this time, heh?"

Reynolds remained seated and watched his client's father turn and walk away. He was dumbfounded by the callousness of this man. And he knew what he needed to do now.

2:00 p.m.
Thursday, August 30, 1956
Dr. Morris Wessel's Office
New Haven, Connecticut

Dr. Morris Wessel was backlogged. His nurse knew what to expect from him. A full waiting room and crying youngsters did not faze him. He was a kind pediatrician and ran an office that could instantly make the most troubled patient feel at ease. His nurse would often tell parents, "That is why his schedule is always full. He is the kindest doctor in town!"

Today, Wessel was a bit harried. He had been unsettled all week, since the Jaspers case was revealed to New Haven and the rest of the nation. He knew about the nurse and her history after having several brief conversations about her with Bob Salinger and some other pediatricians. He couldn't share Salinger's concerns, since he hadn't received any negative reports against Virginia. He had not crossed her off his list of recommended baby nurses and had diplomatically "okayed" her to several parents over the past five or six years. Wessel did add the phrase, "This nurse is on my recommended list, though I still believe that you as a parent should do most of the care for your baby and always trust your heart when you leave him in the care of another." By saying this to every parent that used any baby nurse, Wessel felt he could sleep at night without guilt, but God forbid anything did happen!

He was in the middle of an evaluation when a frantic knock came on the examination room door, which startled him.

"Yes? What is it?"

The door opened, and there stood his nurse and Connie Jeffries.

"Doctor," said his nurse, "I am very sorry to disturb you, but Mrs. Jeffries insisted on coming down to talk with you."

"Yes, I did, Doctor. It's important!"

Wessel set his stethoscope down on the metal table in the exam room. He stood slowly from his wheeled chair and said to his nurse, "Would you mind staying with Ralphie while I go speak briefly with Mrs. Jeffries?"

"Of course, Doctor."

In the hallway, Wessel looked at Mrs. Jefferies and said, "I am in the middle of seeing patients, as you could see. Isn't this something that could have waited until later this afternoon when my office hours are over? My nurse would have gladly scheduled something for you."

"Well, Dr. Wessel, I am very sorry about interrupting you. But I have been in shock the last few days about this Virginia Jaspers case. I can't eat or sleep, and I just had to talk with you about it."

Wessel ran his fingers through his thick, dark hair and looked at the carpeted floor trying to figure out where he fit in with Connie Jefferies' mental collapse.

"Mrs. Jefferies, I am sorry, but I don't understand where I fit in," he said as he looked up at her with questioning eyes.

"Doctor," she said, looking shocked, "don't you remember that I once used the Jaspers woman on your recommendation?"

He hadn't remembered. The inference of what she was saying was now loud and clear to Wessel. *She's come here to blame me,* he thought. Before he had a chance to say anything, the mother blurted out, "You know … you know what might have happened to my baby, to me, to my family if that evil person did something to him?"

"But, Mrs. Jefferies …"

"No thanks to *you,* Dr. Wessel!" she responded.

Wessel's nurse cracked the exam room door open and asked, "Is everything all right, Doctor?"

Connie Jefferies' vocal outburst had carried throughout the entire office.

"No, Helen, everything supposedly is *not* all right. I'll be with Ralphie right away. Mrs. Jefferies was just leaving. Isn't that correct, Mrs. Jefferies?"

The mother tilted her head back with an air and started walking brusquely down the hallway. Wessel followed after her. They walked through the waiting room and out the office door. Parents and children in the waiting room watched the pair as they went by—wondering what the fuss was all about.

Wessel cornered the woman before she headed down the exit stairs. He looked at her intently and calmly and said, "Mrs. Jefferies, I am sorry that you are upset. I had no prior knowledge that Miss Jaspers was an intentional or unintentional child killer. I did not pick you out and wish bad fortune on your family. Instead of coming to my office to scold me in front of my patients, you should, instead, thank your lucky stars that you indeed have a healthy child. Your child is welcome to remain a patient of mine, if you desire. I hope you understand where I am coming from."

Connie Jefferies nodded.

"And one more thing," Wessel continued, "don't you ever interrupt me at my practice again."

When he went back to the exam room, he said to his nurse, "Helen, remind me never to have a mistress. I don't want anybody ever upsetting my office again."

With a surprised expression on her face, his nurse replied, "Yes, Doctor."

6:00 p.m.
Thursday, August 30, 1956
New Haven County Jail
New Haven, Connecticut

Detectives Robert Mulhern and John Widmann rode together in Widmann's car to interview Virginia at the county jail. The two were looking forward to talking with her since there were many unanswered questions that had arisen over the past two days while dozens of parents were interviewed.

"Hey, Widmann, did Berg ever ask Jaspers about the whiskey incident?"

"Which whiskey incident is that?" asked the detective.

"I skipped out home early the other night, and Berg was supposed to ask her if she once offered whiskey to one of the children she took care of."

"Hell if I know."

"Well, it's on my list of questions to ask."

"Yeah, I'm going to be happy to ask her some myself. It'll help me clear some of the paperwork off my desk."

The two rode in silence for a few miles, both lost in thought.

Mulhern soon spoke up. "Boy, was she ever singin' on Monday."

"Like a damn canary, wasn't she?"

"I really didn't think that she would give us *more* than what we wanted, I tell you."

"Well, she's on a roll, so let's get as much from her as we can tonight."

"Yep."

Their vehicle rolled into the county jail parking lot, and the detectives walked to the check-in area. They saw Sheriff Pollard in one of the back rooms and called out to him.

Pollard turned and rolled his eyes when he saw the two. He said, "Oh great, New Haven's finest gracing my walls. And just when I was having a wonderful day."

Mulhern chuckled and teased back, "Bill Pollard, what are you doing here at this hour? I thought you'd be at the fishin' hole right after lunch!"

"Hey, I'm working, which is more than I can say for you beat cops."

Widmann walked up to Pollard and shook hands with him and smiled. "How you doin', Bill?"

"Just fine. I'm feeling lucky too. Ever since you brought your special gal in on Wednesday, we've been up to thirteen residents."

"Hey, you *are* lucky. And I've probably helped put most of them here, haven't I?"

"Probably. Anyway, I wanted to tell you and Mulhern that Jaspers' lawyer just left. I don't know what he spoke with her about, but he was in there for a good forty-five minutes or so."

"Damn, hope he didn't jinx us—we've been on a roll with her blabbing about what she's done over the years."

"Well, I don't know how she'll be today with you. But, I'll tell you one thing, I wish the other twelve that are in here were like her."

"No kidding?"

"Oh sure, she's fit right in. Acting and behaving like any other prisoner. In fact, even better. Polite as all get out. 'Thank you' for this, 'please' for that. You can tell she had a decent upbringing."

"Any of the others giving her a bad time?"

"Nope, not yet anyway. I watch 'em walking around and mingling during rec time and at meals. She talks with the other girls and does just fine."

Pollard then chuckled aloud. "You should see her at meals. If the other girls leave any food on their plates, she asks them if she can have it. Do you believe that? She packs one helluva appetite."

Widmann shook his head from side to side and smiled.

Pollard grabbed his coat from the rack and said, "Well, good luck with her. I guess I will head out now, so you creeps can get to work."

He stopped, patted Widmann on the shoulder, looked at him closely, and said, "It was good seeing you. Let's get out and play some rounds one of these days."

"Sounds great. See you later," said Widmann as he turned away and walked back over to Mulhern.

"Sheriff in a good mood?"

"Yes, he seems to be recovering pretty well, doesn't he?"

"Yeah, it's been a year now, hasn't it?"

The two walked toward Jaspers' cell.

"Well, hello, Virginia! Do you remember me? I'm Detective Mulhern. We last spoke on Monday."

Virginia scowled at Mulhern and said, "Oh, I remember."

Widmann spoke up. "Now, Miss Jaspers, we'd like to ask you some questions. Since you were last interviewed by police, there have been some more allegations against you that we'd like to have cleared up."

"My lawyer was just here, and he told me not to speak with you."

"Well, we really just have a few things to settle, so now ..."

He was cut off by Virginia saying, "My lawyer was just here, and he told me not to speak with you."

"Yeah, sure, didn't you just say that?"

"I did. And I'll say it again, too."

"Now, Ginny, look, let's be reasonable. We are not in court, and you are not pleading the Fifth, so let's get on with our discussion."

Mulhern felt himself starting to perspire. He did not like the position of having to argue with a criminal. His thoughts moved quickly but were also cut off when Virginia called out, "Mr. Mancini! Mr. Mancini! May I have some help here?"

"Jesus H., lady, no need for hysterics. I just ..."

"Mr. Mancini!" Virginia yelled even louder.

One of the assistant jailers ran down to Virginia's cell and informed her that Phil Mancini had the late shift tonight, and he'd be in after she was asleep.

"Well, these cops are trying to question me, and my lawyer told me to call for someone if the cops did just what they are doing!"

The jailer turned to the detectives and shrugged.

Widmann looked at Mulhern and said, "Guess it's the same as asking for her lawyer. Looks like we gotta bug out."

Mulhern grimaced. He was mad. He felt as though he'd hooked the big one, reeled it in, and then it flopped its way back to water as he tried to grab on to it. He looked at Virginia, who turned suddenly away and stared at her cell wall.

"I suppose you didn't feed the Connors baby whiskey?"

Virginia's mouth opened in disgust. "And who said that?"

"Mr. Connors said he caught you doing it and fired you."

"That's a damn lie! I would never do that to a baby."

Now Mulhern was hot. "Oh, you'd shake the stuffing out of a defenseless baby, but you wouldn't give it a nightcap to put it to sleep?"

A voice answered his question in the background, "No, she wouldn't."

The voice belonged to Edward Reynolds.

"Gentlemen, I believe my client has invoked her privilege to have a lawyer present during questioning. I guess I'm glad I forgot my favorite pen and thought to come back for it. 'When the cat's away,' isn't it, gentlemen?"

Widmann and Mulhern looked at each other. Widmann motioned to the direction of the door with his head. Mulhern folded the papers with the names of fifteen persons who stated their infants were harmed while in the nurse's care. These would be questions that would never be answered, issues that would never be put to rest. Outside, Mulhern grabbed a metal trashcan and bashed it down on the sidewalk.

Widmann grinned and told his partner, "Uh, Mulhern, that's littering."

CHAPTER TWENTY-FIVE

"The Jew Baby Got What She Deserved; the Nurse Should Get a Medal!"

12:15 p.m.
Friday, August 31, 1956
New Haven, Connecticut

The wind blew gently on Sheilah Kapsinow as she sat on the ground by Abbe's grave. Her heart felt heavy to her; the sharp stab that had pierced her soul a week ago had now transformed into a dull ache. Sheilah cried as she gently caressed the small mound of dirt that lay on top of her daughter's casket. The plot looked barren. Allen hadn't gotten around to planting the perennials, and the headstone with the lamb at the crest was not ready yet for placement. Harry Weller from the funeral home had promised her that the headstone would be done by Labor Day weekend. Sheilah knew better. The holiday weekend began tomorrow, and for all she knew, Harry was out on the thirteenth green making his par shot. Everything would be closed up, and people would be traveling, sailing, camping, you name it, everything except caring for the dead.

Sheilah tried not to have a negative attitude on the world, but she just couldn't help it. Her trust in anything just and good had been wrested from her violently. Now, she was bitter. *Young and bitter*, she thought.

What was left in her life? *A good-for-nothing drunk of a husband, a dead infant ... and ... two loving children who need me so much,* her thoughts continued. She cried harder now. *I can't give up. God, Abbe, help me through this! I need you, and I need to feel close to you. Why were you taken from me? I can't do this alone. I just can't.*

Sheilah lay back on the ground parallel to the grave, closed her eyes, and wept. Her arm rested on the dirt beside her. Being there was painful, but necessary. Sheilah felt as though she could not leave her daughter alone day in and day out. On the day of Abbe's burial, Sheilah looked across the street from the United Israel Society's cemetery and noticed a brick building that was set back. She could just make out the one large, red word on the sign in the window, which read "Hiring." At the time, she dismissed it, but all weekend, the sign kept repeating over and over in her mind. She knew the office was an insurance group but was curious to discover what type of worker they wanted. On Monday, she drove to the company after dropping the older children off at her parents' house. She spoke with the receptionist at the front desk about her curiosity regarding the sign. She explained to the woman that she didn't know why, exactly, she was drawn to the office, but the fact was that she needed to explore the option further. The receptionist introduced her to Bob Samuels, who was part owner of the insurance group, who explained to Sheilah that because the business was expanding, they would need another secretary. Sheilah was asked if she was interested. She took a brief typing test and was hired on the spot. As she started driving out of the office parking lot to go home, she braked suddenly. The answer to her compulsion to come to this place was staring at her. *I now have a daily connection to Abbe,* she thought. Sheilah decided that she would use her hour lunchtime for daily visits to her daughter's grave.

As she lay next to the mound of dirt, Sheilah watched the clouds float by. She looked at the blue sky and then wondered about the heaven beyond. She questioned silently if the angels were indeed holding baby Abbe in their arms. Instead of feeling comforted, Sheilah felt jealousy, regret, and emptiness. She thought about all the hours that she sat in synagogue and was instructed about God's grace and the goodness of others. She pressed her own being to believe these lessons now as she lay there in the cemetery. *Why struggle so? End it here,* the inner voices beckoned her. Tears dripped sideways across her temples onto the grass. If not for Marcy and Heide, she would check out of this miserable world.

Sheilah then remembered the letters—she had them in her purse, letters from total strangers began to come to the house starting the Monday after Abbe was killed. She read a few and then stockpiled the rest, because it hurt too greatly to read the well wishes of others. Today, she had stuck the three-inch-thick stack of letters in her purse. She had planned on eating a sandwich and reading the letters aloud at the gravesite, but in her grief, she all but forgot them.

She rolled over onto her stomach; the grass felt cool beneath her. After she brushed the dusting of dirt off her right hand and arm, she reached for the letters. The first letter was from an elderly couple. The woman wrote that she and her husband had fourteen grandchildren and that they could not bear the thought of anyone losing a child—especially the way that the Kapsinows had. Sheilah smiled after she was through and carefully refolded it and tucked it in the accompanying envelope. *That one's a keeper,* she thought. She'd need it during her low times.

The next letter was simply addressed to "Kapsinow," not "Mr. and Mrs. Allen Kapsinow," as all the others had been. Sheilah began the letter by reading it aloud and then stopped suddenly as if she didn't want Abbe to hear her. It was a dreadful letter. Sheilah winced and breathed hard after the first paragraph. She pushed herself up to where she was kneeling and began to tear the letter to shreds. She tossed it aside and began to cry.

The letter that was now misshapen, torn, and spat upon held the following words:

> *My dear Kapsinows—*
> *I hate the very thought of you. Your kind makes me sick. Here we have an upstanding member of society getting the shaft by Jews like you. HOW DARE YOU!! And boo-hoo to you for your dead baby. I think the Jew baby got what she deserved; the nurse should get a medal.*

> *Death to all Jews and to you too!*

There were other letters like that as well, though not as cruel and vindictive. Hindsight taught Sheilah that people could be very hateful and ignorant. But, at the time, she was emotionally devastated. It was an issue she could share with no one. So, from then on, she read her letters as if opening a box with a bomb attached. If she sensed any antagonism in the first paragraph, she'd destroy the letter immediately.

Her lunchtime visits to Abbe in September and the following months remained consistent, even on weekends. Sometimes, she would bring the other children, but they would often want to wander among the headstones and play hide and seek. For the most part, she would leave them with her parents. Sheilah's time at Abbe's grave was a personal time; it reflected her commitment to seeing that she was cared for and fueled her growing passion for justice in the case against Virginia. It was on the following day, Saturday, September 1, 1956, that Sheilah pledged to Abbe that she would do everything in her power to block Virginia Jaspers from ever caring for any child again. Sheilah truly believed that if she sat idly by and let the powers that be take charge, then many more children would indeed die and needlessly suffer. She didn't want Abbe to have died in vain—her tiny life was worth more than that.

4:00 p.m.
Friday, August 31, 1956
New Haven, Connecticut

William Jaspers sat at his desk in the personnel office at the New Haven Railroad. He was looking about for things to keep him occupied, even though he had still not sorted through all the mail and other papers that had been left for him during his absence. He had returned to work the day before, just so he could catch up with the paperwork. The long weekend was upon him, and he found it hard to concentrate on anything that lay on his desk. So he stared at the piles and was pensive for most of the day. His secretary, Harriet, knew not to disturb him. She knew of her boss's moods, and today and yesterday, he was in one of them. Yet, this mood was a difficult one for her to decipher. She just left him alone.

Jaspers finally looked at the clock—still an hour before quitting time. He was nervous now, because he wanted to make a phone call and was frozen about doing so as well. He was then reminded that if he put off making the call, he might miss his chance to reach his contact. His heart thumped as he pressed the intercom to Harriet's desk.

The secretary jumped and made an audible gasp. She placed her finger on the answer button and answered in a stuttering, halting manner.

"Please, get me … get me Mr. Crowder on the phone—he's in my Rolodex. Hurry."

CHAPTER TWENTY-SIX

"Do Something, Anything, to Distract the Media"

4:15 p.m.
Friday, August 31, 1956
New Haven, Connecticut

William Jaspers hurriedly picked up the incoming phone call he had been expecting.

"Yes?"

"Bill, it's Crowder. What can I do ye for?"

"Hey, Crowder," Jaspers said as he reached for his handkerchief in his back right pants pocket. "I've been thinking. Well … it's been a long time since we've talked."

Ralph Crowder's forehead wrinkled as he tried to deduce what in the sam hill Bill Jaspers wanted. The two had known each other for years, but it had been several months since they had talked, much less gotten together. Crowder was still on the New Haven police force when Jaspers was in the senate. He would often check files or backgrounds on people whenever the good senator called. He chalked it up to being his civic duty. He also would get a steak dinner, free ball game tickets, and so on, for doing these "favors" for Jaspers. He now wondered what "favor" would be asked of him.

"Yep, sure has been a long time, Bill. Sorry to hear about your girl. Read about it. She is a fine girl, you know."

"Yes … well … that is why I'm calling, Ralph."

"Shoot."

"They're killing me, Ralph."

"Who?"

"The media, my so-called friends, people on the street, people at work, you name it."

"Jesus, Bill, you can't mean everybody!"

"Well, it feels like it. I just want it all to go away."

"And … that's where I fit in?"

"No, er … yes, I mean."

"Bill, we've known each other for a long time—ask me what you want."

Jaspers felt like he'd been led into a candy store, and he was so overwhelmed that he didn't know what to choose first. "I … I … do something, anything, to distract the media. And I don't want any records of her case left."

"Well, hang on, Bill, that's a tall order there, my big boy. Lots of expense and time. Something to distract the media, you say? You mean take the focus somehow off your daughter? Hmmm, I'll have to think about that awhile."

Jaspers shouted, "I don't have time!"

"Whoa, Bill, now calm down. No need to get your shorts in a bind. When do you need this to happen?"

"Immediately, tonight or tomorrow at the latest."

Jaspers felt the long pause at the other end of the phone, and then finally the response came, "Tall order, Bill."

"How much?"

"Tall."

"How much, Goddamn it!"

"Five grand."

Jaspers swallowed hard and blotted his head. He looked over at the picture of Jane and the girls that was on his desk. "Done."

Crowder smiled. It was the easiest money he'd ever made. He wanted to share this fact with Jaspers but thought better of it. He had to think fast, and he had to be creative. He'd worry about the case records later. "Okay, my man. Just watch the papers and see your daughter disappear!"

Jaspers hung up the phone. He was relieved.

Saturday, September 1, 1956
New Haven, Connecticut

Since Virginia Jaspers was not talking, the press hounds were dismayed. William Jaspers was unaware of this, but many reporters had packed their belongings and headed back to their cities in search of a new hot story. The city of New Haven had been made trendy this past week, much to the dislike of Mayor Richard C. Lee. The fifty-three-year-old was still reeling from the effects of the negativity that Jaspers had brought on his city. Conceited as it might be, he still held his people to a standard of truth, honesty, and goodness under his leadership. He even campaigned under this tenet. Yet, now the New Haven reputation had been tarnished. The reputation of Yale could not even smooth this scar. It would take years of winning seasons and educational excellence to do that.

Lee contacted the media for a press conference, since he felt pulled to do something official to try to correct the damage. The sky overhead was gloomy and dark; rain threatened, so Lee held the conference inside the lobby of the city hall building.

He began promptly at 1:00 p.m. Several reporters raced in late and filed into chairs that had been set up earlier that morning. Lee kept talking without missing a beat. That was a virtue of which he was proud; he was not flustered when it came to giving any kind of speech.

"… and so I want to remind you that time is long overdue for a basic study with the object of introducing legislation in the January 1957 session of the General Assembly."

Saul Pett from the Associated Press swore under his breath and leaned toward a fellow reporter who was sitting in front of him.

"Hey, I was at lunch, what's been going on?"

"No shit," said the other reporter as he mimed flicking at his chin.

Pett brushed his chin and a small piece of bologna fell to the carpeted floor.

He repeated his question, "What's he been talking about?"

The reporter leaned back in his chair and told Pett that Lee announced he would appoint a committee to review the problem of unlicensed medical attendants and recommend corrective legislation.

"Why do these things always happen after the fact?" Pett inquired.

The other reporter shrugged his shoulders and turned back around to face the mayor.

Lee continued, "This committee will be headed by Dr. Creighton Barker, who is currently the executive secretary to the State Medical Examining Board. Assisting him will be Francis Looney, director of the New Haven Welfare Department. Also in the group will be doctors, nurses, and members of the general public."

Pett thought, *Welfare? Where were they when the kids needed them?*

Lee concluded, "I am hopeful that such a study not only will eliminate the possibility of the recurrence of such a series of tragedies but will also assist in protecting the reputation of competent people in this field of home nursing who may now be subjected to unwarranted suspicions. Thank you for your time."

When they stood to go, Saul Pett said to the other reporter, "More political talk?"

"No, I really think he means it. He doesn't stand for this crap going on in his city. It is nice that they got that woman."

The reporter tucked his notebook in his vest and grabbed his hat from the floor. He looked at Pett and said, "Something like this better not happen for a long time. The mayor wouldn't be able to take it."

The reporter spoke too soon.

Jacob Johnson reread his interview in the *Hartford Courant*, which had been in the newspaper the night before. He felt proud that the newspaper would choose him as the psychiatrist to be interviewed for a story on the horrendous baby killer in the southern part of the state. One of the editors had simply contacted him two days previously and asked if he would typify the nurse's behavior. Johnson had read enough about the case to comment.

"The whole case really is an incongruity," he began. "You have this caregiver who is acting behaviorally irresponsible and who is now legally responsible for her actions. A person who commits a crime through some deep-seated inner conflict or disturbance may, at the same time, be aware of what he is doing, and therefore be legally responsible."

Johnson thought to himself, *That was one of my better insights yet.* He continued to read comments in the next paragraph. "Any person who does this has strong sadistic impulses. I wonder if she were not very frustrated, and if in her childhood, she was envious of any brothers or sisters or other playmates. Was there a rivalry of any sort? Really, her conflicts are deep-rooted and have been growing as the years went along. Miss Jaspers obviously suffered some frustration in being denied having children. You have to understand that she attempted to share in the happy home of the families she worked for. So she probably suffered an unconscious frustration this way, saying to herself, 'I'm denied this pleasure, these joys,' and the serious and deep conflicts were taken out on little children at the first excuse to give release to her unconscious feelings."

Johnson grimaced slightly as he read the last part of the article. He felt awful for the parents of these children and for society in general that people were out there who would hurt and kill children. All around, it wasn't fair. It was tragic. "It is possible that Miss Jaspers did not feel an annoyance over the children's behavior, as she claimed, but actually has unconscious infanticide impulses. However strong her impulses toward infanticide might have been, there is the question of whether or not she knew what she was doing when mishandling the infants. This question brings us back to where we started with talking about legally responsible actions."

2:00 p.m.
Saturday, September 1, 1956
Sears, Roebuck, and Co. Store
Hamden, Connecticut

Eleanor Ruotolo peeked in her six-week-old daughter's stroller that had been parked at the entranceway of Sears for the past thirty-five minutes. She wanted to check if she was still sleeping. When she looked in, all she saw was baby Cynthia's bonnet, shawl, diaper, and bottle. Her infant had vanished.

"My baby is gone," she cried. "My baby is gone!"

Many shoppers who were nearby rushed to her aid, while she frantically searched under the mattress and around the carriage. She then ran outside to the sidewalk and looked into a covered trashcan nearby. When she became hysterical, she was taken to the store's first-aid room.

Over the store's intercom system, an announcement was made asking for the immediate return of the baby—"with no questions asked." Four thousand shoppers heard the announcement, and all stopped briefly in their tracks. Police were notified and searched the entire three floors of the building. In the sprawling parking lot, every car and truck was examined. Eleanor Ruotolo's baby truly had been abducted.

On Sunday, the story was splashed across the covers of newspapers across the country. Volunteers from all walks of life took pity on Eleanor and Stephen Ruotolo and conducted search parties in the vicinity of the shopping plaza. Boy Scout troops gathered and spread out in a big line, holding hands as they swept across fields in and around Hamden. Rewards were offered. Clues poured in to the police station from people who had been at the Sears store the day the Ruotolo baby disappeared, and a Mass was said that day at Our Lady of Mt. Carmel. Memories were jogged, and bits and pieces came forth for police investigators to assemble. Many of the officers who were assigned to the Jaspers case were pulled from their duties to lend a hand in this new case that now captivated the country.

On Monday, September 3, at his office, William Jaspers was beside himself. He had read about the abduction the day before and had been very nervous about the repercussions of his actions. When he heard Mr. and Mrs. Ruotolo on the radio pleading for the safe return of their baby, he got up from his desk chair, closed his office door, and dialed Ralph Crowder, without his secretary's help this time.

Crowder answered his phone in an upbeat fashion, as though he had already spent Jaspers' money. "Hel-lo!" he said brightly.

"Crowder, what the Christ have you done? My God, that baby better turn up quick or I'll …"

"Hey! Now hold on a darn tootin' minute. What are you asking me?" Crowder asked hastily.

"I said distract the media, not take a Goddamn baby!" Jaspers shouted.

"Whoa, you got your story mixed up, big boy. You'd better check those facts of yours before you start accusing me of kidnapping. In fact, I was still trying to get creative with what I was going to do when the front page of the newspaper did it for me."

"I don't believe you."

"Well, Bill, you've got no choice, do you? Answer me this—how could I have managed to plan such a feat in less than twenty-four hours, since the kidnapping took place on Saturday? Huh?"

Silence was at the other end of the phone.

"That's right—I couldn't. But, you did get your wish, didn't you?"

"I guess."

"Sure you did!"

"You don't get any credit, though, so the deal is off."

"Well, Bill, that's another thing. Seems to me like we have a gentlemen's agreement, don't we? You also said you wanted some records to disappear—meaning as much as I can muster, right? Including victims' hospital records, etc.?"

"Please don't say 'victims.'"

"Hell, Bill, I'm callin' a spade a spade."

Jaspers thought some more and began to sweat.

"Now, the $5,000 doesn't change. A deal is a deal, no matter how it gets done. You wouldn't want this conversation to be shared, now would you?"

"Crowder, that is what I'd expect from you—blackmail."

"Bill, 'blackmail' is such a dirty word. Call it an agreement, and you aren't going to filch on an agreement, right? Oh, by the by, I expect half by the end of the week and the other when all is said and done."

"Fine!" Jaspers cursed and hung up the phone.

Crowder shook his head from side to side and smiled. "What a fool," he said.

CHAPTER TWENTY-SEVEN

"The Babies of New Haven Are Now Safe"

September 20 – October 2, 1956
New Haven, Connecticut

James Corrigan arranged the papers on his desk in a neat, orderly fashion. This matched the ambiance of the rest of his office. In fact, at the end of each day, his inbox was always empty. It was just a trait that he had learned early and still aspired to. He was ready for the small group of reporters that had requested a visit to his office even though he did not have the answer they wanted. The closed hearing in court that morning had clarified a bit more for Corrigan. He was just unsure about what charges he could blame the Jaspers woman for—murder or manslaughter? He truly wondered if there was more to Virginia Jaspers' stories of her abusive outbursts. One question he had was if the act of shaking could actually kill an infant. But after reviewing case files and listening to the testimony at today's hearing, he felt that such a large woman could definitely inflict fatal injuries on very young infants.

Corrigan also questioned intent. For a charge of murder, he knew that Prosecutor Ullman would have to prove intent. It seemed to him that Miss Jaspers had a hair-trigger temper when it came to infants. So, since she was excessively moody, did she intend to cause harm? A murder charge would mean a potential life sentence for the nurse. A manslaughter charge would mean that she would only be charged in two deaths, since the statute of limitations had run out on the Hubbard baby's case.

Corrigan thought back to the court hearing earlier that morning, where Edward Reynolds again made a plea to Judge Henchel for a reduction in bond. The attorney seemed to ignore the fact that his client confessed to multiple crimes and, instead, focused on her release. At the hearing, ME Taylor testified, as did Dr. Salinger and Assistant Police Chief Eagan. They all laid out the facts of the investigation. The police were still completing several interviews that had been ongoing since Jaspers' arrest. After all the key figures had testified, Judge Henchel asked Corrigan if he wanted to change his warrant.

"No, Your Honor, I'd like to leave it as a holding charge of idleness. Today's testimonies have been enlightening, and I expect to have a formal charge in the next one to two weeks."

Reynolds piped up and commented, "Judge, how much longer is my client going to endure time in jail? She was arrested almost one month ago!"

Judge Henchel looked at Reynolds and said, "Mr. Reynolds, I will remind you that a coroner's warrant can hold someone suspected of a crime without use of a specific charge. If Coroner Corrigan says one to two weeks longer, then that's what we will give him. How does your client plead to the count of idleness, Mr. Reynolds?"

"Not guilty, Your Honor," said Reynolds, exasperated.

"Very well, I am keeping her bail at $50,000 and will set another hearing for Monday, October 1. Will that be enough time for you, Mr. Corrigan?"

"Yes, Your Honor, thank you."

"This hearing is now closed," said Henchel as he banged his gavel.

Virginia looked at her attorney with sad eyes. She wanted to ask him what the term "idleness" had to do with her case but dared not since he seemed so upset.

After their meeting with Corrigan, the four reporters who met briefly with him gathered on the street outside his office.

"Welllll," drawled Lonnie Newton. "That was a complete waste of time. What the hell was that? 'No news is good news?'"

"Yeah, you can say that again," complained Skeeter Tyler, who had driven down from Hartford that morning. "First, we are blocked from the hearing, and then we get zilch from the coroner."

Lonnie chuckled and said, "Oh no, we got 'I have to decline to name the witnesses who testified or to say what they told me.' That's what we got!"

Skeeter said, "And ... and don't forget, 'Everything will come out when I issue my formal finding,' even though the creep wouldn't say when that would be!"

Lonnie turned to the others and said, "C'mon guys, let's go get some chow at the greasy spoon around the corner. The best part is that Skeeter's paying!"

"Hey! That's not fair!" said Skeeter.

Lonnie smiled and said, without looking back, "Yeah, life's not fair."

Nurse Charged With Manslaughter – Tuesday, October 2, 1956
New Haven Register

Coroner Finds Responsibility in Baby Deaths

Virginia Jaspers Held to Blame in Two
Instances in Corrigan Finding

A bench warrant charging Miss Virginia Jaspers, a thirty-three-year-old East Haven pediatric nurse, with two counts of manslaughter was issued today by Superior Court Judge William J. Shea.

The warrant was issued shortly after Coroner James J. Corrigan announced a finding in which he held Miss Jaspers criminally responsible for the deaths of two infants under her care. The deaths occurred five years apart.

State's Attorney Abraham S. Ullman said it is "altogether possible" that Miss Jaspers will be presented in Superior Court later today.

When arrested on August 27, Miss Jaspers was held on a technical charge of idleness. Later, she was detained on a coroner's warrant. She is in the New Haven County Jail, unable to raise the bond of $50,000.

In his finding which he announced today, Coroner James J. Corrigan held that Miss Jaspers was criminally responsible for the deaths of 11-day-old Abbe Kapsinow last August and Jennifer Leona Malkan about two months old in 1951.

Third Death

Ullman said that the statute of limitations ruled out a third count against the nurse for still another death she allegedly caused, that of Cynthia Hubbard, infant daughter of Mr. and Mrs. Allen Hubbard of Guilford. Cynthia died in 1948.

The coroner blamed Miss Jaspers' "uncontrollable fits of temper" for the babies' deaths. He noted, "It would not have taken a great deal of effort by the nurse, a 'very robust' woman six feet tall and weighing 220 pounds, to inflict the fatal injuries."

All three infants died after being in the care of Miss Jaspers. The nurse, who is being held under $50,000 bond, lives at 136 Prospect Road, East Haven.

Abbe, daughter of Mr. and Mrs. Allen Kapsinow of 65-H Brookside Avenue, died August 24 from cerebral hemorrhages. Corrigan said that Miss Jaspers confessed she became angered because the baby cried continuously and that she "shook the child strenuously and dropped her onto the mattress of her crib."

Shook Child

Corrigan believed that "shaking the child violently" could have produced the brain hemorrhage.

Jennifer Malkan died December 15, 1951 from asphyxiation. Corrigan quoted Miss Jaspers that she "shook that child sufficiently strongly to cause her head to bob back and forth." The nurse added, Corrigan said, that the baby "lost her breath and her eyes went 'funny' in her head."

The infant was the daughter of Mr. and Mrs. Willard Malkan, formerly of Prospect Street but now living out of town.

Temper Blamed

"Miss Jaspers does not deny that she had done wrong," said Corrigan, adding, "Her only explanation of all of this is in effect that she had an uncontrollable urge to grasp children violently between the elbows and shoulders and shake them when they persisted crying."

Corrigan said there was no need to search deeper for a motive other than "her uncontrolled fits of temper." In a seemingly bitter tone, the coroner declared, "There was no excuse or justification for this woman to have handled the babies so violently that she inflicted fatal injuries upon them."

New Haven mayor Richard Lee stood at the microphone in front of City Hall the afternoon that the manslaughter charge against Virginia was announced. He grinned boldly from ear to ear.

"Ladies and gentlemen of the press and guests, thank you all for coming down to City Hall on this beautiful fall day. As you all have heard, Miss Virginia Jaspers was formally charged today with manslaughter in the deaths of two infants who had been in her care. I was at the court proceeding when the charges were read to her, and she pleaded not guilty. In speaking with investigators in this particular case, along with prosecutors, doctors, members of child welfare, and parents, I know that it has been a very long road for everyone involved. But, I am here today to tell you, to reassure you, that the babies of New Haven are now safe!"

A staccato of hesitant applause began and soon died. Lee knew it was an appeasing statement, especially in light of the Ruotolo baby abduction, but he thought it would sound good and read even better.

The mayor finished his brief speech with, "I assure you that justice will be carried forth in this case. I am overseeing the process myself. I cannot fathom what these parents have gone through and the destruction that one woman has caused on an entire community. May God forgive Miss Jaspers, and may God watch over these parents. Thank you."

In the back of the crowd, Sheilah Kapsinow stood with her children. She felt like shouting out to the mayor, "What are you going to do to prevent this from happening again?" but her depression and respect for her children held her back. She turned away slowly with her children each holding a hand and walked toward her car.

CHAPTER TWENTY-EIGHT

"Guilty, Your Honor"

October 24, 1956
New Haven County Jail
New Haven, Connecticut

As Virginia Jaspers lay on her cot in her jail cell on that Wednesday morning in October 1956, she thought about her life and what she had done to all those children. It was not a time of deep introspection, rather a cursory overview, similar to what a dying person might experience in the final moments of living. Her depression was oppressive at times, but then her jubilant, somewhat manic, times would lift her from the depths of anguish. Virginia worked on a cleaning and mending detail. There were times when she would make a mistake, such as causing a bucket of water to spill on the walkway floor, and she'd cackle with glee, saying, "Oh what a darn klutz I am." Her fellow inmates would look at her with disdain or inquisitiveness and wonder about the large woman's state of mind. Any other inmate would throw the bucket in anger if the mishap happened to her, but not Virginia, she just grabbed her mop and would start singing as she returned to her duties. On the other hand, she would typically cry over the most trivial matter. Jailer Philip Mancini took her behavior with a grain of salt. He knew she was odd and a bit slow. He just guided her as best he could.

Virginia lay on her cot and picked up her Bible. She hoped that there was something in it to help her. Reverend Beakin had visited her the day before. She silently cursed herself for not asking him about a passage that she could use as an aid for court today. She liked the pastor. He came to visit her and pray with her at least once a week. He would also bring freshly baked items from his wife, which she shared with the other girls and the jailers. Reverend Beakin believed in Virginia's goodness. He had known her since she was a tot and found it difficult to think of her as a baby killer, as the community had made her out to be. He would give her advice and counsel each time he visited. "Have faith, Virginia," he'd tell her, as if he were giving a blessing at the close of a church service. As she lay on her cot, she considered his words. They bandied about in her mind. *Have faith.* She didn't have the heart to ask him what to have faith in. The answer was within reach, but she couldn't grasp it. The experience of thinking this way frustrated her to no end.

"I don't know what to do!" she cried aloud.

One of the other inmates said, "Hey … pipe down, will ya?"

Virginia pulled her pillow over her face and returned to wrestling with her thoughts. She knew that if she pled guilty that she would be sent to prison. She didn't mind being in the jail too much. She, of course, would much rather be out, back at home with her parents, but she had more or less adapted. If, on the other hand, she pled innocent and a trial ensued, then she may get off scot-free. Virginia then questioned the reality of this ever occurring. She had confessed—*Plain and simple,* she told herself. *No use hiding behind the fact that nothing at all happened. You got angry and lashed out at those defenseless young creatures! You are wicked. Just wicked!* The voices scolded her.

Virginia wept loudly into her pillow, her face buried deep, her sounds of anguish heard down at the other end of the block.

4:00 p.m.
October 24, 1956
New Haven County Court
New Haven, Connecticut

The gavel held firmly in Judge William J. Shea's hand banged down firmly on the wooden block, which was marred and pitted with age and thousands of court appearances.

The court clerk stood and read, "In the matter of the people of the State of Connecticut against Virginia B. Jaspers …"

Sheriff William Pollard motioned to Virginia to stand after another clerk motioned to him down the hall of the sheriff's office. The court building and sheriff's office stood side by side but was accessible only through a narrow hallway that was restricted to jail and police officials. Pollard kept Virginia in a front office adjacent to the hallway. He stood at the entrance for at least forty minutes waiting for a signal from the clerk, as his wife, Rachel, who worked part-time as a jail matron, waited with the accused. Virginia sat on the hard Formica seat and patiently watched the floor. Mrs. Pollard drank coffee and worked on a crossword. Virginia would look up every now and then to study the matron—she liked the kind way about her. She had always been nice to Virginia and would sometimes play card games with her or share a movie magazine with her. Virginia took to the kindness of others. Her mother had always told her, "Kindness shows the heart and soul of a person." Yet, now, she had more on her mind than playing games, and Mrs. Pollard knew this and respected the silence.

Virginia had slept fitfully the night before, at best, and looked tired. She wore a white blouse and plaid skirt. It was the only nice set of clothes that she had in storage. At least the clothes had been hanging up. Though the style didn't make Virginia look less frumpy, at least they weren't wrinkled. She told herself to remember to take off her topcoat when she got to her place in court. She did not want to appear to be rude in court.

A few minutes before her case was called, Virginia noticed her second attorney Frank Moran appear around the corner of the hallway and wave to her before he pulled himself back to speak with Sheriff Pollard. Virginia raised her right hand to wave back, but her attorney's head had popped out of view mid-wave. Her countenance changed from a curious expression to one of disappointment. She went back to looking at the floor. Rachel Pollard looked up from her crossword in the direction of the hallway. She heard bits and pieces of the conversation, nothing to take note of, and returned to her work.

The court clerk's voice was so loud Virginia jumped when he began speaking. Sheriff Pollard came around the corner and said, "Come on, Virginia. Time to talk with the judge."

"Is it Judge Hershel?" she asked.

"Nope, Judge Shea. Hershel has taken a leave of absence."

"Yes, I was asking, since he wasn't at my last hearing either."

Mrs. Pollard put her hand through one of her arms and gently guided Virginia up and toward the dark hallway. "Mustn't keep anyone waiting, dear."

Virginia grinned slightly and proceeded forward.

The first people she saw when she entered the courtroom were her attorneys. The Pollards dropped her off in their care. Virginia leaned over to Edward Reynolds and whispered in his ear, "I need to speak with you about my charges."

Thinking that it would be another conundrum that he'd need to explain in depth to her, he nipped her request with a hushed, "Not now, Virginia."

Virginia remained steadfast and said, "But ..." aloud, causing the judge's gavel to come crashing down.

Frank Moran leaned forward, looked at his client sternly, and held an index finger to his lips.

"Mr. Reynolds, is anything wrong with your client?"

"No, Your Honor, please excuse the interruption."

"Well, then, let's proceed. Miss Jaspers, you have been charged with two counts of manslaughter in the deaths of infants Abbe Kapsinow and Jennifer Malkan as per the findings of Coroner James Corrigan. How do you plead?"

"Mr. Reynolds," Virginia said as she turned to him.

"Not guilty, Your Honor," said Moran.

"Mr. Moran, it seems that there is something your client wishes to say," said Judge Shea.

"Your Honor, may we have a minute?" Reynolds asked.

Shea waved at the two attorneys in agreement.

Reynolds turned to Virginia and asked in a low, intense voice, "What the hell is it, Virginia?"

"Why didn't you visit me?"

"Where?"

"In jail."

"I have been visiting you. What is this about?"

Moran rolled his eyes and turned away. He couldn't wait to get rid of this case.

"I've changed my mind. I changed it yesterday after my minister and my parents visited me. I want to plead guilty!" A tear formed in the corner of her eye as she spoke. The entire courtroom had heard what she had said.

Reynolds stood back and looked at her as if stunned. He wet his lips quickly with the tip of his tongue and looked toward Moran, as if he had an answer. Moran shrugged. Reynolds looked back at his client and said, "Are you sure?"

She nodded.

Reynolds looked back at Shea and said, "Judge Shea, I think we have a change of plea."

Shea said to Virginia, "You do realize that on each count there is a maximum penalty of a $1,000 fine and fifteen years?"

Virginia nodded but said nothing.

Court Clerk Frank Minnix took the cue and asked Virginia if she wished to change her plea.

Virginia looked forward and answered clearly, "I do."

Judge Shea reread the two counts, and Moran responded for her, "Guilty, Your Honor." Virginia stood silently, with her hands in the pockets of her tan topcoat. She wasn't thinking of vanity now.

The whole matter was over in minutes. There was no drawing out of garrulous arguments between legal sides, no lengthy judicial runnings-on. The former baby nurse took a stance for herself for the first time in her life and pled guilty. Her dazed father led her weeping mother out of the courtroom past a drove of reporters who had regained interest in the case since Corrigan's manslaughter charges. The revelation of today's court appearance stirred up a media fervor like when the case originally broke in August. The headlines read, "Baby Attendant Pleads Guilty; Faces Sentencing November 14."

Back at the jail, Sheriff Pollard walked Virginia to her cell. She remained compliant along the way and spoke no words. When her cell door opened, she obediently entered, like a Labrador going into its cage.

"Proud of you today, Virginia," said the sheriff. "You did the right thing, you know."

Virginia politely returned a "thank you" and lay down on her cot.

"Hungry? I think Mr. Mancini saved some supper for you."

"No, I think I'll read, if that's okay."

"Suit yourself, then. Good night, Virginia."

"Good night, Sheriff."

Virginia reached over to a table by her cot and picked up one of the five religious books that Reverend Beakin had given her. She only read a few paragraphs and found that her eyes kept closing. It was only 6:00 p.m., but she was especially tired.

"Maybe a short nap," she said aloud as she put her book and glasses down, pulled her scratchy wool blanket over her shoulder, and drifted off to sleep.

Virginia was surprised when November 14th rolled around so quickly. She felt refreshed and was ready for what Judge Shea had to say to her.

She had this feeling deep down inside that maybe, just maybe, her father had spoken to him. Regardless, she felt ready.

After she had a large stack of pancakes and three tall glasses of orange juice, the Pollards came for her once again. As they walked from the jail to the courthouse, the colorful leaves flitted about. The air was cool but not frigid. Everything looked and smelled sweet, and the sun shone. *What a lovely day it is*, thought Virginia. The trio went in the main door of the courthouse this time. It seemed strange to Virginia, but she didn't question it. As she entered the front door with the Pollards, she saw some people she knew and gave them a friendly wave. A few reporters asked her questions, but she kept looking ahead, as the Pollards had instructed her.

Inside the courtroom, there stood the clerk, Frank Minnix. He motioned to the Pollards to bring Virginia to the front. The entire room was empty. Virginia thought, *We must be early*, and sat in the front row, where she was directed. The Pollards wished her luck and left the courtroom through the back hallway. As they were almost out of sight, Sheriff Pollard gave his wife a pinch on her rear. Sounds of giggling emanated from the secret hallway. Virginia creased her eyebrows together in wonder. Frank Minnix just looked ahead.

The sound of a crashing gavel startled her, and she made an audible "Oh" sound. Judge Shea looked at Minnix and said, "Next case."

"Yes, Your Honor, the case of the State of Connecticut versus Miss Virginia Belle Jaspers, the charges are two counts of manslaughter."

"Miss Jaspers, how do you plead?"

Virginia stood for the court and grasped the rail in front of her. "Well, Judge, we've been through this already. I pled guilty, and my attorneys, Mr. Reynolds and Mr. Moran, aren't here. Shouldn't we wait for them?"

Judge Shea looked at Virginia and said, "Yes, this *is* the sentencing, isn't it?"

Virginia nodded.

"Well, my lady, I have some good news for you. Your daddy happened to visit me yesterday, and he convinced me to let you go. So that's what I'm going to do."

Virginia was overwhelmed. "Really?" she cried. "Really and truly?"

"Yes. Now go out and go home where your parents will take good care of you."

Virginia gathered her coat and purse and began to turn around, when Judge Shea said, "Oh! I almost forgot. *No more shaking babies!*"

Virginia looked embarrassed and shook her head from side to side. She then turned around and was shocked at what she saw. Her father was dressed as an executioner, complete with a black hood and chain mail across his chest. He held a scythe in one hand. His right hand beckoned her silently, his finger pulling at the air. Virginia looked at his left and saw Sheilah Kapsinow standing poised with a German Luger in her hand. The trigger was cocked, and the gun was yearning to be fired. She looked in back of her and saw Judge Shea cackling at her predicament. When she looked back at her father, she saw him turn to the Kapsinow lady and whisper, "Ready?"

"Noooo!" Virginia yelled and suddenly plunked off her cot onto the jail floor. She scrambled back to bed and immediately began crying into her pillow. Only three hours had passed since she pled guilty.

CHAPTER TWENTY-NINE

"How Can You Live with Yourself?"

November 14, 1956
Office of New Haven Co. Prosecutor
New Haven, Connecticut

State's Attorney Abraham Ullman sat with his size-10 feet propped up on his wooden desk as he read from Virginia Jaspers' file. This was the usual way that his secretary would find him whenever she'd go into his office to ask him a question: feet up and reading. His eyes were glued to the pages as he read intently. Certain key aspects of both the Jaspers' case and of the nurse's personality were jotted down on a pad that lay on a side table next to Ullman. He wanted to make his case for the maximum penalty a good one. He wanted every loose screw securely tightened. This was one of the most important cases of his career, and it seemed that all of Connecticut was watching how he handled it. From all the parents he interviewed and all the stories he'd read in the paper, he knew that providing a safe community, especially for children, was a top priority. He would make a stance that would send a message to anyone prepared to inflict injury on a child to be warned. Abuse would not be tolerated. And if convicted, they should be prepared to face the greatest punishment.

He grinned as he put stars by each point on the pad that he wanted to emphasize to Judge Shea. He felt a sense of pride at the work that he had put into this statement. He had expended far more hours on this case than on most trials that he had worked on in the past. He clunked his feet down from the desk, making a soft thud sound on the floor. He rubbed his ample belly and thought about grabbing a quick midmorning bite before Jaspers' 11:00 a.m. sentencing. He stood and placed his notes in the case file and put the whole lot into his worn briefcase. He walked into the kitchenette just past the desk of his secretary, who was out ill today, and looked for donuts. Finding none, he decided to hurry over to McCann's bakery just across the street. He'd have just enough time for a fry cake and a swill of java.

Sheilah Kapsinow called downstairs to her mother while she checked herself in the mirror. "Mother?" she beckoned.

"Yes?" came the return call.

"Make sure you take the kids to the park. They've been asking me all morning about it."

"Yes. They've asked me as well. We're planning on going right after you leave."

"Which is now. I am so much later than I wanted to be," said Sheilah as she raced down the stairs.

After three quick pecks to her children and mother, Sheilah raced out the door to the car. She gunned the engine and shifted into reverse, but before she took off, she glanced up at the windows. There were the faces of her children, Marcy and Heide, looking out the front door at her through the thin white sheen of the door covering. She paused and looked at them intently. She lifted her left palm to her mouth and blew her children a kiss. They smiled broadly in response and waved to her. She felt lucky to have them and felt very loved. Sheilah's mother came from behind them and lightly placed her hands on their shoulders. The trio watched as Sheilah backed out of the driveway and into the street and headed toward her destination.

Joan looked at Willard and shook her head. She asked him again, "Are you coming with me or not?"

"Joan, as I told you already, I have no interest in seeing the woman who killed our adopted daughter get handed a punishment. I think I can read about that in the newspaper tomorrow."

How callous, Joan thought. "Well, if it's anything to you, I would have liked your company and support."

"I'm sorry, dear. I can't go, and I won't."

There he goes, calling me 'dear' again, she thought. *Guess I'm in this alone.*

Joan walked out of her house and got into the car. She was ready to drive the sixty miles from New Canaan to New Haven. It would be worth it for her to see the resolution of this nightmare. She only wished that she had support from Willard. *No matter.* She shrugged. He would watch the boys, and she would watch the curtain close.

At 10:45, Marvin and Norma Schaefer walked up to the front door of the courthouse. This was a bittersweet day for them. The fact that Virginia was getting her due today was both a blessing and ironic, since she was receiving no punishment for the injury inflicted on their son, Bruce. Still, she was getting what was coming to her, and a life sentence, in the eyes of the Schaefers as well as other parents, was too short for the baby nurse.

When the couple entered the courthouse lobby, there was a small collection of people. Marvin recognized some other parents, town leaders, doctors, and even a few off-duty police officers. One face that he was glad to see was that of Dr. Salinger, who acknowledged the Schaefers right away and came over to them.

"Hi, Doc, you remember my wife, Norma?"

Salinger nodded politely.

"Hey, what gives with the crowd?"

"Well, we all have been speaking with one of the court clerks, who just made an announcement that the sentencing of Miss Jaspers has been postponed until tomorrow."

Marvin stepped backward in shock and said, "What?"

"Yep. It seems that one of her attorneys is tied up with another case in Hartford and can't get away. Judge Shea postponed it."

"Just great! All of us come down here, get all worked up, miss work, and now we have to do this all over again."

Salinger did not smile but shrugged his shoulders and said, "It's the legal way, isn't it?"

November 15, 1956
New Haven County Courthouse
New Haven, Connecticut

"All rise!" said Frank Minnix to the courtroom audience as Judge Shea entered from his chambers.

"In the matter of the State of Connecticut versus Virginia B. Jaspers. This is a sentencing hearing on two counts of manslaughter in the deaths of Abbe Kapsinow and Jennifer Malkan."

Shea nodded and said, "Thank you, Mr. Minnix." He then looked at those in the courtroom and said, "This is a time of sentencing. We will be hearing from several people this morning. Some of the things that they say may be lengthy, so the defendant may take a seat."

Edward Reynolds whispered to Virginia to sit. Normally, defendants would stand throughout the entire sentencing, out of respect for the court, but this sentencing was anything but normal.

"Welcome, Mr. Moran," said Judge Shea sarcastically. "Glad you are with us today."

"Yes ... well ... yes, Judge," stumbled Moran. "I am sorry about yesterday; it was out of my control."

"And out of mine as well," returned the judge.

Virginia squirmed a bit in her seat, though she smiled from time to time. She waved briefly to her parents, whom she found after surreptitiously glancing about over a period of several minutes. Reynolds whispered something to her, and she straightened and turned herself back toward the judge.

"All right, then. Mr. Ullman, you get to go first, don't you?"

Abraham Ullman stood and carried several papers with him as he walked up to the front of the courtroom. All eyes followed him as he prepared himself.

"Thank you, Judge Shea." Ullman took a deep breath and began. "Ladies and Gentlemen, within this court, there sits a criminal here today who should be punished to the utmost letter of the law. She has made such a terrible impact on our society and has broken the trust of hundreds of individuals. Worse yet, she broke a promise to the babies and children she cared for—for over twelve years!

"Let me read to you a document that was signed by the defendant, Miss Virginia B. Jaspers, just before she completed her training program at the St. Agnes Home in West Hartford. In part, it reads, 'I promise to uphold the ideals and tenets which are a part of the St. Agnes Home nursing preparatory program. I furthermore promise to respect the homes of which I am a part, the families for whom I work, and the children for whom I care.' Shaking babies to death, hitting children, feeding them whiskey, breaking their bones ..."

"Objection, Your Honor," Moran piped up. "Miss Jaspers is being sentenced for manslaughter. These other allegations are frivolous and prejudicial."

Marvin Schaefer almost rose from his seat, but his wife calmed him with a touch of her hand.

"Prejudicial? Yes. Frivolous? Tell that to the parents. Mr. Ullman, watch where you go. Continue, please."

"Yes, Your Honor, I apologize. Let me continue by reading from Miss Jaspers' confession." Ullman strode gingerly over to the desk in front of the prosecutor's seat. He grabbed a thin stack of papers and read from the underlined sentences.

"Your Honor and Ladies and Gentlemen, here is what Miss Jaspers said that she did. First of all, in a police interview, she admitted shaking both infants violently, all because they were crying. Little Abbe Kapsinow, who was only eleven days old I remind you, was shaken so hard that her 'eyes went funny in her head.'"

A gasp went out in the back of the hushed courtroom. Judge Shea just smacked his gavel and instructed Ullman to continue. Sheilah stared forward and swallowed hard. Joan stared at the floor.

"She went on to confess that young Jennifer Malkan's 'head bobbed back and forth' under the same treatment. She was a mere three months old."

As Ullman read from her confession, Virginia sat with her bowed head resting in her left hand. Her elbow was propped up on the table in front of her. Reporters made note of this and how her demeanor had changed over the course of thirty minutes.

Ullman pressed forward. "Such a crime as killing an innocent life is about as bad a crime as there is. It is deplorable. And the fact that she did it again and again and again ..."

Moran rose, and Shea waved him back down into his seat. Ullman corrected himself. "Again and again, rather. She knew that what she was doing was wrong. Yet, she failed to stop herself, she failed to get help for these children, and she failed to get out of the practice of nursing. In light of this, Your Honor, the defendant must be substantially punished. These are a serious set of crimes. It will be all to the good of the public—as well as to the accused and to her family—that she be under the supervision of the state for as long a period of time as the law will allow. Thank you."

Ullman retired back to his seat feeling confident that he made as great a petition as he could in the name of the State of Connecticut.

Edward L. Reynolds Jr. stood up and walked to the front of the courtroom. He turned around and faced Virginia, who was now sitting as erect as she could, interested in what her attorney would say on her behalf.

"Judge Shea, Ladies and Gentlemen in attendance, three weeks ago, my client, the defendant, pleaded guilty to two counts of manslaughter in connection with the deaths of eleven-day-old Abbe Kapsinow last August 25 and three-month-old Jennifer Malkan on December 15, 1951. She wants to clear her conscience, accept responsibility, and move forward. Mr. Ullman paints one picture of my client, I'd like to paint a different one.

"Miss Jaspers, who is my age, thirty-three, has had a difficult life in many ways. I have known her since childhood. I grew up a block or so away from her house. I went to school with her, worked for her father, etc. Something I will always remember, as long as I live, were the times, when she was a youngster, when she would often wheel newborn infants around for busy mothers. She has *always* been very fond of babies. And as a professional baby attendant, she was always very much sought out and in demand. It was not unusual for parents to go on two- or three-week vacations and leave Miss Jaspers in charge of their children and home.

"My own sister," Reynolds continued, "tried to engage Miss Jaspers last Christmas, but she was 'booked up' as they say in the business. Her earnings often went into birthday and Christmas gifts for children, and she also had enlargements made of pictures of babies she had cared for. Your Honor, she isn't a monster. She is a woman who had a psychological reaction to crying babies, where she became overwhelmed and didn't know what to do. Miss Jaspers has always been self-conscious about her size, and as a youngster, she never had any social life. So, she entered a world of her own. I am going to ask Mr. Moran to fill in some of that for you and discuss Miss Jaspers' background. Thank you for your attention and consideration."

Reynolds and Moran crossed paths as if they had rehearsed it all week. Moran cleared his throat and continued the appeal. "Your Honor, Miss Jaspers has always been a victim of her own size. I mean, in childhood, she was the butt of jokes and teasing from other children. Cruel things would be said to her. And, you know, after years of this, one gets to start believing it and retreats to a world far away from reality, a make-believe world where you are king, or queen, in this case, of your castle. You are in control in your own way. I spoke with her probation officer the other day, and I quote from his report that Miss Jaspers was a 'physical misfit in society since childhood with the resultant emotional conflicts.'"

Moran stopped and briefly looked at Virginia. She had her arms crossed in front of her and was looking down. When she heard that her attorney had stopped speaking, she looked up in his direction to see what the silence meant. Moran pursed his lips and slowly said, "Your

Honor, I ask ... well, I ask that you take pity on her. She's had a rough life emotionally."

Many of the parents in the courtroom began whispering fervently like a collection of sparrows. The judge's gavel quieted them.

"When considering this woman's size, I'd like for you to also consider her handling of the infants she cared for. I propose that she handled them in the customary way, except that her tremendous physical vigor was responsible for the injuries. She was a victim of her own strength."

"Objection!" rang out from the prosecutor. "I have spoken with medical authorities that such shaking of a newborn infant was just as effective as if the baby had been struck a blow on the head."

More gasps and whispers emerged from the crowd, and there was another gavel smack.

Judge Shea said, "Okay, Mr. Moran, it is an interesting theory, but let's proceed to something else. A medical debate is not customary at a sentencing hearing."

"Yes, Your Honor," replied Moran, looking over at Reynolds, who was spinning his index finger sideways toward him. Moran took the hint and wrapped up. "In conclusion, Mr. Reynolds and I are asking for the minimum term of confinement with a long period of probation for Miss Jaspers. Thank you for your time."

The judge looked over at Ullman and asked if he had anything further to add to his recommendations.

"No, Your Honor."

"Then the court will be in recess for approximately one hour, while I make my decision."

Clerk Minnix jumped up from his seat and shouted, "All rise!"

Most people in court ended up staying in their seats waiting for the final sentence to be handed down. Several reporters, police officers, and doctors went out in the lobby for a smoke and to talk. The parents sat in silence. Some prayed silently, some read, all were hopeful. Virginia sat quietly and either stared at the floor or looked behind her at her parents. Her sister, Betty, came in about halfway through Moran's oration. She had questioned whether or not she should observe her sister's fate. But then a mix of grief and guilt got the best of her, and she drove to New Haven. She, like her parents, had faith that Virginia would be spared a lengthy punishment.

Just as he said, about an hour later, Judge Shea reentered the courtroom. When everyone took their places after the obligatory "All rise!" not a sound was heard. Virginia and her attorneys were leaning forward, anxiously awaiting a word from the judge.

"Miss Jaspers," he began.

"Yes, sir?" answered Virginia. She then realized that she did not need to answer after Edward Reynolds touched her shoulder and shook his head from side to side.

Judge Shea took a tolerant breath and began again without repeating her name. "You were entrusted by those who taught and guided you from the St. Agnes School to care for all the children whom you nursed. It is also a fact that when you enter a couple's home to care for their baby or child, that you treat everyone with the utmost respect and dignity. Unfortunately, for many families, you did not do this. In fact, your actions caused the deaths of at least two infants, the two for whose deaths you are charged with manslaughter. I cannot think of a more heinous crime than deliberately causing the death of a child. Mr. Moran raised the question that these deaths for which you are charged may have been accidental. Well, accidental or not, you told no one. You did not seek help. You hid the truth. For that, you should be ashamed. I cannot use either your size or your rough childhood as an excuse for your behavior as an adult. That would not be fair to the parents.

"In light of everything I've said, Miss Virginia Jaspers, I sentence you to serve ten to twenty-two years at the State Prison for Women at Niantic. There is minimum of seven years of prison that will be served before you may be eligible for parole. Is there anything you wish to say?"

At that, Virginia broke down and sobbed. She shook her head and looked down, her hands covering her face.

"I'll take that as a 'no,' Counselor?"

Reynolds nodded. Virginia began to wail.

Shea pounded the gavel and rose. Minnix directed the participants. Virginia remained seated, half-lying across the table in front of her.

Sheilah Kapsinow calmly gathered her blue purse that lay beside her on the courtroom bench and walked out to the center aisle. At the end of the aisle stood Joan Brainerd with an outstretched hand.

"Hi, Mrs. Kapsinow. I'm Joan, Jennifer Malkan's mother."

Sheilah took only the front half of Joan's hand and limply shook it. She looked away blankly and said, "Yes, I've seen your pictures in the paper, concerts and all."

Joan blushed slightly and said, "Well." She then changed the topic and said, "Wasn't that grand about the sentencing?"

Sheilah kept moving with the crowd toward the door. She looked at the sea of reporters that had collected like spawning salmon at the front door. "Yeah ... grand."

Joan continued. "It has been an emotionally difficult time these past few months, and ..."

She was cut off by Sheilah, who turned to her suddenly and asked, "How can you live with yourself?"

Joan took her question to mean, *How can you tolerate this grief and carry on from day to day?* So, she answered, "Well, I get support from my friends and family. I focus on my children, I sing, and so on. It helps me cope." She smiled and nodded at Sheilah.

Sheilah stopped looking at her and headed for the side door. "I'm going to go out this way, I guess."

"Well, it was nice meeting you," said Joan.

"Likewise," Sheilah said politely and walked down the dark side corridor of the courthouse lobby.

She didn't feel badly for asking Joan the question. It was one of the many questions that burned in her mind and soured her soul. The question continued to nag at her as she ran over to her car after she burst out the side door of the building. *How can people be like that? They get a baby, they lose a baby, and then they carry on as if nothing happened.* She remembered watching Willard Malkan laughing at something outside the police station the day they were all brought down to the police station, the week that Jaspers was arrested. She remembered overhearing Joan's father being introduced to a police officer by Willard that same morning. The conversation topic numbed her. She wanted to spit in all their eyes. *How dare they!*

"Officer Jedson, this is Ted Brainerd, Joan's father."

"Hey, great to meet you. You know, tough break about the baby. I feel for Joan and Willard, of course."

"Well, my daughter is a tough one. She can stand up to the best of challenges. And besides, they can always get another baby. Isn't that right, Willard?"

CHAPTER THIRTY

"Oh My God, There's That Woman"

January 1957 – April 1958
New Haven, Connecticut

Connecticut state legislators met in mid-January 1957, after their lengthy Christmas/New Year's break. One of their first orders of business was to discuss, and ultimately pass, a bill that required specific training of women who professionally care for children. William Jaspers and New Haven mayor, Richard Lee, were in attendance when the bill was signed. The bill stipulated that those who care for children have a specific number of hours of both training and supervised experienced prior to performing private duty. The bill did not inconvenience St. Agnes Home. There were plenty of nuns trained in childcare to assist in the supervisory functions that the state now required. What the home was not prepared for was the certified letter notice in April 1958 that Miss Virginia B. Jaspers would be joining their ranks again.

The Women's Prison at Niantic in Connecticut was the only prison for female inmates in that state. Virginia was a model prisoner. She carried out her prison functions without complaint and interacted with the other inmates on a friendly basis. Virginia's biggest challenge was when she first arrived. She was mocked and scorned by many inmates.

They not only judged her size and appearance, but her criminal acts as well. She was called "baby killer," "fat-assed pig," "daddy's girl," and so on. Some of the girls in the prison avoided her, as they were fearful of what she was capable of doing. Other girls came on to Virginia sexually.

The good news about her impending release came in January 1958 during a visit with her parents.

"Now, Ginny, I don't want you to get your hopes up," began William Jaspers, "but I may have convinced Judge Shea to release you early."

"Oh, Daddy, how early?"

"Well," he said, looking at Jane Jaspers secretively, "it could be as early as this spring!"

Virginia yelped lightly and put her hand up to her mouth.

One of the guards came over to the trio and asked if everything was all right.

"Oh, sure," said the elder Jaspers, "just a bit of good news."

"Well, Virginia, please refrain from such outbursts, you know better," cautioned the guard.

"Yes, I know, I'm terribly sorry," said Virginia.

William continued. "Ginny, I made a proposal to Judge Shea that you would go to live at St. Agnes Home again for a short time."

"Oh, Daddy," moaned Virginia, "would I have to go there?"

"For Christ's sake, Virginia, this is a chance of a lifetime, don't even think about …"

He was cut off by his wife touching his arm and saying, "Now, Bill, watch your heart, and remember what the doctor said. And watch your tone here."

William Jaspers looked around and then bent down a bit and whispered to his daughter, "Don't you see this is a good thing? This is your *freedom*."

"Yes, Daddy, I know. And I appreciate what you have done for me. I am just very anxious to get home, that's all."

"And you *will*, honey. We are only talking for about three or four months of community service at St. Agnes, and then you'll be able to come home for good. I'm trying to make it that you will be able to come home on weekends while you're at St. Agnes."

Virginia smiled broadly. She was very pleased. The thought of being out of prison made her excited.

"And when do you think I'll be able to start caring for children again?"

The Jaspers looked at each other as if they had expected this question.

"Well, dear," began William, "I don't think you will ever be able to be a nurse again."

"What? Well … why not? I was a good nurse."

"Yes … you were," her father stammered, "but there were the obvious problems that you had with infants."

"Yes, but I'm beyond that now. I've matured. I've been in prison!"

"Ginny," Jane Jaspers interjected, "the Kapsinow mother has also made it difficult for you to ever care for children again. She's hired a lawyer and that lawyer met with Judge Shea. Well, honey, it's part of the agreement with the judge. He won't let you out without it."

"That cursed woman!" Virginia said aloud. Several other inmates in the visitation room turned in her direction.

"We both wanted you out of here. We couldn't stand seeing you live in a place like this. You're no criminal. This is the only way."

Virginia thought about the whole arrangement for the rest of the day. Pediatric nursing had been her entire life. Now, she was stripped from performing the only duties she had ever loved. Her insight and foresight were limited. She felt more victimized than liberated.

Gerald Hershey picked up his office phone and dialed Sheilah Kapsinow. He was looking forward to sharing his news with her.

"Sheilah? Hi, Jerry Hershey here. Got some great news for you."

"Hi, Mr. Hershey, what is it?" asked Sheilah, putting a finger to her mouth to hush Heide, who was in the middle of playing with her plastic doll figures.

"Well, we were able to get the judge to agree to include a statement in Jaspers' release that she never professionally care for another child again. I met with him and Mr. Reynolds myself this morning."

Sheilah was silent. She didn't know what to say, much less feel.

"Hello? Sheilah? Are you there?"

"Yes, Mr. Hershey, I'm here. When is she getting out?"

"Well, they haven't finalized it yet, since they have to figure out something with her parole officer. But they told me they were shooting for a few months from now—April or May. Why are you asking?"

"I just wanted to prepare myself when and if I see her on the street."

"As some free legal advice, I'd caution that you stay away from her."

"Oh, I have no intention of trying to see her. I just wanted to prepare myself. Yes, I would love to rip her heart out, as I once told a newspaperman, but I'll never stoop to her level. And, you know, murder *is* her level."

Gerald Hershey agreed with Sheilah and closed the conversation politely but quickly. He was somewhat unnerved by the whole affair and wanted to wrap it up.

Sheilah began her mission on the day that Virginia was sentenced; when she raced out of the courthouse and got into her car, she drove until she spotted an attorney sign that hung in front of a stately house. The sign belonged to Hershey. He had been a lawyer in New Haven for only about three months, having practiced in Bridgeport for several years prior. At first sight, Sheilah was wary of him. He wore dark horn-rimmed glasses and appeared bookish. He was also very confident. It was not a flattering attribute to Sheilah, but she felt that an act of fate had brought them together, so she hired him after he agreed to take on the case. Though he was fast to submit a letter to the judge, the whole mess dragged out for over a year. It was Judge Shea who put Hershey's block together with Jaspers' plea for release. It all came together in early spring 1958. It was bittersweet for Sheilah. She had achieved her one wish that she had battled for for eighteen months, yet her opponent won freedom. It didn't seem fair.

Marvin Schaefer walked in downtown New Haven on the third Saturday in April. He had just eaten his lunch in the park square that was adjacent to many of the main buildings of New Haven. It was one practice that he had recently begun, but something that was therapeutic for him—to eat his lunch once a week in the park and watch birds, squirrels, and people. He knew that he needed to get out of the office regularly. His weekend real estate work often brought him to New Haven, so his weekly routine in the park fit nicely into his schedule.

Today, he had arranged with Norma to go with her to a movie at the Strand Theater in New Haven to see a new Troy Donahue film. He told her that he would meet her outside at 1:15 for the 2:00 matinee. As he stood waiting for his wife, he looked up at the sky. The air was crisp and fragrant. The day was very sunny, a perfect day. He took time to notice nature around him—much more than before. Since the Jaspers' fiasco, he now appreciated the special moments of life. This was one of the reasons why he and Norma were making it a point to take time for themselves.

A line was beginning to form outside the theater, and it was close to 1:15, so Marvin got in line as well to wait to purchase movie tickets. About five minutes later, Norma appeared from around the corner.

"Sorry, I'm late. There are a ton of shoppers for some reason and traffic was terrible."

"That's okay, sweetie. As long as I don't miss the movie previews, I'm fine," kidded Marvin, leaning forward to give his wife a kiss.

Norma clung to Marvin's arm as the line slowly moved forward. They talked about Bruce, the beautiful weather, and how their mornings had been. Just before they reached the ticket booth, they both heard laughter. It wasn't any laughter; it was a certain type of laughter that made the couple look at each other in fear.

The woman in the ticket booth asked, "How many?"

Marvin was frozen. He listened and stared ahead, like a deer in the brush on the side of a road. Norma made no sound either.

"How many tickets, please?" implored the ticket woman.

Marvin's concentration was broken, and he quickly replied, "Two."

After paying for the tickets, Marvin leaned his head slowly backward and looked down the line. The cackling continued, and Marvin's eyes tracked down the source—Virginia Jaspers standing about thirty feet away. She was also standing in line for the movie.

Marvin grabbed Norma and said, "Come on," pulling her into the theater. His emotions ran wild. He was both angry and nervous. His thoughts ran even faster. He wondered if he was seeing things. Why was Virginia Jaspers in New Haven, or *any* city for that matter? How and when did she get out of prison?

After he and Norma found their seats, he sat down and remained quiet. He didn't have to talk with her about seeing the nurse. He knew that Norma saw her too. He looked at the back of the seat in front of him and stewed. He couldn't settle his mind.

Virginia was with another woman that the Schaefers didn't know and proceeded to sit down about fifteen rows ahead of them. Virginia carried a large bucket of popcorn and a large drink. The previews had just started, and Marvin just stared at his nemesis. He'd have to talk with someone about this. He'd have to report her as an escaped convict. Yeah, that's what he'd do, report her. Then they'd take her back to the four-by-six cell where she belonged! *But ... why would she show herself out in public? What nerve she had! I better just calm down and do something to stop her,* he thought. Marvin had no direction and no plan. He was just reacting. He thought about Bruce and his tiny leg and the tongue depressor splint. How he hated Jaspers! His son was now a very active three-year-old, but what she did to his family would never be forgotten or forgiven.

Fifteen minutes into the movie, he found himself staring ahead and not focusing on the screen. Norma leaned over and said, "I can't concentrate either. Let's go."

Her words were a relief to Marvin, as he was not enjoying himself at all. He smiled at his wife, patted her hand, and stood up. As they were going up the aisle, Marvin looked back once more, his smile turned to a glare.

"Come on, Joan," her mother called to her from downstairs.

"Mother, there is no race. We are simply going shopping."

"Yes, but the sale starts this morning."

God forbid we not save an extra 10 percent, thought Joan sarcastically.

The two women were soon in the station wagon heading for their local Sears and Roebuck store. It was the final Saturday in April 1958.

Joan was, in fact, looking forward to this shopping day with her mother. She did not get out of the house too often, since she was busy with the boys. Willard opted to take them to a local park in New Canaan and then to lunch. Joan's mother wanted to go to the Sears store near her in New Haven, so Joan drove nearly an hour to the city that created painful memories for her. She had only been back once since the sentencing, and she did that with great trepidation. In planning today's trip, she told herself to shake off her negative thoughts and live life without fear. It was just negative energy wasted. *No more bad luck following my family and me. Live positively. Jennifer would have wanted that.*

Joan's mother headed right for the dresses. It was a new style for older women that Joan thought was God-awful. Joan spent some time in the shoe department, then in hosiery, and finally in lingerie. The two women met up with each other around 11:30 a.m. and decided to go for a bite to eat at the restaurant inside the store. All tables were full, so Joan left her name with the cashier. As they waited to be called, Joan and her mother looked in the book department that was adjacent to the restaurant. Joan went down the magazine aisle, and her mother was just around the corner from her looking at romance novels.

Joan about dropped her magazine when she heard her mother exclaim, "Oh my God, there's that woman!" She felt the palpitations of her heart, and she stared ahead. She knew which woman her mother had seen. Joan's head turned very slightly to the left in order to maximize her hearing. She held her breath and waited. It seemed like a lifetime when her mother finally called to her, "Joan?" She wheeled around and saw her mother standing at the end of the magazine aisle; she was pointing to her left. Joan walked slowly toward her, and as she reached the spot where her mother stood, she followed the invisible line to where she was being directed.

In the restaurant inside Sears and Roebuck, Virginia sat laughing up a storm with her sister Betty. In front of her was a large, half-eaten strawberry sundae. Nothing was wrong with her appetite. Her chin had several drips of vanilla on it, and she had a drop on her blouse. It didn't matter, though. She had been free for several weeks now, and she was on one of her "weekend furloughs" as her father called them. She enjoyed such time away from the home. It meant that she could spend time with her family and get reacquainted with friends and relatives. Today was special—it was one that she decided to devote to her sister. Her baby sister who stood by her throughout the "terrible ordeal," as she now regularly called it. Life was grand, indeed. By August, there would be no more St. Agnes, no more people telling her where she could and could not go, only life to be explored. Maybe she'd travel some. Maybe she'd go out to Hollywood to meet some famous people. *Maybe ... well, enough dreaming for now. Let's just enjoy this ice cream!*

Joan wept in her car during the entire trip home to New Canaan. She didn't say a word to her mother, except for a "thank you" for her time and company. The two had left Sears quickly and quietly. Joan's mother tried to speak with her in the car, but when she saw Joan's face, she remained silent.

When she walked into her house, Willard knew there was something afoul. His initial thought was that Joan had had some sort of row with her mother, which he vocalized as, "You two girls arguing over dress sizes again?"

Joan bent over and kissed her sons, who were scrambling for her attention. Both asked, "What's wrong, Mommy?" when they noticed her dampened eyes.

She looked angrily at Willard. His joking at a time like this was pitiful. She wanted to wrap her arms around her boys and walk them straight out to the car and leave forever. But, instead, she drew from her depths and said to him, "Virginia Jaspers is out of prison, and I saw her today. I don't know how this happened. I don't know why no one let us know, but the fact is that she is out. I can't talk right now. I need some time to figure this out and work with it in my head." She looked down at her children and said, "Boys, I love you so much. Right now, Mommy is going to lie down, since I haven't been feeling well. I should be better by dinner. Go outside and play in the backyard, and I will see you in few hours." She kissed their heads and they scrambled off to play.

Willard looked at her and said, "I'm sorry for what I said, Joan. I didn't know."

Joan smiled ever so slightly and said, "I forgive you. I'll see you in a few hours."

She ambled slowly upstairs to their bedroom and shut the door behind her. After kicking off her shoes, she pulled down the sheets of her bed and slid in between them. They were cool and brought a feeling of relief to her injured soul. She closed her eyes tightly and rested. Sleep never came. Visions of Virginia crept in and annoyingly stirred her. Joan countered with thoughts of Jennifer's sweet face. This barrage of images continued for several minutes until Joan whipped aside the sheets in frustration. She sat up and rested on the edge of the bed, staring at the floor, thinking of what she could do next. She walked over to her window and looked down at her children happily playing. The flower buds were blooming; the world around her was becoming green, awakening from the sleep of winter. The lilac bush caught her eye—by next weekend, it would be in full bloom. She thought to herself that she'd have to take a moment to enjoy the fragrance after dinner. She then looked up at the blue sky and said aloud to Jennifer, "I miss you, dear. I miss you." Joan walked over to the slant-top desk that stood in the corner of their bedroom and withdrew a piece of paper and a pen from the top drawer. She sat and wrote, and wrote. This would be how she would make it through her sad moments. And this would be how she would make it through the rest of her life—this, and her music.

Lilacs in the Rain

I've never seen the leaves so wet
As yesterday's rain began,
I'll never, no never more, forget
The innocence so quickly gone.

If you ever come to visit me
I'll always know you're near.

The sweet sound that calls to me,
the sweet fragrance in the air.

The lilac reminds me of you, my love,
Your life left in my care
God took you and brought you up above,
A twig broken, my heart not spared.

The buds of beauty lasting much too brief,
ne'er to come again,
And nothing, no nothing, spares my grief
Like lilacs in the rain.

Epilogue

"They Are Like Lilacs in the Rain"

Fifty-one years ago, a story that shocked the nation sprang forth. It has long been forgotten to society, but not by the families of the victims. My interest in this saga began in 1998, while researching the medical condition known as shaken baby syndrome, better known as SBS. The physician who coined this term, Dr. John Caffey, used the story of Virginia Jaspers in his first and second articles about SBS. He had made reference to a 1956 *Newsweek* article about the case. I decided to read that particular article and thus began my journey to unearth this compelling tale. The majority of the records pertaining to the Jaspers case have been lost or destroyed.

Cynthia Hubbard—Stephen Hubbard knew that he had a younger sister who died before he was born, but he knew no details. His parents never shared any information about her—just that she had died. Stephen, as an adult, figured that she had most likely died of SIDS, or "crib death" as it was called in his parents' day. A year after Stephen was born, Allen and Eleanor had another girl, whom they named Cynthia. Such a practice of reusing dead children's names sounds odd today but was quite a common practice decades ago. Stephen never knew that his older sister was murdered. Eleanor died in 1969, and Allen died in 1985. Today, Stephen operates Connecticut Cycle Works in North Haven, Connecticut.

Jennifer Malkan—Forty-eight years after her death, her mother, Joan Brainerd, found out the details of her burial. The particulars were taken care of by Willard, as is described in this story, but Joan was never informed about them, nor did she ask. Jennifer was cremated and interred in a small plot in Mountain Grove Cemetery in Bridgeport. Beecher and Bennett Funeral Home took care of the arrangements. Upon hearing this information, Joan spoke with the funeral home and made plans to visit Jennifer's grave.

Joan and Willard divorced in 1974. He died in the 1980s, and Joan has been remarried for many years. She focused on raising her sons. Joan never returned to concert touring, though she formed a singing group with her husband in the community in which she lives and teaches voice lessons.

It was many years before Joan could even talk about Jennifer's death. She recounts the time when one of her grown sons found some newspaper clippings about the Jaspers case and asked Joan about it. It was after this that she could talk openly, without falling apart. About five years ago, Joan heard the oratorio that she sang the night she heard about Jennifer's death. She said she was able to listen to it, but the emotions connected with the musical piece were raw. Joan said she doesn't blame the adoption agency or St. Agnes Home or anyone else for what happened to Jennifer. She does, though, blame all of society. All the signs of danger were present with Virginia Jaspers, yet people looked the other way, did not listen, and failed to act.

Bruce and Marvin Schaefer—Though obviously not remembering the time when his nurse broke his leg, Bruce enjoys telling about the tongue depressor that was used for his splint. He still works with his father's real estate appraisal business. To this day, Marvin has an emotionally difficult time talking about the abuse that his son endured. He carries a degree of guilt for having hired Virginia Jaspers in the first place. He also reminisces fondly of Dr. Robert Salinger, who failed in his attempts to get legal notice of the dangerous person that Jaspers was. He agrees with the idea that William Jaspers carried a great deal of power and influence in and around New Haven. It was largely because of this authority that the tragedies were not stopped sooner.

Sheilah Kapsinow—Sheilah and Allen Kapsinow divorced in the 1960s. Sheilah later remarried and is now Sheilah Edmunds. She has significant health problems, many of which she attributes to the emotional pain of dealing with Abbe's death. Sheilah spends time once a month to help raise money for child abuse prevention. She and this author contacted Yale-New Haven Hospital for Abbe's hospital records and found that they do not exist.

Dr. Robert Salinger—He is now deceased. Several New Haven pediatricians, including Dr. Stilson and Dr. Wessel, remember Dr. Salinger as a kind man and a thorough medical practitioner. Everyone who speaks of him says that this story would have a very different ending with more infant deaths had it not been for the tenacity and courage of this doctor.

Dr. Laurence Michel—He has retired in Florida. Though Dr. Michel never again had an SBS case in his career, the Jaspers case was one that he frequently discussed with others over the years, both on a professional and personal basis.

Edward L. Reynolds—He died in 2000 after a long career as a private attorney and probate judge.

Harold Berg and Bernard Lawlor—They are the only two police officers from the original investigating team that are still alive. Both do not have clear memories of the case.

St. Agnes Home—The Pediatric Nursing School closed in 1962, though the home continued with its baby program until 1972. No one knows the effects that the Jaspers case had on the success or downfall of the nursing program. Few nuns are alive that were a part of the program when Virginia Jaspers attended. There is no record or remembrance of her.

Virginia Jaspers—While researching this story, I discovered that few records directly connected to Jaspers exist. The women's prison has no records that she was ever a prisoner behind their walls. The New Haven police have no records. Besides newspaper accounts, the only other detail of Jaspers' arrest and conviction was her docket number (10866) and personal accounts by parents and professionals.

Virginia Jaspers died in April 2004 at the age of eighty years. In 1999, I had a personal encounter with her. Several months before I stopped in New Haven, while on vacation, I was able to obtain Virginia Jaspers' address and phone number. I called her and asked about her case and childcare, in general, in the 1950s. She did not want to talk. One rainy summer day, when in New Haven, I found her apartment building. She buzzed me in after I told her that I had a delivery for her. I walked up the steps to the second floor. She was coming out of her apartment as I entered the rotunda area. She was smiling and then stepped back in surprise when she realized that I was not a deliveryman. I had my hand extended and told her that I wanted to meet her and needed a minute of her time. Instead, she said, "That was a dirty trick!" and she moved back toward her apartment. She knew who I was. I asked if she wanted to talk, and she said, "No," and began to shut her door. I took a moment to visually take in her features. She was hunched over. She was not as imposing a figure as she had been in her youth. Her hair was disheveled, and she wore a bathrobe without slippers. I made a point to look at her hands and bare feet—both sets were quite large. I wanted to inspect her hands, as they were the weapons that killed and injured so many infants and children. Going back to my car and family, I thought about her potential. The outcome could have been so different for her. Had she just used the training that was imparted to her at St. Agnes, had she just had the emotional wherewithal, etc., this story never would have been written.

July 1999
New Haven, Connecticut

After visiting Jaspers, we drove down to Whalley Avenue on the outskirts of New Haven to the Jewish cemetery. After a great deal of time looking, we found Abbe Kapsinow's tiny grave, complete with an engraved lamb. I stood and thought about Sheilah spending her lunches here. I thought about an innocent life lost. I thought about the "Lilacs in the Rain" poem and its meaning—rain as a representation of sadness, lilacs that are fragrant and beautiful like infants, and the combination of the two—rain, ironically, making the lilacs more fragrant, and the lilacs lasting for such a short time, like when an infant's life is cut short. I thought about how while walking in other cemeteries, we might not think about the tragedies that lie in the ground beneath the lambs. How many other stories like Abbe's haven't been told? How many other little souls are calling us?

Printed in the United States
200232BV00004B/365/A